More praise for
Coaching Your Kids to Be Leaders

"This book is a must for parents who have an interest in their children. I am sure that will be all of you. It will give you all the answers."
—Chuck Tanner, manager, Pittsburgh Pirates, 1979 World Series Champs

"A book that is long overdue. This is powerful leadership information for every parent, teacher, and coach."
—Jack Canfield, coauthor, Chicken Soup for the Soul Series

"Pat Williams has done all of us a service with his fabulous new book. The stories and illustrations are superb. A powerful read for young and old alike."
—Jerry Reinsdorf, chairman, Chicago White Sox & Chicago Bulls

"The term 'leadership' is one of the most complex in the English language. Business, education, and sports are all looking for leaders but coming up short. This book enters a whole new arena. Finding the reason why and starting the development at an early age—leadership can be taught. Read and share this information with your kids."
—Chuck Daly, Hall of Fame basketball coach

"As a coach, I've been helping to develop leaders for over 30 years. Pat Williams's new book is packed with powerful information on this important topic. I wish I could've read it at the start of my career."
—Jim Calhoun, head basketball coach, University of Connecticut,
NCAA Champions 1999, 2004

"With all the overwhelming choices kids have to make today . . . I am grateful Pat Williams wrote this book to give our youth specific direction on how to become a leader. *Coaching Your Kids to Be Leaders* can serve as a 'guidebook' for parents and teachers interested in teaching children how to develop character by learning such things as honesty and integrity. This is a book with specific instruction based on true life stories from successful, ethical leaders of today. If we can teach these basic principles, along with the Christian principles contained throughout the book . . . we will all look forward to a generation of great leaders!"
—David A. Brandon, chairman and
chief executive officer, Domino's Pizza

"Anything and everything we can do to benefit our kids must have the highest priority. That's why it's so important that you read Pat Williams's new book."
—Tony La Russa, manager, St. Louis Cardinals

"Where will the next generation of leaders come from? That's an extremely important question, and Pat Williams has tackled it head-on in this riveting new book. Please read it carefully and spread the word."

—Doug DeVos, president, Alticor, Inc.

"Pat Williams brings to light the tremendous importance of coaching your kids to become future leaders of character. This insightful book will inspire you to see your children and your role as parent in a whole new way."

—Larry Julian, author of *God Is My CEO*

"Pat Williams's book is a must-read for every parent who wants their offspring to grow into solid citizenship and to have a positive influence on others. There is a great need for this kind of book in our unsettled world. Williams supports his main tenets on leadership development with interesting anecdotes from some of the foremost leaders in today's multi-faceted society. He writes in an easy-to-read and understandable manner. This book is a page-turner that the reader will linger over and savor as he finishes it."

—Dr. Jack Ramsay, Hall of Fame basketball coach & ESPN broadcaster

"I'm excited about Pat Williams's excellent new book on leadership. I believe leadership skills can be nurtured in youngsters, and Pat shows us how to fully develop their potential. I highly recommend *Coaching Your Kids to Be Leaders*."

—Mark Richt, head football coach, University of Georgia

"If you are looking for a clear, concise, practical book on leadership you don't have to look any further. I would encourage anyone who is willing to find insights into what it takes to become a leader to read *Coaching Your Kids to Be Leaders*. This book covers the elementary disciplines in what it takes to excel as a leader, which includes the biblical truths of servanthood, character, risk taking, and more. You'll be referring to this book again and again for yourself and for those you will have the opportunity to mentor."

—Dr. Charles F. Stanley, senior pastor, First Baptist Church, Atlanta

"There seems to be very little originality these days—everyone seems to just follow along with the crowd. Pat Williams shows us how to motivate and equip our youth to be effective leaders."

—Danny Wuerffel, 1996 Heisman Trophy winner and director of
development, Desire St. Ministries

Coaching
Your Kids to Be Leaders

■ ■ ■

The Keys to Unlocking Their Potential

Pat Williams
WITH JIM DENNEY

WARNER
Faith®

NEW YORK BOSTON NASHVILLE

I dedicate this book to my friend Jay Strack,
who helps train more young leaders than any
person in the country.

Scriptures noted NIV are taken from the HOLY BIBLE: NEW
INTERNATIONAL VERSION®. Copyright © 1973, 1978, 1984 by
International Bible Society. Used by permission of Zondervan Publishing
House. All rights reserved.
  Scriptures noted AMP are taken from the Amplified® Bible.
Copyright © 1954, 1962, 1965, 1987 by The Lockman Foundation.
Used by permission.

Warner Faith
Time Warner Book Group
1271 Avenue of the Americas, New York, NY 10020

Visit our website at www.twbookmark.com

Warner Faith® and the Warner Faith logo are
trademarks of Time Warner Book Group Inc.

Printed in the United States of America

First Warner Books printing: January 2005

10 9 8 7 6 5 4 3 2

Library of Congress Cataloging-in-Publication Data
Williams, Pat, 1940–
  Coaching your kids to be leaders : the keys to unlocking their
potential / Pat Williams. — 1st Warner Faith ed.
    p. cm.
  ISBN 0-446-53349-1
  1. Parenting—Religious aspects—Christianity.   2. Leadership—
Religious aspects—Christianity.   3. Leadership in children.
I. Title.
  BV4529.W573   2004
  248.8'45—dc22   2004009580

▪ Contents ▪

Contents

▪ Foreword ▪

by John Wooden

John Wooden is the winningest coach in college basketball history. While at Purdue University in 1932, he was named College Player of the Year. He began his long, legendary career as head coach of the UCLA Bruins in 1948. Under his leadership, UCLA won ten national championships in twelve years, collecting 664 wins for a .804 average.

Named Coach of the Year six times, John Wooden doesn't consider himself so much a coach as a teacher of leadership principles and character qualities. "I'm an English teacher at heart," he told me. When I asked him when he retired from coaching, he replied, "I retired from teaching in 1975."

Well, he may be officially retired—but I know for a fact that Coach Wooden is still teaching and still coaching, because I am one of his pupils.

—Pat Williams

I have been around young people my whole life. From coaching high school basketball players in Kentucky and Indiana to coaching college players at Indiana State and UCLA, I have had the privilege of working with some outstanding young leaders. One of the great thrills of my career has been to see so many of my players go on to become leaders in sports, business, government, the military, and the church.

I have always believed and taught that the game of basketball is of small importance compared with the totality of the life we live. The true importance of basketball is this: Every great virtue and principle that applies on the basketball court is completely transferable to everyday life.

Whether in the sports arena, in the corner office, in the government office, on the battlefield, or in the pulpit, leadership is still leadership, character is character, and servanthood is servanthood.

For as long as I can remember, I have been a student of great leaders. I have analyzed the character qualities, skills, and attitudes needed to be a leader. The future of our nation and our world will be determined by the caliber of young leaders we are developing right now. Because nothing is more important than developing young leaders of vision, competence, and character, I believe that *Coaching Your Kids to Be Leaders* is an indispensable addition to your leadership library.

Pat and I have known each other for many years. While I was coaching at UCLA, he was in the NBA, working as general manager of the 76ers, the Bulls, the Hawks, and the Orlando Magic. I have long known him to be a serious student of leadership and a committed Christian.

I have truly come to know Pat as a friend in the past several years. He came to me and told me he wanted to write a book about my life and views called *How to Be Like Coach*. Well, I was flattered by his interest, of course, but the most satisfying outcome of all of this is that I have gotten to know Pat as a man of accomplishment, integrity, and faith.

He is a veteran of over forty years in professional sports and the father of nineteen children—four by birth, fourteen by international adoption, and one by remarriage. Both his career and his family life have been focused on the challenge of motivating and mentoring young people to become leaders. His credentials to write this book are impeccable.

When Pat asked me to contribute my stories and insights to this project, I responded immediately. I knew that this would be an important book. But I had no idea the depth and breadth of insight that would be collected in these pages until Pat sent me the completed manuscript.

In researching this book, Pat Williams has turned over every rock, interviewed some of the great leaders of our time, seeking stories and insights into how to identify, train, equip, mentor, and motivate young leaders. Pat has crafted a book that truly stands alone. He has exhaustively and intensively explored a topic that has long been neglected.

Pat has been a guest in my home on two occasions, and I always love to see him because he brings such energy and enthusiasm to everything he does. You'll find that same energy crackling on every page of this book. *Coaching Your Kids to Be Leaders* is a joy to read, filled with powerful, insightful stories, and brimming with ideas and principles that you can instantly put to good use.

Whether you are a parent, teacher, coach, pastor, mentor, or youth worker, this book will change the way you look at the challenge of training young leaders—and it just might change your world.

▪ Introduction ▪

by Charles W. Colson

Chuck Colson is the founder of Prison Fellowship and the author of such books as Born Again, Loving God, *and* How Shall We Now Live? *In 2001, he received the Mark O. Hatfield Leadership Award, honoring those who demonstrate uncommon leadership reflecting the values of Christian higher education.*

He was special counsel to President Nixon from 1969 to 1973, and though he had no role in the Watergate break-in or cover-up, he admitted wrongdoing in the White House effort to discredit Daniel Ellsberg (who leaked the top-secret "Pentagon Papers"). For that, he served seven months in prison. Chuck's fall from power had a profound effect on his life. He came to faith in Jesus Christ, and was transformed in his love for others, including his political enemies.

Chuck was moved by his prison experience to launch Prison Fellowship, an organization he oversees to this day. Prison Fellowship has had a profound impact on the lives of thousands of prisoners, their families, and society as a whole. He has devoted his post-Watergate life to Prison Fellowship. All of his book royalties go to support this ministry.

I asked Chuck Colson about the influences that shaped him as a leader. His responses were so instructive that I asked him to turn his thoughts into an introduction for this book, and he graciously consented.

—Pat Williams

It was quite a journey from my boyhood in Boston to the White House in Washington to a federal prison in Alabama. Along the way, I have learned many profound lessons about leadership—what leadership consists of, how it is developed, and how it should be used.

The first person to encourage me to develop my leadership capacity was my dad. He taught me to work hard, set goals, get out front, and lead. I was also influenced by a teacher in prep school who continually encouraged me while I was on the debating team. I didn't know I had any ability as a public speaker until I went out for debating (at my dad's urging). As I gained experience, my confidence grew, and I became a pretty good debater.

In prep school, I was turned down for a position on the school magazine, so I started a campus newspaper to compete with the magazine. Within a few months, the newspaper's readership surpassed that of the school magazine. Before the year was out, the magazine absorbed the newspaper and made me editor. At the time, I didn't think of what I was doing as leadership. I simply set out to do what needed to be done. I recruited people to help, and we got it done together. Looking back, I realize that it was my first real leadership role.

After graduating with honors from Brown University, I joined the Marine Corps. It was in the Corps that I first became a serious student of leadership. The Marines taught me the fundamental principles of leadership, and those lessons have guided me in every role I've held ever since. I would recommend the Corps to any young person who seeks to become a leader, and who thinks he or she is good enough to enlist.

My Marine officers continually challenged me to work harder and expect more of myself. One night on the obstacle course, I almost passed out while running three miles with a full eighty-pound pack. One of the majors in charge of the course (who was heavily decorated and just back from Korea) found me exhausted on the ground, wracked with nausea. He stood over me and barked, "Colson, if you're not good enough, we'll get somebody else to carry your pack." I was so infuriated I jumped up and ran another two miles to the barracks.

In the Marines, I learned that an authentic leader achieves objectives through people by becoming their servant. Servanthood, in the Marines, is the essence of leadership. In the field, Marine officers always feed their troops first—they never eat until every one of their men has been fed. I was commissioned as a lieutenant during the Korean War, and I felt an enormous responsibility for men that I would lead into battle.

In the years since I became a Christian, I have been amazed to discover that most of the leadership principles I learned in the Marine Corps are actually biblical principles. In 2 Samuel 23, David, the great warrior-king, was in the cave stronghold of Adullam with his soldiers and the Philistine forces were encamped in the valley near Bethlehem. David's forces had run out of water, and he was thirsty. Three of his men heard him complain of thirst, so they broke through the Philistine lines at great personal risk and drew water from a well outside of Bethlehem.

When the men brought the water back to David, he poured the water out on the ground, saying, "Is it not the blood of men who went at the risk of their lives?" He wanted his men to know that their safety meant far more to him than his thirst or his comfort.

The Bible is filled with examples of leaders who led through servant-hood. My favorite example is the story in 2 Kings 6, when the prophet Elisha was besieged by the army of the Arameans. Elisha's servant rose up early in the morning and saw that he and the prophet were surrounded by an army with horses and chariots. The servant despaired, but Elisha calmly replied, "Don't be afraid. Those who are with us are more than those who are with them."

Then the prophet prayed, "O Lord, open his eyes so he may see." And God opened the servant's eyes, and the man saw that the hills were filled with the horses and fiery chariots of the army of the Lord. God's army far outnumbered the army of the king of Aram. Elisha saw what his servant couldn't see because Elisha was a prophet, a man of vision.

As Pat Williams makes clear in this book, vision is the first key to authentic leadership. Leaders must be able to see what others do not see, then have the courage and boldness to lead others to act upon that vision.

Wherever you find enduring and momentous accomplishments in history, you will find a man or woman of vision—a leader with the courage to call others to a cause that changes the course of history.

After the Korean War, I returned to civilian life, earned a doctorate in law, and opened a successful law firm. I got involved in politics and became the youngest administrative assistant in the U.S. Senate. When I was thirty-nine years old, President Nixon asked me to serve in the White House.

Every day, I worked with the most powerful leaders on the planet. Dr. Henry Kissinger began each of his national security briefings with the words, "The decisions we make today will change the course of human history." We believed those words. We were convinced that we were going to change the world.

That, of course, was before Watergate.

Looking back, I can see that all of the splendid leadership ability in the Nixon White House did not really change the history of humanity—certainly not in the way we had hoped. Even with all of the resources of the most powerful nation on earth, we failed to improve the way people lived their lives. It was a bitter lesson.

I believe that we in the Nixon White House failed in our mission because many of us—myself included—misunderstood the true nature and purpose of leadership. We thought that leadership was about *power*. In reality, leadership is about such issues as vision, servanthood, integrity, and character—the very issues that Pat Williams has been exploring in this book.

As the Watergate scandal unfolded, I went to prison, where I received some startling and unexpected lessons in leadership. I became involved in a prayer group—a group that consisted of a couple of drug dealers, a stock swindler, a car thief, and a former White House official. We went to our knees together and asked to be led by the Carpenter from Nazareth, just as He led the Twelve.

Today, I thank God for that prison and for those fellow prisoners who led me into a deeper understanding of what it means to follow Jesus Christ. I thank God that I was humbled and stripped of power, so that I could learn lessons in leadership from the greatest Leader who ever led. Perhaps the most important leadership lesson I learned is that Jesus led by serving.

There is no more effective leadership model than the model of a servant. There is no more rewarding way to live than to lead by serving others. When the end of life approaches, the most rewarding memories you will have are of those times when God has used you to touch the lives of others.

This is the heart of authentic leadership. This is the message we must teach to those young people who will be tomorrow's leaders: True meaning and joy in life are found through following in the footsteps of the Carpenter, through putting ourselves second and others first.

A leader is, above all, a servant.

Coaching

Your Kids to Be Leaders

PART I

■ ■ ■

To Build Leaders, Start Early

| 1 |

Urgently Needed: Young Leaders

I was a young leader, but I didn't know it.

When I was in high school, sports was my passion. I played quarterback on the football team—a leadership position. I played point guard on the basketball team—a leadership position. I played catcher on the baseball team—a leadership position. But during those years that I was busy being a leader at my high school, I never thought about what it meant to be a leader. What's more, no adult ever mentored, taught, or coached me in the practice and principles of leadership.

After high school, I went to college at Wake Forest University in Winston-Salem, North Carolina. At the start of my junior year, I was tossed headfirst into an experience that galvanized me as a leader. It occurred in November 1960, and it had to do with a basketball game.

In those days, freshmen were not eligible for the varsity basketball team, so every November there would be a big game in which the freshman team would play the varsity team. The game, held in the Coliseum in Winston-Salem, was open to the public.

Five days before the game, Jerry Steele, the president of the Monogram Club, our lettermen's organization, came to me and said, "Williams, we've got to put this game on and you're in charge."

"In charge of what?"

"In charge of everything," he said. And he meant that literally. Even though the game was just five days away, nobody had done one thing to make it happen.

I opened my mouth to argue—then I shut it. Jerry Steele was a six-foot eight-inch, 240-pound basketball player, all of which added up to a very persuasive personality. So I agreed to be volunteered.

I spent the next five days putting together a basketball show for the whole community. I worked on various promotions and got the publicity information to the local radio and TV stations and the newspapers. I planned a halftime show and brought in a band from a local high school. I auditioned a singer for the national anthem. I located a color guard for the start of the game. I brought in cheerleaders. I printed and sold the tickets. In short, I was doing the same things I would later do as an NBA executive. It was on-the-job leadership training.

The job was far too big for one guy, so I learned very quickly the importance of delegating. I grabbed volunteers (not all of them willing!) wherever I could find them. I buttonholed and recruited; I wheeled and dealed; I became a leader!

How did it come off? I remember that game as if it was yesterday. Everything happened right on schedule, and everybody had a great time. When it was over, I was walking two inches off the ground. I was so pleased with myself that my grin barely fit on my face. It was one of the most satisfying and energizing experiences of my life. I received accolades from the athletics director, the students, the players, the coach, and people in the community.

That night, as I went to bed, I realized something I had never known before: I was a leader!

■ The Seven Keys to Unlocking Leadership Potential

Looking back, I see that this one event opened the door for every other leadership role I've held during these past forty-odd years. Everything I've done as a leader, as a promoter, as a general manager, as a sports executive, had its genesis in that one event. Jerry Steele tossed me that responsibility as if it was a live grenade. He thought he was giving me a job nobody else would want, nobody else would take. But I passed the test. Little did Jerry realize that he had a big hand in launching my career as a leader.

In the years since then, I have become fascinated with the subject of leadership. Some of the most effective and influential leaders in the world of sports and the world of business, including baseball executive and promoter Bill Veeck, Philadelphia Phillies owner Bob Carpenter, and Orlando Magic owner Rich DeVos, have instructed and mentored me. Other leaders who have had a big influence on my life include businessman and minor-league baseball owner R. E. Littlejohn; former major league catcher and Miami Marlins manager Andy Seminick (I caught for the minor-league Marlins in 1962–63); my college baseball coach, Jack Stallings; my high school football coach, Bob DeGroat; and my high school baseball coach (who was also a former Phillies farmhand), Peanuts Riley. These leaders and mentors not only modeled leadership in my life, but they also set a high bar for me to live up to. I wanted them to be proud of me and pleased with my work. They motivated me to be a leader.

Finally, I distilled everything I had learned about leadership in a book called *The Paradox of Power*, which was published in the fall of 2002 by Warner Books. This book had quite an impact, and I received literally hundreds of letters from readers who were excited about the concepts and principles in that book. After the book had been out for a few months, I received a call from my publisher at Warner, Rolf Zettersten. "Pat," he said, "I've just come from an editorial meeting, and we have an idea for a book we'd like you to write."

Well, that was something new in my experience! Usually, I came up with book ideas and tried to find a publisher who would agree to publish them. Here was my publisher coming to *me* with a book idea!

"This book would be a natural follow-up to *The Paradox of Power*," Rolf continued. "Pat, what's the number one desire of every parent for his or her children? What's the number one desire of every teacher, coach, pastor, and youth worker concerning the young people they are guiding and mentoring?"

Well, I am the father of nineteen children (four by birth, fourteen by international adoption, and one by remarriage), and the first answer that came to mind was that they stay out of trouble! But I knew that Rolf was getting at something much deeper than that.

"I know," I said. "Our number one desire is that they become leaders."

"Precisely," Rolf said. "We thought that with all the young people you have raised in your home, and with all the study you have put into the issue of leadership, you would be uniquely qualified to write a book on how to develop leadership skills in young people."

I thought, *Wow! Does this idea hit me where I live or what?* Developing young leaders has been one of my top goals, not only as a parent nineteen times over, but as a sports manager, a speaker, and a volunteer in my church. What's more, in my travels across the country, I have sensed a hunger throughout our society for fresh insights into the challenge of training and motivating young people to be leaders.

My next question was: Where would these fresh insights come from? The answer came to me in a flash: from leaders themselves. I realized that to write this book, I needed to chase down hundreds of leaders and distill the best of those stories into this book. I was convinced that the essential principles of training and motivating young leaders would emerge from those hundreds of interviews—and I was right.

I spent twelve months sending out letters and making phone calls, gathering stories, insights, and ideas from leaders around the country. I sent out more than a thousand questionnaires to leaders in every walk of life—business, sports, government, the military, education, religion, and on and on. A friend of mine, author-journalist Larry Guest, calls me "the Prince of Overkill," and I am—I can't help myself. Once I started collecting ideas and stories from the first wave of respondents, I got so excited about what I was reading that I had to send out more and more questionnaires. When the smoke had cleared, I had mailed more than nine thousand questionnaires.

Before I was finished, I had received stories and insights from more than eight hundred leaders, from Florida's Governor Jeb Bush to Democratic presidential nominee George McGovern to San Antonio Spurs head coach Gregg Popovich to leadership guru John Maxwell. While answers to my questionnaires were still pouring in, I saw patterns and trends emerging. Many of these leaders had youthful experiences and influences in common. Many talked about the same components of authentic leadership. Though their stories were different, the principles for inspiring, instructing, and motivating young leaders were the same. So I got together with my writing partner, Jim Denney, and we hammered out the structure for this book—a structure that was based entirely on the results of this research, not on any preconceived notions.

In short, this book was written in the trenches. It comes straight from the real-life experiences of real leaders. So you can be sure that these insights are true and these principles work. If you apply these insights and principles to your relationships with young leaders, you *will* see results in young lives.

At the beginning of this project, I suspected that the same seven principles of leadership that formed the basis of my previous book, *The Paradox of Power*, would apply to the challenge of training and motivating young leaders. My research confirmed this to be true. The essential principles of leadership do not change, whether they are practiced in the Oval Office, the corner office, or the office of the sophomore class president at Herbert Hoover High.

The essence of a leader is embodied in these seven keys to unlocking leadership potential. It is up to us as parents, coaches, teachers, pastors, youth group advisors, and mentors to inspire and motivate young leaders to build these seven qualities into their lives. The seven qualities of effective leaders are:

1. *Vision.* Every leader, young or old, must have a vision. A vision defines what success looks like. The leader and the entire team compete for, struggle for, and sacrifice for a vision. We must learn how to challenge and inspire young people to become young visionaries.

2. *Communication.* Every leader must be able to communicate the vision to the entire team—and must do so effectively and persuasively so that all the team members will buy into it. We need to give young people opportunities to build their communication skills—and their confidence.

3. *People skills.* Whether young or old, leaders must know how to motivate people, resolve conflicts, listen, acknowledge, affirm, praise, and build community. In other words, leaders need people skills—the ability to work effectively with people in order to inspire them to achieve a goal.

4. *Character.* People admire and follow leaders who exhibit genuine character. As John Maxwell observed, "People buy into the leader before they buy into the leader's vision." So young leaders need to build good character traits into their lives, including a strong work ethic, humility, honesty, integrity, personal responsibility, social responsibility, self-discipline, courage, kindness, fairness, tolerance, and respect for others.

5. *Competence.* Notice that the first seven letters of *competence* are *c-o-m-p-e-t-e*. A group or team with a competent leader can compete and win. Competence comes from having experience (a proven track record), learning how to delegate, and approaching every task with a commitment to excellence.

6. *Boldness.* It's fourth-and-one, and you're forty yards from the goal line. Do you gather up your courage and reach for one more hard-fought yard—or do you punt? To become leaders, young people must learn how to overcome shyness, timidity, and a tendency to play it safe. Without risk, there is no adventure. You can't be a leader without boldness.

7. *Servanthood.* True leadership is not about being "the boss" but about being a servant. Young people need to be mentored, inspired, and challenged to see their leadership roles not as opportunities to expand their egos, but as opportunities to serve others and God.

These seven qualities provide a solid foundation for any leader, young or old. They are the foundation of this book.

■ Why We Need Leaders

We live in an increasingly dangerous world—a world that often seems to be drifting toward a dark and uncertain future. Our civilization seems hemmed in on every side by the threat of economic catastrophe, ecological destruction, racial and ethnic clashes, religious warfare, nuclear, biological, and chemical terror, cyber attacks, social and political instability, poverty, urban blight, crime, drugs, alcoholism, ignorance and illiteracy, population pressure, and unknown threats from emerging technologies.

"If today's kids do not become leaders, where does society go?" asked Dr. Larry McCarthy, associate professor at the Stillman School of Business Management, Seton Hall University. "We constantly need to replenish the world's coterie of leaders. The current leaders move on, move up, or die off, yet the world's problems continue to grow. Where do we turn, then, if we have no new generation of leaders ready to step up to the challenges of our world?"

My friend Jay Strack, president of Student Leadership University, is America's number one authority on developing young leaders. "We have been hit between the eyes as parents, educators, and coaches," he said, "with the fact that our kids are woefully unprepared to deal with real life. Corporations are spending millions of dollars training young people how to lead. It's a huge industry. Our universities and the military are realizing that the young people who stream into their halls and barracks are not well prepared to lead. We have produced a generation that is neither deep nor wide in leadership ability. Many parents are beginning to realize just how ill-prepared their kids are to face life's challenges and make good decisions."

Let me tell you about a young leader named Danny Rohrbough. Danny was fifteen years old, a high school freshman who loved computers, stereos, and big-screen TVs. He often helped out his dad in the family electronics business. He eagerly looked forward to getting his driver's permit.

On one warm spring day, Danny Rohrbough and more than four hundred of his fellow students were eating lunch in the high school cafeteria. Suddenly, the students were startled by the sound of gunfire just outside the building. Two male students in black trench coats were stalking the grounds, guns raised, firing at students. They killed a seventeen-year-old girl who was eating her lunch. Then they shot a young man sitting next to her eight times, leaving him alive but permanently paralyzed.

The two killers then went down some stairs and entered the cafeteria. When the students in the cafeteria saw the armed boys, they fled. The killers tried to detonate some butane-powered bombs in the cafeteria, but they failed to explode.

Danny Rohrbough was in the crowd of students who made it out of the cafeteria, running for safety. But unlike the other students, Danny stopped, went back, and held the door open so that his fellow students could get out of the cafeteria faster. He stood there holding the door until one of the two killers saw him, took aim, and shot him three times. Danny staggered a few steps down the walk, then stumbled and fell.

He died on the sidewalk, just a few steps from safety.

The gunfire and screams continued. The gunmen killed twelve students and a teacher that day. It was Tuesday, April 20, 1999, and the school was Columbine High School in Littleton, Colorado.

Several days later, Danny Rohrbough was remembered at his funeral as both a leader and a servant, a young man who held the door open, showing his fellow students the way to life and safety and a future. He laid down his life for his friends. The minister at his funeral said, "Danny might have lived if he had made a different choice. Yet he chose to stand and hold the door so that others might make it to safety. They made it. Danny didn't."

A high school senior named Nick also spoke at the funeral. He said, "I never knew Danny, but I wish I had. I owe him everything." Then, his voice choking, he raised his eyes toward the rafters and added, "Thank you for saving my life."

Danny Rohrbough could have chosen safety. He chose leadership instead. He demonstrated boldness, character, and a servant's heart. He held the door so that others could walk through and live.

The world is a dangerous place. That is why we need more young people like Danny Rohrbough. The world needs young people who are willing to lead, willing to serve their generation, willing to boldly stand at the crossroads of history and hold open the door to the future.

That is the challenge before us. As parents, coaches, teachers, and mentors, we have the task of inspiring and motivating a generation to take Danny Rohrbough's place at the door so that they can lead our world to hope, to life, to the future.

So turn the page with me. Let's learn together how to change our world by changing lives. Let's discover what it means to coach our kids to be leaders.

| 2 |

Leadership Training
Starts at Home

My seventeen-year-old son, Alan, is the youngest of our nineteen kids. Born in Brazil, Alan attends a Christian high school in the Orlando area. He's a terrific kid—friendly, outgoing, and good-natured. He has only one problem, but it's a biggie: Alan is a cutup, a disrupter. He doesn't mean to cause problems—he just can't seem to help himself. It's a good week if I get just three phone calls from the school about his behavior.

Again and again, I have had to sit him down and say, "Alan, you need to be a leader. Your teachers and your principal tell me that you have leadership potential, and I know you have leadership potential. We all want you to be a leader, and we know you can do it."

"But," Alan invariably replied, "I don't *want* to be a leader."

I don't have to ask him why he doesn't because the reason is obvious: A leader can't be a cutup. A leader has to set a good example for the other young people in the class. A leader has to lead all the time, not just when he feels like it.

Just when I was beginning to think I would never get through to him, something changed. Alan came home from school with exciting news—

so exciting that he looked as if he was about to burst. "Guess what?" he said. "My coach wants me to be the captain of the basketball team!"

"Wow!" I said. "That's terrific, Alan! Congratulations! I'm proud of you! Hey, do you know what this means?"

Alan looked at me with startled eyes. "No. What does it mean?"

"What do you have to do to be the captain of the team?" I asked.

He gulped. "You mean, I have to *lead*?"

"That's right," I said.

In a high, stunned voice he said, "You mean, I'm a *leader*?"

I said, "That's right, Alan. You're a leader."

Amazed, he repeated it to himself: "I'm a *leader*!"

I can't say that the calls from school have stopped altogether, but I have definitely seen a change in Alan. He has truly grown into this big, new leadership role his coach has given him—and he *likes* it. He is getting accolades and affirmation that he never got before as a cutup and a disrupter—and he likes all of that, too.

Leadership training begins at home. Though every youngster needs many leadership trainers, including teachers, coaches, mentors, Sunday school teachers, and youth group advisors, the earliest and most influential leadership training comes from Mom and Dad.

■ Preparing Kids for a Life of Leadership

John Maxwell's name is synonymous with leadership. The author of more than twenty books, including the *New York Times* best-seller *The 21 Irrefutable Laws of Leadership*, John has devoted most of his life to researching and proclaiming leadership principles through writing and speaking. Born in Ohio, the son of a pastor, John decided at the tender age of three that he wanted to be a pastor like his father. At seventeen, he began his preparation for ministry at the Circleville (Ohio) Bible College.

John began his ministry at a tiny rural church in Indiana, and he went on to serve other, larger churches. Along the way, he became fascinated with how leaders lead—what are the ingredients of leadership, how one learns to become a leader, and so forth. In 1985, John founded an organization called The INJOY Group, devoted to the study and dissemination of leadership principles. In 1995, he resigned as pastor of a church that had tripled in size under his leadership, and he devoted himself full-time to INJOY. Today, he reaches and teaches millions of people every year through his books, audio and video products, and personal appearances.

I asked John Maxwell about the source of his fascination with leadership. "My parents," he replied. "I learned about leadership in the home. My father believed in personal growth. He practiced personal growth and leadership on a daily basis, and he planned and taught personal growth and leadership for my brother, my sister, and me.

"When we were little, Mom and Dad read to us constantly. As we got older, we read a lot. At each stage of our development, my parents introduced us to new books. By the time I was in the third grade, I was required to read for thirty minutes every day. At first, I read stories from the Bible. But as I grew, my parents gave me other books to read, such as *The Power of Positive Thinking* by Norman Vincent Peale and *How to Win Friends and Influence People* by Dale Carnegie.

"My parents picked the books, and they paid me part of my allowance to read them. Each night at dinner during our family time, we discussed our reading. We were encouraged to share not only the facts that we had learned but also our opinions. As we got older, we were allowed to pick some of our own books to read with Dad's approval. I read every weekday until I graduated from high school."

Candace Long is a singer, songwriter, producer, entrepreneur, advertising executive, and playwright (author of the original musical *A Time to Dance*). She is also a once-divorced, once-widowed mom. To sum it all up, Candace Long is a leader. She has been a leading force in the entertainment industry for creating more behind-the-camera jobs for women. In 1993, she founded Quadra Entertainment, a company with a mission to create film and television scripts that emphasize roles for women.

Candace told me, "My parents always instilled in me the notion that I could do anything I set out to do. Their affirmation and confidence in me were the keys to developing my own confidence. My peers recognized that I didn't follow the crowd easily—I liked to chart my own course. When I was young, I noticed that my siblings and younger cousins always looked to me to lead them in activities. Throughout school, I was called on because I had a great sense of responsibility and a conscientious approach to life.

"I wasn't so much a take-charge, follow-me sort of leader. My temperament, which is more understated, takes a while to be noticed. But once it is, people have always looked to me for leadership."

As a parent, Candace Long is encouraging the leadership qualities of her son. "My son has an assertive personality, which is a good quality in a leader," she explained. "But like most personality traits, that assertiveness can have its downside. I have tried to affirm his God-given leadership gifts while also encouraging him to be sensitive to others. More than anything, I have prayed for him and I've encouraged him to read good books. After he read Dale Carnegie's classic *How to Win Friends and Influence People*, he said, 'Mom, this is the best book I've ever read!'

"My son strayed away from his leadership goals for a while when he was in high school. It was a tough time for me and for him—I went through both a divorce and widowhood in the space of a few years. The hurt of those experiences left their mark on him. But with time and prayer, he has been turning around and renewing his interest in becoming a leader. It's a thrill to watch his leadership knowledge and confidence grow."

During the writing of this book, I had the opportunity to sit down with Ericka Dunlap, Miss America of 2004 and a former Miss Florida. The subject of our conversation: parents and young leaders. "My parents were the key to my leadership position," Ericka said. "They were supportive of me as a young girl. I entered my first pageant when I was six. My mom encouraged me but never pushed me. I played soccer in seventh grade and I wasn't any good, but my mom was there to support me all the way.

"These days, I meet a lot of kids who say, 'Ericka, my parents don't come to my games or activities. They're real busy, and they don't have time for my events.' Kids take away a message that other pursuits and activities are more important than that recital or concert or Little League game. Kids need to know they are number one on their parents' list of priorities. It's vital that parents know what their children are doing, and that they are actively involved in their kids' lives. When kids know their parents care, their confidence and self-esteem soar."

You may be thinking, *I don't have time to go to all my kids' activities! Pat, you just don't know what it's like having this many kids!* Well, how many kids are we talking about? A pair? Two pair? Three of a kind? I'll bet my full house beats anything you've got.

You see, in the Williamses' household, we have nineteen kids, so I've been to a lot of games, recitals, and pageants. In fact, I'm willing to bet I've seen more youth sporting events than any other dad in history. Most of my kids are grown now, but from 1980 to 1998, it seemed that about half my waking hours were spent on the bleachers at Little League games. Every morning at breakfast I'd hear the same question: "Dad, are you coming to my game tonight?" If I can do it, you can do it.

There is an ancient biblical admonition: "Train a child in the way he should go, and when he is old he will not turn from it" (Prov. 22:6). In other words, training must start early. If you want to raise young people to be leaders, you must begin teaching and modeling leadership from the very earliest years of their lives.

■ The Making of a "Renaissance Jock"

My parents began preparing me for the leadership life I now lead from my very earliest years. My dad, Jim Williams, gave me my first baseball glove when I was three years old. He took me to my first big-league game in 1947 when I was seven years old—the Philadelphia Athletics hosting the Cleveland Indians in a doubleheader at Shibe Park. I gobbled down hot dogs and yelled my head off and had a great time. That day, I was hooked on sports for life. I left that park with a vision of a life in sports.

Throughout my boyhood, I hardly went anywhere without a bat, ball, and two baseball gloves. Why two gloves? Because I might run into a kid who didn't have his glove with him. Wherever I went, I wanted to be prepared for a game of catch.

I marked off my strike zone with tape on the full-length mirror in my room, and I practiced my swing in front of that mirror. Once, my dog got in the way of my swing, and I cracked him in the head with the bat! Poor Happy was never quite the same after that.

Mom and Dad were baseball fans. If I wasn't playing catch with Dad, then my mother, Ellen Williams, filled in. I had set up two rocks in the front yard, one for the pitcher's mound, the other for home plate. One day when I was seven, I was practicing pitching with my mom. I was at the pitching rock, and Mom was in her batting stance at the home plate rock. I unleashed my fastball, and Mom swung the bat, connecting with a loud crack. She lined it straight back at me, nailing me square in the eye. I hit the ground as if I'd been shot. Everything went black.

Well, Mom thought she had killed me, but I recovered. Years later, I kidded her and said, "I should have gotten back on my feet and thrown you a brushback pitch. You were really crowding the plate!" But it wasn't funny that day. I ended up with a black eye and a splitting headache.

The important thing is that Mom and Dad encouraged my mania for sports—and sports provided many opportunities for young people to learn the fundamentals of leadership. Mom and Dad used my passion for sports as a way of teaching me all sorts of life lessons. My dad was a teacher and coach at a private all-grade school. Some of my earliest memories were of being around my dad in the locker room or on the bench by the field. I watched him coach, I listened to his motivational speeches, and I absorbed his values and his leadership example. My mom talked sports with me, played catch with me in the yard, and used those times to teach me lessons about life.

Through sports, I first learned (in a rudimentary way) about the seven keys of leadership. I gained a sense of what it means to have a *vision* for the future. Coaches give their teams a vision of winning games and celebrating championship seasons. I learned the importance of *communication* with your teammates and the value of good *people skills*—skills for resolving conflicts and building team spirit.

Through sports, I learned about *character* qualities that build trust and instill confidence—a strong work ethic, a humble spirit, a commitment to honesty and integrity, and more. I learned the importance of *competence* (the ability to compete and complete tasks with excellence) and *boldness* (the willingness to take risks in order to succeed). Most of all, my early involvement in team sports taught me the power of an attitude of *servanthood*—success takes place not as we feed our egos, but as we put the good of the team above ourselves and willingly serve one another on the team.

I even learned how to read and do arithmetic from baseball. I practically inhaled the sports pages of the *New York Times*. I learned math by checking the box scores, keeping tabs on batting averages, and studying the won-lost columns. I also devoured the stats and player bios printed on the backs of baseball cards.

But my parents didn't want to raise a sports geek. They wanted me to be a well-rounded human being—and they wanted me to be a leader in any arena of life I would ever be involved in. Mom exposed me to many positive influences, from Scouting to the arts. Mom often took my sisters and me to New York and Philadelphia to visit museums, attend concerts, go to the zoo, and watch Broadway shows. I didn't have a lick of musical talent, but to this day, I can enjoy and intelligently discuss everything from Gilbert and Sullivan to the whole Broadway scene. My friend Jerry Jenkins once called me a "renaissance jock," and I think that's a good description of the well-rounded way my parents raised me.

Mom was a fanatic about reading, and I vividly recall sitting with her while she read aloud to me when I was a little boy. I've been a compulsive reader ever since. In fact, I would say that my entire life has been shaped by good books. The power of a book is amazing. When you open a book, you open the mind and heart of another human being, and you can't help being changed by the encounter.

My life was changed at the age of seven by one of the first books I ever read, *Pop Warner's Book for Boys*, a book my dad gave me. It was filled with advice for young athletes: caring for your body, maintaining a winner's attitude, playing the game of football, and being a team leader. I found it to be not only a great book about the game of football, but also a foundational book about the game of life. The lessons I learned from that book at such an early age continue to reverberate in my life.

Leaders are readers. A young person who doesn't read can't truly lead. As parents, we have a duty to our kids to model and teach good reading habits.

■ Parents: A Child's First Teachers, Mentors, and Coaches

My mom and dad were leaders.

Soon after my dad's return from World War II, my parents were expecting their fourth child. I already had two sisters, so I was praying for a brother. But on a cold and snowy day in February 1947, a third girl was born to our family. Her name was Mary Ellen.

It was immediately obvious to the doctors and my parents that something was wrong with Mary Ellen. She was born mentally retarded due to a condition then called mongoloidism. Today this condition is called Down's syndrome, and we know that it is caused by an irregular number of chromosomes. In the 1940s and 1950s, families with a mentally retarded child felt stigmatized. It was as if the parents had somehow failed in the biological process.

At that time, there was very little help for families like ours. There were no counselors or agencies to offer support and information. Very little research was being done about the medical and social issues of kids with special needs.

But as I look back, I realize that my mom and dad led the way. They got out in front of this issue and began fund-raising and educating the community about the problems faced by kids who had mental retardation. They talked about the issue in media interviews. My dad, with the help of Phillies owner Bob Carpenter, started the Delaware All-Star High School Football Game to raise funds for research. The first game was held in 1956, and to this day, almost fifty years later, the event (now called the Blue-Gold Game) is held annually to benefit the Delaware Foundation for Retarded Children.

My mom continued to be active in mental health causes well into her eighties, as well as be a leader in her church. Mom and Dad were leaders in the Democratic Party in Delaware. I remember how they walked the precincts for Adlai Stevenson in 1952 and 1956. Throughout my boyhood, our house was a beehive of leadership activity and a home to committee meetings, board meetings, and planning sessions for the various causes that my parents supported.

My parents, Jim and Ellen Williams, continually practiced leadership. Their example established in my mind the notion that leadership is simply something that we do. It is expected. It is a part of our lives. Mom and Dad didn't spend much time preaching leadership to me—they were too busy *doing* it. So I absorbed their example, and leadership became a natural part of my life.

How important are parents (or early caregivers) in preparing young people to become leaders? When we look closely at the early lives of leaders, we find that the influence of parents is indispensable to children's understanding of the leadership role. Children look up to their parents as their primary examples and role models. Children want to please their parents and win their approval.

When we have children under our care, their minds, emotions, and futures are entrusted to us. It's a heavy responsibility. Our influence on them from their earliest years will shape the course of their entire lives.

I asked leaders from the business, sports, education, and organizational arenas to share with me their stories and insights about how their parents prepared them to lead, and how they are preparing their own children to lead. Here are some of those stories and insights:

General Tommy Franks, who led our armed forces in Iraq in 2003, told me that his father taught him by example. "My dad was a quiet, thoughtful man," he said, "barely a high school graduate. We lived in a trailer house, and my dad was a mechanic who worked six days a week. He never had a rocking chair on his front porch. My dad's main message to me was this: 'You do what you want to do.' I learned from my dad that you don't need to talk a lot to lead. We would go quail hunting out in West Texas when I was a kid. It would be December and January, and the cold wind was whipping around wildly. My dad would be the first one out of the truck, maybe fifteen different times, and everyone else would follow him."

Cameron Strang, a young publishing executive in Orlando, told me that "leadership skills are instilled, not inherited. It starts with your parents. My mom and dad encouraged me to take risks and not to be afraid of failure. I want to pass along the same philosophy to my children."

Former Phillies pitcher Dickie Noles was my teammate at a recent Phillies Dream Week event in Clearwater, Florida. If you don't know what Dream Week is all about, sportswriter Bob Andelman described it as a place where "up to a hundred doctors, lawyers, entrepreneurs, and lifelong fans with an average age of forty-two pay $3,300 each to spend seven days in the presence of aging baseball stars, playing ball, over-using dormant muscles, and chortling over endless bawdy stories and tall tales." Well, I don't go in much for bawdy stories, so Dickie and I just sat on the bench for a while and talked about kids and leadership.

"Setting the right example is the key to developing young leaders,"

Dickie said. "I have twin boys who are now fifteen, and they are pretty good athletes. Whenever I hear a coach or some other parent tell me that my boys are respectful and well behaved, I feel like I am doing my job. Those two boys are not mine—they belong to God. I believe that God has entrusted them to me until they are old enough to make it on their own. For the time I have them with me, I'm responsible for teaching them everything I can about how to live a successful, effective life. How I model leadership to them now will largely determine how well they will do in life."

B. J. Armstrong, a former NBA guard, told me, "As a leader, you can only give to others what's been given to you. If you have seen examples of leadership, you can then give it to others. My parents did that for me."

Matt Guokas, broadcaster and former head coach of the Orlando Magic, recalls that his dad was a role model, both as a basketball player and as a great human being. "My dad, Matt Guokas, Sr., was a former player with the Philadelphia Warriors," he told me. "He would show up at our practices and games, and he'd talk to the team and show us the proper way to play. I looked up to him and wanted to be like my dad. As a result of an automobile accident, he had an artificial leg, but he used it to his advantage in coaching us kids. He'd be at the practices and be the permanent center. He'd give us his fancy passes, always feeding us the ball, never taking a shot himself, so that we would learn about ball movement, court awareness, shooting, and teamwork."

Bill Bradley is a former basketball star who went on to become a United States senator. When he was growing up in Crystal City, Missouri, his parents gave him the strength to not be influenced by the crowd. "In fact," he told me, "I would go against what the crowd wanted and just say no. Pretty soon *they* would be following *me*. My parents had created the context in which I could say no.

"One summer as a teenager, I played baseball for an American Legion team. We were in a tournament down in the boot heel of Missouri, and we stopped at a restaurant. There were a couple of black players on the team, and the restaurant refused to serve them. I stood up and said, 'Let's get out of here.' Everyone followed me out the front door."

Dick Vermeil, head coach of the Kansas City Chiefs, said, "My dad ran a garage that was twenty-five yards from our house. I couldn't get away from his presence. I was constantly aware that he was evaluating my conduct—though not in an overbearing or overly critical way. I knew that he had certain expectations of me and he wanted me to grow up to become a certain kind of person. He would often praise something I did, and it was exhilarating to get that positive comment from him. Whenever I'd leave the house, he'd say, 'Remember, you're a Vermeil, so live up to it.' That was Dad's way of giving me a standard of integrity to aspire to, and it gave me a strong sense of responsibility and accountability for my actions."

Matt Certo is the president and cofounder of WebSolvers, Inc., an Internet design company. He started his company with a single computer on his dorm room desk, and it has grown into a $2 million business with more than a dozen employees. Asked where he learned the fundamentals of leadership, Matt Certo gave all the credit to his mom and dad.

"I remember my parents instilling a 'be a leader, not a follower' ethic in me," Matt stated. "I'm twenty-seven now, but I remember hearing that line as early as kindergarten. Though I now realize that the world needs followers as well as leaders, in my young mind, I saw the delineation between 'leader' and 'follower' as the equivalent of 'right' versus 'wrong.' That's how strongly my parents encouraged a leadership mentality in me. It oriented my mind toward independent thinking and away from following the crowd.

"My dad, Sam Certo, coached my basketball teams. He had me play the point guard position, and he explained my role as the person who (*a*) brought the ball up the floor and (*b*) served as the coach's voice on the floor. I knew that it was my job to get the team into the offense, to recognize when we were off track, and to influence my teammates to follow suit. In my mind, I was taking the steps necessary to winning basketball games. In Dad's mind, I was developing as a leader.

"One of the lessons Dad taught me through the game of basketball involved the responsibility I had as a leader. In one game, I fouled out—and I didn't like the call! I threw a fit with the referee. Dad—my coach—took me aside and really let me know how I had blown it as a leader. Most important, he used that incident as a turning point in my understanding of my role as a leader. He said, 'When you get what you think is a bad call from a referee, you have a choice. You can embrace your responsibility as a leader and submit to the referee's decision—or you can lose your cool. But if you lose your cool, you also lose the respect of others—and you ultimately lose your influence on them. At that point, you cease to be a leader.'

"Dad was building a foundation for leadership in my life from day one. He was continually pointing out leadership examples to me, both positive and negative examples. Day after day, he explained to me the implications of constructive and destructive leadership behaviors.

"There are three things parents must do in order to instill leadership ability in their children. First: Parents should take time to understand what their children are passionate about. My father used basketball to teach leadership principles to me. Other parents might use their child's love of science or writing.

"Second: Parents should take time to understand a child's daily challenges, then extract leadership lessons from those challenges. That's what my father did in that basketball game where I fouled out. He showed me that I didn't just have an attitude issue or a behavior issue—I had a leadership issue, and my attitude and behavior were undermining my leadership.

"Third: Parents should point to daily examples of leadership—both positive and negative examples. This can take place by pointing out a positive or negative leadership role model on TV or in a public setting.

"I value group efforts, team efforts, because it's all I know. I was born into a big family, so teamwork is my element, and I love it. In my family everything was shared. Each child in the family did not have his or her own bathroom, TV, or phone. Do you know what it's like to stand in line behind eight other people to use the bathroom? What about one phone line for six talkative girls? I was last in the pecking order, so I rarely got to watch what I wanted on TV and I never sat in the front seat of our car until I was much older. I had to share a full-size bed with two of my sisters who always got all the covers.

"But that's how I learned the value of teamwork. I'm grateful for all of those experiences because they taught me the meaning of such team concepts as sacrifice and loyalty and cooperation. My parents made the greatest sacrifices of all. Watching them made more of an impact on my life than anything. I learned that leaders are servants—self-sacrificing servants.

"My parents are people of a strong faith. The most important thing to them was seeing to it that their children enter the kingdom of heaven. How they lived showed me how to be like Jesus Christ.

"My parents also exemplified an incredible work ethic—which, again, is a crucial part of being a great leader. My mother never allowed me to quit anything—she wanted me to be a finisher. I have never met anyone like her. My dad is a man of integrity, discipline, and genuine humility. My parents are both true servants of Christ. Through their example, they introduced me to the greatest coach and leader of all, Jesus Christ. Ultimately, He is the one I want to be like."

Dan Wood, executive director of the National Christian College Athletic Association, talked about his youth: "I was the youngest of five children raised in a country pastor's home. I didn't see myself as a leader, but I was nurtured and taught to be responsible. My earliest recollection of seeing myself in a leadership role involved leading in various situations at church and Sunday school. I served as a class secretary, which meant collecting the offering and taking roll each Sunday. I enjoyed the responsibility, and I inherited that role with each class promotion.

"Later, as a teen, I served as president of our youth group. Outside of church, I was the captain of various sports teams and usually ended up in a leadership role at summer camp. As I look back, I think that term *ended up* seems to follow those whom others see as leaders. I didn't seek out leadership roles in my youth—I ended up in those roles. People seemed to see leadership qualities in me long before I saw them in myself, and long before I ever sought to become a leader. So I believe it's important for parents and other adults to affirm leadership abilities in young people so that those young people will catch a vision of themselves as leaders.

"Dad and Mom were my first leadership coaches. They encouraged me to practice my budding leadership skills. They instilled in me a love for Jesus Christ—who, of course, is the greatest leader the world has ever known. I committed my life to Jesus as a young child, and to this day He continues to lead me and shape my life more than any other role model I know.

"Everything I have ever learned about leadership has its basis in the lessons I learned from my parents in the home. Everything I've learned along the way from teachers, pastors, speakers, authors, and coaches is just corollary—it reminds me and confirms everything my parents taught me during those early years. To this day, whenever someone compliments or recognizes some leadership ability of mine, my response has always been, 'I'll tell my parents you said that'—or, since my dad passed away in 1997, 'I'll tell my mom you said that.' Everything I have ever done as a leader in any capacity is a tribute not to me, but to the two godly people who raised me."

"The first people we emulate and learn from are our parents," said Steve Alford, head basketball coach at the University of Iowa. "Parents are crucial shapers of young leaders because they have the eyes and ears of their young people on a daily basis. When I was a boy, I constantly watched my father. He was a high school coach at the time, so I saw him lead his team every day. I would watch him set up practice plans, organize the time and place, and then I would watch the players execute the plan he created. Most children emulate what they see and hear as they watch their parents in real-life situations, so parents need to be aware of the kind of example they set."

Of all the influences on a child's life, parents rank number one. Parents are a child's first teachers, mentors, and coaches.

■ Building the Confidence to Lead

The essence of leadership is confidence. When a leader exudes boldness and confidence, the confidence of the entire team or organization soars. So our job as parents is to raise confident children. We must raise them to believe that they can achieve anything they set their minds on.

Mike Gannaway, chairman and CEO of Pillowtex, Inc., agreed: "Self-confidence is the first critical area of leadership. Confidence is contagious. If a leader is confident, it lifts the spirits and abilities of the entire organization or team. I'm grateful that my parents first gave me the room to gain confidence in myself. The confidence I learned in the home became a foundation that other mentors in my life—my teachers, my first employer—could build on. Adults should encourage young people to gain confidence in themselves and to value the skills they have to do certain things well."

Many times, we parents think we are being involved when we are actually being intrusive—and our intrusiveness gets in the way of building our kids' confidence. Larry McCarthy, associate professor at the Stillman School of Business Management at Seton Hall University, said, "Parents can build confidence in young people by giving them responsibility—then letting them rise or fall on their own. Too many times I have seen parents get involved in their children's activities to a point where they are not really needed or wanted. They are smothering and stifling their kids. Go away, Mom and Dad! Kids learn confidence by doing it themselves.

"I was born in Cork, Ireland, and I came from a culture and an era where parents allowed the volunteer scoutmaster to run the Boy Scouts; they allowed the volunteer coaches to run the basketball club or the rugby team. I am amazed by the involvement of American parents in *everything* their kids do. While it's good that parents take an interest in their kids' activities, I actually find it quite appalling and off-putting to have so many parents around everything their kids do, often intruding and taking over and preventing kids from developing their own skills and self-confidence. One of the best things parents can do to build their children's confidence is to cut the apron strings and let kids sink or swim on their own."

Most kids have a great deal of inertia. In physics, *inertia* is defined as "the tendency of an object to remain at rest." Objects—whether bricks or young people—tend to remain pretty much as they are unless an outside force acts on them. Our job as parents is to be the outside force that overcomes our kids' inertia.

No great deeds were ever achieved inside a comfort zone. So as parents, we need to prod, encourage, nag, and shove our kids out of their comfort zones. We have to help them overcome their inertia so that they will gain the confidence and the spirit of adventure that all true leaders have.

Joe Dean, Jr., is director of athletics at Birmingham Southern College. He told me, "My father was a born leader who inspired me to step out of the box, so to speak—to get out of my comfort zone and strive for success in all areas of life. He often told me that he was the captain of every team he ever played on, and that message inspired me to want to be a leader as well.

"While serving as the athletics director at Louisiana State University, my dad had to hire a football coach—a moment of decision that created statewide interest and enormous pressure from the fans and the media. His statement to the press was, 'I was born to make this decision.' That was his attitude about his leadership responsibilities, and his strong, confident attitude has been a major influence on me in my role today as a community leader and athletics director."

Just as Joe Dean's father encouraged him to "step out of the box," the comfort zone where most kids are content to remain, Joe is now encouraging his own children to take that step. "I have always felt that the most important thing parents can do for their children," he said, "is to put them in educational and extracurricular environments where their children can flourish. My wife and I always watched very closely the friends and associates our children developed; we encouraged their friendships with other children who were well-motivated young people with good values.

"We also required our children to get involved in at least one extracurricular activity. We didn't care if it was sports, music, dance, church youth activities, or whatever—we just felt that involvement in a group or team would enhance their chances to develop confidence and leadership skills.

"When we lived in Orlando, I strongly encouraged my daughter Leslie to take gymnastics. She was about eight years old, and she complained about going all the time. She didn't want to step outside that box. But I would pick her up at the gym at the end of the day and rave about the progress she was making on the balance beam or tumbling or some other skill.

"One day, Leslie informed me that her gymnastics coach wanted her to compete in a gymnastics meet in Orlando. She didn't want to, but I cheered her on and finally she agreed—but under one condition: We, her parents, could not attend. I said, 'Leslie, that's out of the question. Your mother and I are paying a lot of money for those gymnastics lessons. We deserve to go and watch you perform at the meet.' She said, 'Well, okay, you can come—but you are *not* going to videotape it!' I said, 'Okay.'

"On the day of the meet, after we dropped Leslie off at the gym, I asked my wife, 'Did you bring the camcorder?' She said, 'Yes, I have it right here.' How could we not tape her first big meet? We proceeded into the gym to watch and videotape this big occasion in our child's life. I walked all over the gym that day, following Leslie's every move with the camcorder.

"After the meet was over and Leslie had her collection of blue and red ribbons for winning various events, she rushed over to me and said excitedly, 'Did you get a video of me on the balance beam?'

"The moral of this story is that sometimes you have to push kids to step out of the box, to move out of their comfort zone and into the adventure of life. Once they take that step, they realize how exciting it is to discover what they can do. Every time they take that step, their confidence grows."

WebSolvers founder Matt Certo summed up the issue of confidence building this way: "Parents should continually nurture leadership traits in their children by building their confidence and encouraging them to act boldly and take risks. My dad was a great confidence builder. By the time I went to college, he had me thinking that I could truly accomplish things that others thought I couldn't.

"When I was nineteen and I told my dad I wanted to start a business, he immediately looked for ways to support me. When I mentioned this dream to other people, they told me I was wasting my time, but my dad told me I could accomplish anything I committed myself to achieving.

"The White House invited me to visit President Bush last summer, which was quite an honor. Dad pulled me aside before I boarded the plane. He could see that I was extremely nervous about the trip. He told me to take a deep breath and recognize the fact that I *belonged* where I was going. That changed my whole perspective.

"I had planned to take my camera with me to the event, but after Dad's comments, I opted to leave my camera in the hotel room. If I had taken my camera, I would have gone with the mind-set of an observer. Dad helped me think of myself not as an observer, but as a participant—as someone who belonged there. When I saw myself on C-SPAN a few days later, I was struck by how calm and relaxed I looked. That sense of calm was the result of the confidence that Dad's words had instilled in me."

Young people need many teachers, mentors, and trainers along the way as they grow to become leaders, but parents lay the foundation for every experience that follows. The strongest foundation we can lay is a foundation of confidence and faith—faith in God and faith in themselves.

■ No Telling How Far It Will Take Them

Rich DeVos is my boss and my friend. He was born in 1926, three years before the start of the Great Depression. Rich's parents, Simon and Ethel DeVos, raised him to have a positive and proactive attitude toward life. "We grew up poor," Rich recalled, "but we were certainly no poorer than most other people in the depression. During the week, my father sacked flour in a grocer's back room, and on Saturdays he sold socks and underwear in a men's store.

"My father raised me to be a leader. He told me, 'Own your own business, son. That's the only way to control your own future. Own it, work hard at it, set high goals for yourself, and never give up, no matter what obstacles come your way.'"

Rich DeVos took his father's advice to heart. He not only owned his own business, but along with his boyhood friend and business partner, Jay Van Andel, Rich built a business empire. Rich and Jay founded the Amway Corporation, which is now one of the Alticor family of companies. Today, Alticor does business in more than eighty countries and rings up nearly $7 billion in sales every year. Rich is also the principal owner of the organization I work for, the Orlando Magic.

And it all began when Rich's father told him, "Own your own business, son." The training of young leaders begins in the home—and there's no telling how far it will take them!

| 3 |

The Nature of Leadership

Picture this: You're twenty years old. The Navy hands you a boat with a crew of twenty, saying, "You're in charge now. You're responsible to complete your mission and keep these twenty men alive." With that, the Navy sends you into battle. You are kicked around by typhoons. Enemy airplanes dive at your boat in waves of suicide attacks. You are shelled by artillery from the shore. And you ask yourself, "Can I really do this? Am I really a leader?" That was the question young Jack McCloskey asked himself in April 1945.

Jack is the former general manager of the Detroit Pistons and currently a scout and consultant with the Toronto Raptors. "I was in the South Pacific," he told me, "the twenty-year-old skipper of the LCT 1326, a tank landing craft. Our job was to hit the beach and unload vehicles as part of the invasion force that was liberating Japanese-held islands in the Pacific. I had very little experience in handling a Navy ship, so I had a meeting with the crew of twenty men, plus my new executive officer, who knew far less about commanding ships than I did. I explained to my men that I had to learn from their experience, and I assured them that I was going to get them all home safely. They were magnificent, and we had an excellent team chemistry. Even though they were my teachers, they still respected my authority.

"We took part in two invasions. The first was the assault on Okinawa. It was pretty rough. We got battered by several typhoons along the way, plus we also had to dodge kamikazes—Japanese suicide aircraft. I had to make some very tough decisions during that invasion."

As an amateur historian, I know that Jack McCloskey's description of the Okinawa invasion is a considerable understatement. It was, in fact, the largest amphibious invasion of war in the Pacific, and it used more ships, troops, vehicles, bombs, and artillery than any other operation in the war against Japan. More people were killed in the battle of Okinawa than were killed in the atomic bombings of Hiroshima and Nagasaki combined. Thirty-four Allied ships were sunk, mostly by kamikaze attacks, and 763 Allied aircraft were lost. Picture twenty-year-old Jack McCloskey commanding his LCT through that man-made storm of death and destruction.

"The second invasion we took part in," Jack explained, "was at Ie Shima, a small island northwest of Okinawa—the island where war correspondent Ernie Pyle was killed. As we were preparing to hit Ie Shima, the oldest member of our crew asked to meet with me. He was forty years old, and his problem was that he believed he could not go through another invasion. We had already survived several typhoons and dodged a lot of kamikazes. He felt like we were pushing our luck, and he just wanted to get back alive to his small Texas farm.

"Here I was, half his age, and I was reassuring him that we would make it. I told him I would get him home as soon as possible. After I told him that, he said, 'Skipper, you got us through some tough times. I know you'll get us through this next invasion.' His trust in me gave me a lot of confidence. It assured me that I was their leader and their friend. We all made it through."

■ What Is Leadership?

Leadership is the ability to achieve goals through people. Leaders get things done—not through their own effort, but through the combined efforts of people. A military leader achieves victory on the battlefield through his soldiers. A coach achieves victory on the athletic field through the players on the team. A political leader achieves a visionary goal through the people of his or her administration.

To measure the effectiveness of a leader, don't look at the leader. Look at the followers. Look at the organization. Look at the results. Ultimately, it doesn't matter whether the leader is articulate, charming, or busy all the time. In the final analysis, the only question that truly matters is this: Does that leader achieve results through people?

José Abreu, secretary of transportation for the state of Florida, told me, "Whether I'm leading the Florida Department of Transportation or coaching a team of Little Leaguers, my task is essentially the same. My job is to shape consensus and build team unity so that the team can achieve its goals.

"I used to coach my son's Little League team in Hialeah. It was a team of overachievers. Nobody thought our team had the talent to go undefeated, yet there was one season in which we won every game we played. During one of the games that season, I overheard a parent of one of the boys on the opposing team. 'Look at those kids!' he said, referring to our team. 'Look at the way they follow instructions! I don't know if I'd want my son to be on his team. They look more like synchronized sewing machines than real people.'

"That parent meant it as a disparaging remark. He saw the kids on our team as robots. But they weren't robots. They were a team! They took direction; they were coordinated; they acted as one. I took that comment as a compliment to my ability to get our team to win games when no one thought they could."

A leader gets things done through people. Does this mean the people in the organization or team feel used or manipulated? Do they feel as if they are being treated like robots? Absolutely not! People admire leaders who challenge and direct them to achieve great things. It's an exhilarating experience to be a part of a team effort, to make progress toward an envisioned goal, and to know that you have a leader who is taking you to that goal.

On the playground, in the classroom, in the hallways, on the court or playing field, in the youth group, on the streets and in the alleyways, young people are looking for young leaders to follow. Who is the young leader they will find and take their cues from? Will it be the young student government leader who also leads the girls' Bible study at Starbucks on Tuesday nights? Will it be the fifteen-year-old snowboarding champ who competes in the Extreme Olympics, then talks to youth rallies about faith and morality?

Or will it be the angry young man with a trench coat on his back, a grudge in his heart, and a closet full of guns and ammunition? Or will it be the gang leader who is looking for young hearts and minds to follow him down a dead-end street of drug abuse and drive-by shootings?

Young people want to be led. What kind of leader will they find? We need to raise up young leaders with a positive vision and the skills to communicate that vision, with good character and good people skills, with boldness and competent ability, and with servantlike hearts. If we do not train a generation of the right kind of leaders, we will lose this generation to the wrong kind of leaders.

■ Formal versus Informal Leadership

There are two basic kinds of leadership—formal and informal. Formal leadership refers to an official position of authority. Informal leadership refers to an intangible but very real sense of authority and command that is exercised by a person with leadership ability, whether that person is in an official position of authority. Ideally, authority and position should be given to people who also possess recognized leadership ability. When there is a mismatch between the formal leadership and the informal leadership in a team or organization, the result can be destructive.

We see an example of this principle in the motion picture *The Caine Mutiny*. Aboard a Navy ship, the *Caine*, the formal leader is Captain Queeg, played by Humphrey Bogart. Queeg is eccentric, demanding, vain, and dictatorial. He tells his crew: "There's the right way, the wrong way, the Navy way, and my way. Do it my way, and we'll get along just fine." The crew, however, doesn't trust Queeg as a leader. The sailors suspect that he is unstable, even psychotic. He focuses all of his attention on meaningless details (untucked shirttails and missing strawberries) while making huge errors in judgment that nearly sink the ship.

Having lost faith in the formal leader of the ship, the crew rallies around an informal leader, Lieutenant Maryk, played by Van Johnson. The sailors see Maryk as a man of sound judgment, stability, duty, loyalty, character, and competence. In short, he has all of the leadership qualities that Captain Queeg seems to lack. The result: During a storm, when Captain Queeg appears to lose his nerve, the crew supports Maryk and mutinies against Captain Queeg.

Though the scenario in *The Caine Mutiny* is an extreme case, clashes between formal and informal leadership take place all the time. In sports teams, a certain player with strong natural leadership abilities sometimes challenges the formal leadership of the coach. In churches, a layman with recognized leadership ability sometimes arises and challenges the formal leadership of the pastor. In a military unit, an experienced, battle-scarred sergeant occasionally challenges the formal leadership of an academy-trained captain. A mismatch between formal and informal leadership usually produces chaos, confusion, and conflict.

People can tell when a formal leader lacks the ability to lead. Given the choice between an incompetent formal leader and a competent informal leader, people will follow the competent informal leader every time. So it is important that we put people with authentic leadership ability into formal leadership positions.

Michael Means, CEO of Health First, Inc., told me, "My first real leadership opportunity came through the military. After joining the U.S. Army Reserve in 1971, I was sent to basic training at Fort Lewis, Washington. On the first day of basic training, I was selected as a platoon guide, probably because I was six feet four inches and had a degree in business administration from the University of Florida. I am fairly confident that my selection had nothing to do with any inherent leadership skills on my part. Like most opportunities, the mantle of leadership was simply thrust upon me.

"I learned through that experience that a position of leadership is a privilege, a responsibility, and an honor that should never be taken for granted or abused. Authentic leadership is not the result of having a job title or having a place on a formal organizational chart. It's what you do with that job title that matters. A leadership position must be earned, and it must be re-earned every day. If we fail to earn it, it can be quickly taken away."

Fay Vincent, the former commissioner of baseball, told me: "I was fifteen or sixteen and a student at Hotchless Prep School. One day the headmaster said to me, 'Fay, the boys will follow you and want to follow you, but you are not a leader.' No one had ever said that to me and it really hit me hard. From that point on, I started to think of myself as a leader."

Former Dodgers general manager E. J. "Buzzie" Bavasi spoke of his experiences: "I didn't realize I had any leadership ability until July 1944. I was in the infantry, a staff sergeant, and we had to take a hill called Monte Battaglia, which appropriately enough means 'Battle Mountain' in English. We needed the hill to establish an observation post overlooking the Po Valley. So we went up the hill with sixteen men, and we came back down with four. A young lieutenant ordered me to go back up the hill and bring back two machine guns. Well, we had absolutely no intention of going up that hill again. The machine guns were ruined, and we had lost a dozen men.

"I explained this to the lieutenant, but he insisted that we go, stating that the guns were worth twelve hundred dollars. I asked him for his home address. He asked why. I said, 'I'll have my mother send you a check.' With that, the whole platoon was in an uproar. I then realized what it took to be a leader. The lieutenant may have had the rank to order us up that hill—but he didn't have the leadership ability. And we didn't go back up that hill."

Formal leadership is based on position, authority, and rank. A formal leader is usually empowered to control outcomes by distributing rewards (such as bonuses and incentive awards) and punishments (such as demotion or firing). A person who has the position and rank of a leader but lacks the abilities of a leader is a boss, not a leader. Bosses exercise control through fear, intimidation, and punishment. Bosses may be able to accomplish short-term goals, but over the long haul, they are not able to inspire the motivation and loyalty that produce a cohesive, successful team or organization.

Bosses *push* their people. They demand, order, threaten, and bully people to get results. Authentic leaders *pull* their people. They inspire, motivate, and draw people along in order to achieve results.

"The benefit of becoming a leader," Dr. John C. Maxwell told me, "is not that you will be able to tell people what to do. This is a misconception among adults as well as children. In reality, with leadership comes responsibility. The benefit of being a leader lies in being able to work with others, encouraging and equipping them, and together seeing something great achieved. Although we admire people who seem to be solo achievers—presidents, war heroes, inventors, athletes, and movie stars—the truth is that no individual has ever done anything of significant value on his or her own. Significant accomplishment always requires teamwork. And being a leader means working with a team. It is not easy to be a great leader, but only great leaders inspire great accomplishments."

■ Many Ways to Be a Leader

Is there such a thing as a "leadership personality type"? I put this question to Don Lund, former head baseball coach at the University of Michigan. "No," he replied. "There are all kinds of leadership styles and leadership personalities. Some people lead by jumping up and down and screaming all the time. Others are able to get equally good results with a softly spoken word every now and then. Some leaders are charismatic and articulate. Others are plainspoken. There's no one way to lead. All kinds of personalities can become leaders."

Vini Jacquery is the founder of International Reach, an organization that works with street children in Brazil. I spent a week with Vini in 1992, and we became very good friends. He played a key role in facilitating the adoption of our four Brazilian kids.

"Typically," Vini told me, "we equate leadership with being a *director*—managing people, giving orders, holding people accountable for the results, and so forth. That's definitely one style. But there are others.

"A great leader can also be a *persuader*. Billy Graham was a great persuader through his speaking. C. S. Lewis was a great persuader through his writing. Persuaders are leaders.

"A great leader can also be a *unifier*. A unifier doesn't bark orders. He or she usually does not seek or achieve great visibility. Unifiers generally work quietly, even self-effacingly to melt differences and bring people together.

"A great leader can be a *perfecter*. A perfecter refines and implements the ideas of other people. A good example of a perfecter is an assistant coach. The assistant coach is *a* leader, but not *the* leader. The head coach defines the overall vision, goals, and strategy, but delegates responsibility for perfecting and implementing that strategy to assistant coaches. In football, you'll have such assistants as offensive and defensive coordinators, special teams coaches, and so forth. They are leaders within their area of specialization, but their job is to support and implement the strategy of the head coach.

"All of these different styles reflect different personality types, different experience and preparation, different emphases, but they are all forms of leadership. Often, the most effective leaders are the ones who make the least noise and draw the least attention to themselves."

■ Why Be a Leader?

I have often heard young people say, "Why should I be a leader? Leadership is hard work. I'd rather be a follower." I've heard words like these from some of my kids. How do you answer a question like that?

"I tell young people, 'It feels good to be a leader!'" said Steve Gilbert, football coach at Jacksonville University. "Success and failure are part of the adventure of life. Young people need to see that good leaders are important in their community—and there are great rewards for being a good leader. Those rewards include a sense of satisfaction and a feeling that what you are doing is meaningful and significant. You don't always win when you lead, but that's okay. Young people should be rewarded and encouraged for stepping up and leading, no matter whether they succeed or fail."

Stan Morrison, athletics director at the University of California at Riverside, offered this opinion: "Young people need to understand that the rewards of leadership far outweigh the rewards of following. As parents, teachers, and coaches, we need to help them see that there are few things in life more exciting and uplifting than leadership—the challenge of determining their own destiny and even the destiny of their entire team or organization."

Young people who are given leadership responsibility are rewarded with increased self-esteem and confidence that will carry them throughout their lives. Donna Lopiano, Ph.D., executive director of Women's Sports Foundation, recalled, "At a very young age, I realized I could lead. I was always the best athlete on my street, the one who was looked up to by the other kids, even though I was a girl. I was usually made a team captain by other kids on the street. In school, I organized kids' games during recess because I wanted to play. I had self-confidence and good communication skills, and I wanted to get the games organized so that we could start quickly and have more time to play the game.

"Leadership is a function of opportunity and experience, so I believe in giving young people a lot of opportunities to gain the experience of leadership. Everyone should have a chance to be captain of the team, to teach a class, and so forth. We should never assume that this boy or that girl can't be a leader.

"At the same time we are giving kids opportunities to lead, we also need to give them training and instruction on how to lead so that they can improve their basic people skills, organizational skills, and communication skills. I'm convinced that virtually any young person can be a leader in a style that fits his or her personality. So we should approach every youngster with an attitude that says, 'I believe in you. I know you can be a leader. Go out and lead, and I'll be here to help you and support you.'"

As a father of nineteen, I have found again and again that kids can usually learn to lead at a much earlier age than we expect. We tend to think of training young people to lead when they get into junior high or high school. But I have long suspected that young people can begin learning to lead as early as elementary school. Basketball star Diana Taurasi told me, "There is no age barrier on being a leader." Some leaders I interviewed confirmed that was true in their lives.

Jamie Brown is special assistant to the president, White House Office of Legislative Affairs. Prior to her present appointment, she was assistant attorney general at the Department of Justice, where she was a leader in our government's war on terrorism and our homeland security strategy. She told me, "I realized I had leadership potential as early as the second grade, when my teacher provided opportunities to lead. She let small groups of students prepare skits or puppet shows for chapel, and I would write the skit, recruit friends for the different parts, and run the rehearsals.

"My parents taught my sister and me to believe that we could be leaders—that we could accomplish anything we put our minds to. One of their favorite sayings to us was, 'Most people do what is expected of them. Successful people do more.'

"The Bible tells us, 'Don't let anyone look down on you because you are young, but set an example for the believers in speech, in life, in love, in faith and in purity' (1 Tim. 4:12). This is great advice for all young leaders. There are things that young people are positioned to do that adults are not. For example, young leaders can have a far greater influence and positive impact on their peers than adults can. If kids say, 'I'm too young to make a difference,' they may be squandering a beautiful leadership opportunity—and they could be missing out on God's plan for their lives."

Lisa Maile has been honored as one of central Florida's top ten businesswomen and entrepreneurs. She founded Lisa Maile Image, Modeling, and Acting in 1982. But long before she became a businesswoman, before she graduated summa cum laude from the University of Central Florida, before she was student body vice president and valedictorian at her high school, Lisa Maile was a young leader.

"My first memory of leading," she said, "involved my third grade class at Clark Street School in Worcester, Massachusetts. For some reason (probably immature infatuation), the boys were extremely cruel and constantly picked on all of us girls. So I encouraged the girls to organize and we founded the Boy Haters of America Club.

"Despite the name of our club, my dad supported my early leadership ambitions. He made membership ribbons for us all, and I was elected president of the club. My friends and I took the club very seriously because we knew that by organizing, we could force the boys to treat us with more respect! I discovered that I truly enjoyed leading my female comrades—and I didn't mind the attention garnered from those little boys either.

"In elementary school, I noticed students would really listen when I made a speech—though public speaking was difficult for me at first. In junior high, after studying acting, I felt more comfortable in leadership. I became involved in student government in junior high, and I continued that involvement through high school. Those experiences became my launching pad for leadership in adulthood."

Born in 1911, Buck O'Neil was a standout first baseman and clutch hitter in Negro League baseball. In 1946, his .353 batting average was the best in the Negro National League. In 1962, fifteen years after Jackie Robinson broke baseball's color barrier as a player, Buck O'Neil broke the color barrier for coaches when he was hired to coach for the Chicago Cubs.

"I knew I was a leader in grade school in Sarasota, Florida," Buck told me. "Kids would always follow my lead. My mother, father, and grandmother all influenced me as a young leader. They taught me to be self-reliant, and I took up their advice as a kid. I found that when you show initiative and do a lot of things for yourself, people will want to help you succeed, and they will do a lot of things for you.

"As a boy, I was impressed with the leadership of John McGraw [Hall of Fame baseball manager, the Baltimore Orioles and New York Giants] and Connie Mack [Hall of Fame baseball manager, the Pittsburgh Pirates and Philadelphia Athletics]. Mr. Mack wore a business suit and would direct the club right from the bench. Then there was Rube Foster, the great Negro League manager. I can still see him sitting on the bench smoking his pipe and blowing smoke rings. He was giving signals with the smoke rings. I never did figure out what they meant, but that's what he was doing.

"Young people can be leaders, so pay attention to them. Give them a chance. They have some wonderful ideas—ideas that we grown-ups would never think of. As adults, we tend to think that we know more than youngsters, but that's not necessarily so. There is something within most children that enables them to step up and lead—if they're given the opportunity. The more chances they have to lead, the more their abilities and confidence will develop and grow."

Young leaders are often surprised to find that even people who are much older are willing to follow their leadership. This realization is a big confidence builder for young people. James White is the fire chief of Winter Park, Florida, where I live. I asked him about his early experiences with leadership, and he said, "My first opportunity to lead people was as a safety patrol in eighth grade. I was made captain and was given a great deal of responsibility. It was a real eye-opener to find that people listened to my ideas and took my direction. I discovered what it felt like to accomplish goals through other people. Once you prove that you are competent and successful as a leader, you find that more and more people are willing to trust you and follow you.

"When I arrived in Winter Park, one of the first people I met at the fire department was a man who had begun his career the year I was born. He had no problem following my leadership. Age doesn't matter—people want to be led. If you respect people, if you demonstrate confidence and competence, if you offer a sound plan and wise direction for the future, people will follow you regardless of your age."

Marriott Vacation Club executive Larry Birkes told me, "In 1959, at age eleven, I began working for my father's trucking company in St. Louis. The truck depots were not located in the best parts of town, so after school I'd ride the bus to midtown St. Louis near the Union Station, then run past the taverns and all the strangely dressed ladies (these 'ladies of the evening' worked at all hours), and finally arrived at the garage that housed my dad's trucks and office. He depended on me to be there at the specified time, so I could take over dispatching while he made deliveries.

"During the summer I would ride with the drivers (the owner's kid) and often confront them (as only a kid can do) about why we would take so many breaks. My father had taught me right from wrong and the value of hard work, so I decided to hold the drivers accountable by asking a lot of embarrassing questions about their behavior and how it affected the business. So I began exercising leadership with adults when I was eleven.

"There's a saying that if you are not the lead dog, the scenery never changes. Leaders get to do things and see things that most people miss. I spent twenty years as a naval officer, ten of them as a Navy rescue pilot, credited with seventy-one rescues. If I had not chosen a life of leadership, I never would have had the experience of saving seventy-one lives.

"While an ensign in the Navy, I was given a division of eighty men, the First Lieutenant's Division, a group of what was referred to at the time as 'McNamara's 100,000'—individuals who were essentially given the choice to either go to jail or join the service. These guys had nothing to be proud of, and life had been very hard for them. I took charge of that division and, with the help of my chief boatswain's mate, turned it into a division to be proud of. In fact, our division marched in such perfect precision during a change of command that we received a standing ovation. The First Lieutenant's Division went from being a joke to being the place to be if you wanted to be the best and get promoted.

"I learned a lot about leadership in the Navy, but the most basic and foundational leadership lessons of all were the ones I learned as an eleven-year-old kid, riding with the drivers for my dad's trucking company."

Clyde King was a right-handed relief pitcher with the Brooklyn Dodgers in the 1950s who went on to manage three major league teams, the Giants, the Braves, and the Yankees. As a player for the Dodgers organization, he worked for Branch Rickey, the visionary baseball executive who invented the modern farm system and broke baseball's color barrier by signing Jackie Robinson, the major leagues' first African-American player. Clyde King told me how Branch Rickey gave him a leadership opportunity that transformed Clyde's self-image.

"I was a minor-league pitcher with the Dodgers AAA club in Montreal, the Royals," Clyde said. "Mr. Branch Rickey asked me to come to spring training early and instruct some major league pitchers on how to hold runners on base. He wanted me to show them a pickoff move to first. Can you imagine, me—a minor-league player—teaching big leaguers? Wow! Mr. Rickey, who was like a father to me, instilled confidence in me by giving me this opportunity. At the end of the spring training, I knew I could be a leader."

I have associated the name "Shula" with leadership for many years. I first met legendary NFL coach Don Shula in 1958, when I was a high school football player and Shula was an assistant coach at the University of Virginia (he had come to scout one of my teammates at the Delaware

All-Star Football Game). Today, Don's son, Mike Shula, is continuing the Shula coaching tradition as head football coach at the University of Alabama.

"In grade school," Mike Shula recalled, "we would choose sides for pickup games—and I was always the one who did the choosing. So the desire to be a leader came early in life, and my father and brother taught me a lot about how to be a leader in football and in life. Most important, they taught me how a leader should treat people.

"I started coaching at age twenty-two, and the guys I coached were as old as thirty-three. It took me ten years to reach an age where the people I coached were younger than I was. I quickly realized, however, that your age isn't nearly as important as the type of person you are. If you have wisdom, confidence, and experience, people will place their trust in you and follow you anywhere."

■ Leadership Is for Everyone

The Honorable Mel Martinez was Secretary of Housing and Urban Development in the George W. Bush administration before resigning in 2003 to run for the U.S. Senate from Florida. Born in Cuba, Mr. Martinez has devoted much of his career to the needs of urban populations and has led in the cause of helping the working poor obtain affordable housing. "Leadership is not for the few; it's for everyone," he told me. "All children should be given an opportunity to lead. I don't believe that we should be too quick to select this one or that one for leadership while eliminating opportunities for the rest. We should operate on the assumption that every child has the capacity for leadership in one way or another."

I agree with the wise words of Mel Martinez. Many people mistakenly assume that leadership is a rare gift that is bestowed on a lucky few. My experience and years of study and observation tell me that leadership is a set of learnable skills. Many people mistakenly assume that leadership should be wielded only at the top of an organizational pyramid. In reality, leadership can and should be exercised at every level of every organization or team—in the mail room as well as the corner office.

Many people believe that a person must have an elusive quality called charisma to be a leader—that a leader must be a spellbinding speaker with almost superhuman charm and attractiveness. Well, a dash of charisma certainly doesn't hurt, but this world has known many gifted leaders (Abraham Lincoln, Mother Teresa, and Mahatma Gandhi come to mind) who demonstrated leadership ability and personal power that had nothing to do with attractiveness and charismatic charm.

Many people believe that leadership is about acquiring and wielding power. In reality, leadership is about empowering others to achieve the goals and vision of the team. People hate to be bossed. They love to be inspired and motivated; in other words, they love to be led.

Leadership is for everyone, including children. All young people have some capacity for leadership. Some can be loud, vocal leaders; others can be quiet, soft-spoken leaders. Any young person can become a leader, according to his or her own style and personality.

Our job is to give them the training, the support, the encouragement, the confidence, the motivation, and the opportunities to lead. When we turn them loose and let them lead, they will be amazed at what they can achieve as leaders—and so will we.

In the next chapter, we will examine the question of whether leaders are born or made, and find out how we can discover and build upon the leadership strengths of young people.

| 4 |

How to Identify
Young Leaders

Daniel "Rudy" Ruettinger dreamed of playing football for Notre Dame. Unfortunately, Rudy's small physique (five feet seven inches and 165 pounds) made him an unlikely prospect for the legendary Fighting Irish. A learning disability (undiagnosed dyslexia) and a lackluster academic record made his chances seem even more remote. Rudy's own family and friends told him to forget his dream.

Only two people encouraged Rudy in his quest. One was his football coach, Gordon Gillespie, who was impressed that Rudy led the team in tackles, even though he lacked size and natural ability.

Rudy's other encourager was a close friend from school who died in an industrial accident soon after graduation. The death of his friend impressed Rudy with the fact that life is uncertain and people should pursue their goals while they can.

So Rudy went to South Bend, Indiana, in quest of his dream. The first person he met upon his arrival was Father John Cavanaugh, the president of the university. Father Cavanaugh took a special interest in Rudy and helped him get into Holy Cross, a community college affiliated with the university. Rudy worked hard, improved his grades, and kept applying. He was accepted on his third try in 1974.

After being admitted to Notre Dame, Rudy went to see football coach Ara Parseghian and informed him that he intended to earn a spot on the team. Parseghian allowed Rudy to play on the practice squad, where he endured taunting and physical abuse from the much bigger players. Sometimes Rudy was hit so hard, he didn't know who he was—but he kept getting up and coming back for more. Some players hated Rudy and hit him all the harder because his intensity and courage made them look bad. Eventually, Rudy earned their respect and admiration. His character and commitment made him a leader.

One day, Rudy went to Coach Parseghian and asked to dress out for one game. The coach was reluctant. Rudy had a lot of heart—but he just didn't have the size and ability needed to compete. "Coach," Rudy said, "I don't want to be a starter. I just want to run through that tunnel and take the field. I've paid the price. I've earned it."

Coach Parseghian couldn't argue with that. He promised to let Rudy dress for one game before Rudy graduated—but Parseghian left Notre Dame a few months later. Parseghian's replacement, Coach Dan Devine, refused to honor Parseghian's promise to let Rudy suit up for a game. Two days before the final home game of Rudy's senior year, one of Rudy's teammates went to Coach Devine and offered to give Rudy his spot on the team. Reluctantly, Coach Devine agreed.

On November 8, 1975, Rudy suited up, ran through the tunnel, and took the field in a game against visiting Georgia Tech. Rudy could hardly believe it—his dream had come true. He wore the uniform of the legendary Fighting Irish.

Near the end of the game, Coach Devine rewarded Rudy's persistence by sending him out for the final play. Rudy lined up at left defensive end. It was not a melodramatic, last-ditch play to win the game—Notre Dame had already sealed the win. But it was the moment that Rudy had dreamed of, and he was determined to make the play count.

With five seconds left to play, the ball was snapped, Rudy came around the corner, caught the Georgia Tech quarterback by surprise, and sacked him. When the game ended, Rudy became the only football player in Notre Dame history to be carried off the field on the shoulders of his teammates. His story was dramatized in the 1993 motion picture *Rudy*, starring Sean Astin.

The lesson of Rudy Ruettinger's life is that we should never discount the leadership potential of any young person. That runty little kid that you've been ignoring just might be the all-important sparkplug your team needs to succeed. Every young person has more leadership potential than we know—and every young person deserves a shot at greatness.

■ Are Leaders Born—or Made?

When I was doing my research and interviews for this book, I put one question to every person I talked to: "Are leaders born—or are they made?" Some said that leaders are born that way—it's genetic; it's a fixed and immutable trait. Most, however, were convinced that leaders are *made*, and that every young person has at least *some* leadership ability. Virtually any young person can become a leader on some level.

The leadership experts seem to agree with this view. Legendary NFL coach Vince Lombardi put it this way: "Leaders aren't born; they are made. And they are made just like anything else, through hard work. And that's the price we'll have to pay to achieve that goal, or any goal." In 1942 General Eisenhower wrote to his son John, a student at West Point: "The only quality that can be developed by studious reflection and practice is the leadership of men."

Todd Duncan, CEO of the leadership training organization the Duncan Group, explained that leadership "takes a lifetime to achieve. The pursuit is where the growth is. Too many people try to become a leader in a day instead of leading daily. You can't pay $5.95 and become a leader. Too many people think that leadership comes in a package. You've got to be a leader on the inside first, before you can lead on the outside."

I asked Dwight Bain if leaders are born or made. Dwight is a nationally recognized speaker, counselor, and motivational coach, and the founder of LifeWorks Coaching Club. He told me, "Babies are born. Leaders are developed. People get old and die. Leaders live on forever. As a life coach, I challenge everyone to take an active role in educating, encouraging, equipping, and empowering young people to become leaders."

Without question, some people have more natural talents than others. Some people seem ready and able to take charge of any situation, even from a very early age.

Marianne Horinko was appointed acting administrator of the Environmental Protection Agency by President Bush in July 2003. She recently shared her story with me: "My mom told me I was born with my hands on my hips, asking, 'Who's in charge?' My parents always made me feel that my potential was limitless as long as I worked hard, got good grades, and had as much education as I could afford. I've been privileged to have excellent teachers and bosses who mentored me and, in many cases, became lifelong friends.

"My junior year in high school, I tried out for the school play, *Fiddler on the Roof.* I was surprised to find out I had landed the lead role as Tseitel, the eldest daughter. The music director told us candidly why each of us got our particular roles. Everyone else got this role or that role because of a combination of physical traits, acting ability, and vocal talent—everybody except me. The director said I got the role of Tseitel because I was smart and I looked like I knew what I was doing! It was leadership ability, not stage presence, that got me the part."

While some kids seem to have a natural ability to take charge, others have other natural leadership gifts. Some are naturally gifted public speakers, organizers, or motivators. Gifts and abilities are not distributed equally across the entire population.

Yet a look at the roster of the world's great leaders reveals that many (if not most) of them showed very little obvious leadership talent when they were young. Few demonstrated skill in public speaking. They had, at best, a few rudimentary talents and abilities, then they worked very hard throughout their lives to improve themselves and sharpen their leadership skills. Some of the world's most notable leaders have, in fact, overcome enormous obstacles and personal disabilities to achieve greatness.

The Old Testament leader Moses told God that he could not lead the people of Israel because "I have never been eloquent" and "I am slow of speech and tongue" (Exod. 4:10). Some scholars believe (based on archeological and historical evidence) that the phrase "slow of speech and tongue" refers to a speech impediment and possibly a cleft palate. Whether that was the case, it is clear that Moses was not a confident public speaker and had no personal charisma. Even so, Moses holds a place as one of history's greatest leaders—a leader who was made, not born.

Demosthenes (384–322 B.C.) was a noted orator and leader in ancient Greece. In his youth, Demosthenes suffered from a serious speech impediment that he overcame by doing a number of exercises, such as practicing his diction with a mouth full of pebbles. He made his living as a writer, speaker, and shaper of public opinion, and he rallied his countrymen against Philip II and the armies of Macedonia. Demosthenes was not a born leader; he *forced* himself to become a leader.

Thomas Jefferson was one of our nation's greatest leaders, the third president of the United States—and a man without any real charisma. Though an elegant thinker and an eloquent writer, he was a mediocre public speaker. Why? Because speaking in front of groups filled him with terror. His knees shook and his voice quaked at the thought of public speaking—a fear that remained with him to the end of his days.

Late in life, Jefferson complained to a close friend that he was outraged over the Continental Congress's revision of his original draft of the Declaration of Independence. When his friend asked why he didn't rise up and defend his original draft, Jefferson confessed that doing so would have meant facing the terror of speaking in public—and he would rather let his beloved Declaration of Independence be botched than face that fear. Despite his limitations as a public speaker, Jefferson forced himself to take a leadership role in the founding and governing of our country. As a leader, he was made, not born.

Winston Churchill suffered from an embarrassing speech impediment as a boy. He spoke with a lisp, and he had difficulty pronouncing the letter *s*. Though he worked hard to overcome this impediment throughout his life, he never fully overcame it. When they hear his recorded voice, most people consider it part of his mannerism, the Churchill persona—but he considered it a liability. Though his speech impediment impaired his confidence as a public speaker, he became known as one of history's most resolute and decisive leaders—and, ironically, one of the twentieth century's most compelling public speakers. Why? Because he worked a lifetime to overcome his disability. Winston Churchill was not born a leader; he willed himself to become one.

The evidence shows that leadership is not a gift. It's a set of learnable skills. Many leaders who appear "blessed" with a "gift" of leadership have worked hard at developing their innate talents, acquiring new skills, and learning the principles of leadership. A danger of the "leaders are born, not made" myth is that people with natural leadership talents may become complacent and fail to work at becoming a more skilled and effective leader. Another (and even more serious) danger of that myth is that we may foreclose leadership opportunities to young people whose leadership potential is not instantly apparent. We risk missing out on all the contributions they might have made if only we had given them the chance and the encouragement to prove what they could do.

■ Our Job: To Hold Up a Mirror

The Honorable Edwin Meese served as the seventy-fifth attorney general of the United States (February 1985 to August 1988) and is the author of the memoir *With Reagan: The Inside Story* (1992). When I put the "born versus made" question to Mr. Meese, he replied, "Some people may seem to be born leaders, but most people derive their leadership skills through training and experience. Having spent over thirty years in the Army Reserve, I have observed how effective leadership training has turned 'ordinary' people into successful leaders. Even born leaders are better if they study the art of leadership and the habits of leaders who have distinguished themselves."

Toni Jennings is the first woman lieutenant governor in Florida history, as well as a successful businesswoman. She said, "It's not always easy to spot the leader in a group of children. Frequently, the leader is the talkative one, the one who says, 'Let's do this,' or 'Let's go there.' But adults need to look beyond the obvious leaders to the quieter ones, because they can be leaders, too. The quiet leaders often grow up to become the calm and steady hand who solves problems in a crisis. My advice is to treat every child as a potential leader. If you give children encouragement and the chance to lead, they usually rise to the occasion and surprise everyone—including themselves!—with their leadership ability."

Dr. Richard E. Lapchick is a human rights activist, scholar, author, founder of Northeastern University's Center for the Study of Sport in Society (Boston), and current director of the DeVos Sport Business Management Program at the University of Central Florida. He told me, "I would advise any adult who has a responsibility for young people— whether that adult is a parent, coach, counselor, or teacher—to treat every single young person as a potential leader. When we talk to young people, we should talk about the problems confronting society in a way that encourages them to seek solutions. We should say, 'You can make a contribution. You don't have to change the whole world. Just reach out to one person at a time, and in the process you'll make a big difference in the world.'"

As parents, teachers, coaches, and mentors, our job is to hold up a mirror to young leaders so that they can see themselves and their leadership ability more clearly. Many young people lack the confidence to take on a leadership challenge until someone else tells them, "I believe in you. I see you as a leader. I know you have the skills to tackle this challenge."

In June 1962, I graduated from Wake Forest and played my final college baseball game at a regional tournament in Gastonia, North Carolina. My family drove down from Delaware for the final game, my mother and sisters in one car, my father in a separate car. After the game, Mom drove one car back to Wilmington and Dad took my sister Carol to Washington, D.C. I took the team bus back to Wake Forest, then drove back to Wilmington with friends.

When my friends and I pulled into the driveway, Mom came out and gave me the horrible news: My father had been killed in a single-car accident after dropping Carol off in Washington. I was devastated. I couldn't believe that my dad was no longer in the world. There were so many things I wished I had said to him.

Within days of the funeral, I had a phone conversation with Bob Carpenter, owner of the Philadelphia Phillies and a longtime family friend. He offered his condolences—and then he offered me a chance to play pro ball with the Phillies farm club in Miami. I finally had a chance to make my dreams of a baseball career come true, but it hurt that I couldn't share that moment with my father.

"Are you broke?" Bob Carpenter asked.

"Yes, sir," I said.

"We'll give you a five-hundred-dollar signing bonus and four hundred a month," he said. "Be in my office tomorrow and we'll sign the contract."

The next morning, I signed the contract and was all set to drive to Miami. But before I left his office, Mr. Carpenter told me, "Keep your eyes and ears open, both on and off the field." That's all he said—but I would later discover that those words were the key to my future.

It turned out that a Phillies scout, Wes Livengood, had watched me play for Wake Forest and had sent up reports about me: "Williams is a good catcher. He handles himself well, runs the club nicely, but he's not much of a hitter. He won't make it into the big leagues as a player, but has a future in the front office."

Bob Carpenter had been following those reports, and unbeknownst to me, he already had mapped out the next few years of my future: I would play in the minors for a couple of years, then move to the front office. That's why he told me to be observant. He was sending me to Miami to begin my training as a sports executive.

As it turned out, my career followed the general outline Mr. Carpenter had in mind for me (though I ended up in the NBA instead of Major League Baseball). I played two years in Miami, 1962 and 1963. Then, when I was twenty-four, the Phillies organization gave me the opportunity to move into sports administration, making me general manager of a Phillies farm club in South Carolina.

Bob Carpenter gave me good advice for all of us who are coaching young people to be leaders: Keep your eyes open for potential young leaders. Keep your ears open to what they are saying about their interests, ambitions, and dreams. Then give them opportunities to lead.

■ How to Spot Leadership Ability

Another question I asked in my research was this: "How do you spot a leader in a group of young people? What traits do you look for?" The leaders I interviewed provided a wealth of insight. Based on these interviews, I have assembled a list of twenty-five traits to look for (or issues to be aware of) in potential young leaders. When you find these positive traits, encourage these young leaders, give them opportunities to serve, train them, and mentor them. Here is the list:

1. *Look for young people with excellent character traits.* Randall James, president of First Orlando Foundation, told me, "Watch for young people who demonstrate the character traits of a good leader. They take the initiative and undertake tasks without having to be told. They prove themselves dependable and reliable, are committed and dedicated, and want to serve others. They have integrity and maturity, and they control their

anger. When you find young people of strong character, encourage them to take advantage of every leadership opportunity presented to them—and encourage them to use their talents and abilities to serve God."

2. *Look for young people who boldly speak up.* Congresswoman Carolyn Kilpatrick of the Thirteenth Congressional District of Michigan told me, "Kids with strong leadership ability are the first with an opinion on a topic. They take the lead in seeking to mold opinion and consensus. Leaders are not wishy-washy; they express what they believe."

   And John Paxson, general manager of the Chicago Bulls, told me, "Leaders are people who boldly speak their minds. How many kids sit in a classroom and know the answer but are afraid to speak up? They're afraid of what their peers might think of them. But a leader doesn't even think about it. A leader speaks up. That kind of boldness transfers to other arenas. The kid who's not afraid to give the answer in class is not afraid to call to his teammates and say, 'I'm open! Gimme the ball!' He's not afraid to take the shot when the game is on the line because he's a leader."

3. *Look for young people with creative ideas.* Congressman Mark A. Foley is a representative from Florida's Sixteenth Congressional District, a member of the House Ways and Means Committee, and cochairman of the Missing and Exploited Children's Caucus. Congressman Foley offered this advice: "I believe in listening to the ideas of young people. We should never dismiss or ignore someone simply because of his or her youth. Some of the best and most creative ideas come from young people, so let's recognize them, support them, guide them, and enthusiastically affirm them. We need new ideas and fresh, energetic leadership, so we should give creative young people a chance to lead."

Sir Nick Scheele, president and COO of the Ford Motor Company, told me, "When I was a college freshman in northern England, I was selected to organize a weeklong series of charity fund-raising events called Rag Week. At the time I was not sure why I was elected, except that I was relatively outspoken, organized, and I got things done. One of my jobs was to book talent for a concert, so I contacted a number of talent agents and finally booked a little-known group with an oddly misspelled name: the Beatles. That was just weeks before their singles hit the charts and turned them into a sensation on both sides of the Atlantic.

"When I returned from holiday break, the Beatles' agent called and cancelled their campus appearance—they were already too big for our little campus concert. So we booked another group that was on its way up—Eric Burdon and the Animals (the three bands that spearheaded the so-called British Invasion of the '60s were the Beatles, the Rolling Stones, and the Animals). The concert and fund-raising activities were extremely successful because we were flexible and creative in seeking rising stars for our entertainment."

4. *Look for problem solvers.* Dr. John MacArthur is pastor-teacher of Grace Community Church in Sun Valley, California, president of The Master's College and Seminary, and a noted author and speaker. "In looking for young leaders," he said, "I want to see the ability to solve problems. I need problem solvers around me, not people who just bring more problems to my desk. I need people who can evaluate a situation and see if there is an issue that needs attention. I need people who can spot problems on their own, then mobilize the people and resources to solve those problems."

5. *Look for young people with the courage to take a stand.* Jim Livengood, athletics director at the University of Arizona, told me,

"Look for young people who are not afraid to take a stand, regardless of how others look at them. Find youngsters who are more interested in being right than being popular." And Christian songwriter-performer Bill Gaither stated, "Good leaders lead. They do the right thing and ignore peer pressure. They don't take a popularity poll before making a decision. They just want to do the right thing."

6. *Look for youngsters with people skills.* Bob Seddon, long-time baseball coach at the University of Pennsylvania, explained, "A people person can easily be identified in youth. When you spot a young people person, you've identified a young leader. Give that person some responsibility and encouragement!"

Another term to describe people skills is *emotional intelligence.* Psychologist Daniel Goleman introduced this concept in his 1995 book *Emotional Intelligence.* According to Goleman, a person's emotional quotient (EQ) is a more reliable predictor of success than that person's intelligence quotient (IQ). People with a high EQ are better equipped to empathize with, understand, relate to, and connect with other people.

Dick Batchelor is a former Florida state representative, a political analyst, and founder of the Dick Batchelor Management Group, Inc. "When we seek to identify young people who can lead," he told me, "we tend to look at the IQ traits, the intelligence-oriented traits. But I believe we should not overlook the EQ traits. There are children who demonstrate an ability to communicate with their peers, connect with them and organize them for almost any activity, and then coach them to the fruition of the project. These children have excellent people skills, excellent leadership skills, though in some cases they may not test out as geniuses on an IQ test.

"It is a mistake to automatically equate IQ with leadership ability while overlooking kids with a high EQ. Children who can relate to and connect with their peers on an EQ level should be recognized and given the opportunity to cultivate their skills as leaders."

7. *Look for young people who are unstoppable.* Spot the ones who persevere and recover from their mistakes. T. K. Wetherell, president of Florida State University, said, "Leadership is usually revealed and applied during critical times. Look for young people who get up and keep going after they make a mistake. Encourage them; spend time with them; build their confidence and their willingness to take risks to achieve great things."

8. *Look for young people with a passion.* Passion, emotion, enthusiasm, intensity—these are contagious qualities. If a leader is fired up, the whole team soon catches that same fire. Jim Beattie, executive vice president of the Baltimore Orioles, told me, "I would try to identify a child with a passion for his or her pursuits. A young leader is someone who pursues an interest or a goal with an intense focus. A person who can inspire this passion and focus in others is a leader." And Steve Scanlon of the executive coaching firm Building Champions stated, "Watch the kid whose face lights up when he talks about his passion. Nurture that young leader and feed that interest. Affirm him and confirm him. Put him in situations where he can talk about that passion and communicate it to others."

9. *Look for effective young communicators.* "I believe that leadership is seventy-five percent verbal," said Dr. John MacArthur. "A young leader has to be able to speak to people and persuade them, to excite them and sell them on the importance of a goal, a project, or an idea."

Bob Harlan, president of the Green Bay Packers, told me, "The ability to communicate well is a great leadership skill. One of our three sons, Kevin, got a job while he was a junior in high school, broadcasting the school's football games. I could see a great potential in Kevin as a communicator, and I encouraged him in developing his skills. I listened to all of his broadcasts, I took notes, and I went over the notes with him. He was teachable and eager to learn.

"Kevin's high school broadcasting stint was a great confidence builder and a growing experience for him. He went on to Kansas and majored in broadcasting. Since then, he has broadcast games for both the NBA and the NFL. I believe that when young people demonstrate leadership ability, the key is to be available and supportive, but not push."

10. *Look for young people who are eager to listen and learn.* Former New York Yankees manager Clyde King said, "You can recognize leadership potential in youngsters by observing the one who pays close attention to you when you speak. The future leaders will be up front in order to hear. They ask questions. They are the first to arrive and the last to leave."

Former baseball commissioner Peter Ueberroth told me, "Potential leaders are the ones asking questions. They have great curiosity and crave knowledge. They ask for directions because they are going somewhere in their lives."

Former NBA star and college coach Jeff Mullins told me a story about the need for young leaders who listen. "When I tried out for my high school basketball team in Lexington, Kentucky," he said, "the coach demonstrated how he wanted lay-ups to be made—right-hand lay-ups from the right side, left-hand from the left. He picked someone to demonstrate the right-handed lay-up, and then looked for someone to demonstrate the left. I had never shot a lefty lay-up in my life, so I shrank back and hid. Wouldn't you know it? The coach picked me.

"I tried the left-handed lay-up, missed it badly, and was sure I had blown my chance at making the team. I had also humiliated myself in front of a hundred of my peers.

"Later in the practice, we scrimmaged on the court, and I stole a wing pass on the left side. All the way down the court, all I could think was, *I can make an easy lay-up with my right hand—but Coach said, 'Left hand from the left side.'* I was wide open for an easy right-handed lay-up, but I put the ball up with my left hand—and missed horribly. I instantly regretted my decision, certain that I had sealed my doom.

"But then the coach ran out and pointed to me and shouted, 'I want this man on my team because he follows instructions.' Suddenly, I felt ten feet tall, and I was glad I listened."

11. *Look for young people who refuse to quit.* Jerry McMorris, owner of the Colorado Rockies baseball team, said, "Leaders don't quit. We all face defeats from time to time, whether in sports or business or some other arena in life. So one of the most important qualities a leader can have is perseverance. When you find a young person who refuses to quit, you've found someone who's already halfway to becoming a leader. Our job as adults is to help build kids' confidence, to nourish their determination and persistence so that they won't give up on themselves when things get tough. When young leaders refuse to give up, they begin to win more consistently in life."

12. *Look for a confident attitude.* Don Miers, former director of Lakeland (Florida) operations for the Detroit Tigers, said, "Look for the young person who is confident, outspoken, and not afraid to stand out. Look for the one who speaks his mind—not just among his peers, but to his elders. I'm not suggesting that this young person should be disrespectful or demonstrate a cocky attitude—a courteous and respectful manner is also part of being a leader. But a young leader should be willing to challenge the consensus and ask questions of authority figures while boldly offering new ideas and insights."

13. *Look for an inquiring mind.* "The youngster who boldly asks

questions," said Don Miers, "demonstrates a willingness to think for herself. She doesn't want to be spoon-fed. She's inquisitive; she's an independent thinker; she's willing to look at a problem or a question from a new angle. People who think for themselves are called leaders."

14. *Look for young people who show up early.* "I've always liked coaching the young person who shows up early for practice or a game," said Don Miers. "That shows he's interested, enthusiastic, and excited about being involved with our activity. When young people show up early, they often want some time and attention for some one-on-one conversation or coaching. When I see a young person who is that eager to improve his game, I give him as much time, support, and advice as I can."

15. *Look for young people who are cool under pressure.* Carl Franks, former head football coach at Duke University, told me, "Look for youngsters who don't panic, who keep their cool and take time to think, who are patient, and who don't get rattled under pressure."

16. *Look for young people who are eager to work hard.* I interviewed former U.S. senator Paul Simon by mail a few months before he died following heart surgery in December 2003. Senator Simon is remembered for his jaunty bow ties, his career as a crusading newspaper owner, his two terms in the U.S. Senate, and his unsuccessful bid for the White House. "Over the years," he wrote, "I have had the chance to meet and work with many leaders in this country and in other countries. I have known several U.S. presidents. There are several key words that I associate with leadership: *creativity, a willingness to volunteer and serve others, a willingness to take a risk.* But I think one of the most important indicators of true leadership potential is a willingness, even an eagerness, to work hard."

Orlando Magic forward Grant Hill is a five-time NBA All-Star. He recently told me that a broken nose opened his eyes to the importance of a strong work ethic: "I was a freshman at Duke University, eighteen years old. During one game in December, I broke my nose very badly—splattered it all over my face. Over the Christmas break, I ended up spending three nights at Coach Mike Krzyzewski's house. With the injury, it was very difficult for me to sleep, and I woke up many times during the night.

"I woke up once at about three or four in the morning and I looked out my bedroom door—and there in the next room was Coach K. He was hunkered down in front of a video screen, watching game film of our next opponent. I thought, *Man! I had no idea coaches had to get up that early and work that hard to prepare for a game!* It was quite a lesson to an eighteen-year-old basketball player about the amount of work it takes to be a leader."

Bob Johnson, founder and CEO of Black Entertainment Television (BET), told me, "I look for young people who are not afraid of hard work. I want them to get in the trenches with me and not just be nine-to-fivers. I want young people who will look at their job as a mission. Call them 'go-to guys' because no matter what the assignment, they'll get it done. Give me three hardworking young leaders, and I will change the world."

17. *Look for mental toughness.* Jack McKeon, manager of the Florida Marlins, told me, "Look for young people who will play hurt. That means mental and physical toughness. Leaders get hurt. They are in the cross fire. They are under pressure. They get criticized—and a lot of the criticism they face is unfair. They have to keep leading when other people would quit. They have to play through the pain. When you find a young person with

the mental, physical, and spiritual toughness to play hurt, you've got a young leader."

18. *Look for a sense of humor.* This much-overlooked quality can actually be an important indicator of leadership ability. Humor is a great tension reliever in pressure situations. Effective leaders use humor to convey hope and optimism and to break tension and keep a team's mind-set loose and confident. When I asked Minnesota Vikings head coach Mike Tice what to look for in a young leader, the first thing he said was, "A sense of humor. Most great leaders have a great sense of humor."

19. *Look for young people who are ready to take charge.* Jack McKeon told me, "When you are looking for leaders, you want that young player who wants the ball, who stays cool when the whole game is on his shoulders. You want a young person who doesn't shrink from responsibility, accountability, and risk. You want a young person with the confidence to take charge."

Diana Taurasi said, "My coach at Connecticut, Geno Auriemma, taught us about being responsible. You are responsible for all you say and do, so don't put it on anyone else."

Terry Bowden, college football coach and ABC college football analyst, said, "All four of us Bowdens—Steve, Tommy, Jeff, and me—have a quarterback camp in Alabama every summer. We'll have three or four hundred youngsters from the ninth through twelfth grades. We run through drills during the day, then at night it's time for Bowden Ball. The kids play pickup games, and we leave them on their own. All of us Bowdens are up on the hill in lawn chairs, watching the kids. We can spot the leaders quickly because the others gravitate toward them. We get our best evaluation on the quarterbacks by sitting back and seeing which QBs take charge and run their teams."

20. *Look for young people who can follow directions and obey orders.* At first glance, this advice seems like a paradox or even out-

and-out nonsense. Why should leaders need to obey? In reality, a person is not qualified to give orders until he or she has demonstrated an understanding of the value of obedience and a cohesive team effort. As Benjamin Franklin once said, "He that cannot obey, cannot command."

James White, chief of the Winter Park, Florida, fire department, told me, "I have coached my daughters' softball teams for more than five years. We have been very successful, winning several local and state tournaments. I've found that the young people on the team who listen attentively and who follow your coaching are the ones who become quality leaders on the team. The best followers always make the best leaders."

21. *Look for an attitude of inclusiveness and cooperation.* Authentic leaders like to involve the entire team; they do not isolate themselves like the Lone Ranger. Dr. Rita Bornstein, former president of Rollins College, told me, "Look for young people who include others in their deliberations and actions. Encourage an inclusive approach to problem solving, and affirm young leaders when they demonstrate a spirit of cooperation and a team attitude."

22. *Look beyond "problem behavior."* William Donohue, president of the Catholic League for Religious and Civil Rights, told me, "Youngsters who show early signs of leadership are often very expressive individuals. You hope that they express this leadership ability in good conduct—but some exuberant young leaders express their leadership ability through misbehavior. Adults make a big mistake when they dismiss young people as potential leaders merely because they exhibit problem behavior."

Jay Strack, president of Student Leadership University, said, "We tend to look at our kids in terms of whether they embarrass us or not. If we have a high-maintenance child, we think, *That kid is just a lot of trouble.* We need to start seeing kids for their potential and not just their problems."

Dr. John E. Haggai, founder of the Haggai Institute, told me, "Dwight L. Moody, the famous American evangelist, said, 'If you want to find someone who will rock the world, find a mischievous child whose energies have been harnessed.' It has been my observation that children with a lot of drive and leadership ability oftentimes lack discipline. It is important that the trait of discipline be instilled in them and that they come to understand that it is one thing to capture the attention of people and it's another thing to maintain their respect after you have captured their attention."

23. *Look for a positive, uncomplaining attitude.* Rick Hartzell, athletics director at the University of Northern Iowa, told me, "Great leaders don't waste time and energy on complaining. They focus on positive reinforcement, not a negative attitude. I learned this lesson the hard way when I was a quarterback on my high school football team. I felt I was getting hit, hurried, and sacked too much, so I complained to the coach about my offensive line. I said the offensive linemen were doing a poor job of blocking. So my coach—who is my close friend and mentor to this day—took the ball out of my hands and said, 'Okay, you play offensive line for the next fifteen plays, and I'm sure that the blocking will improve.'

"Well, that put a stop to my complaining. That's a great technique to use whenever a young leader is becoming too negative and critical about others. That experience taught me that a leader has to delegate and trust his teammates to carry out their assignments to the best of their ability. I also learned that positive reinforcement inspires better performance than criticizing and complaining."

24. *Don't mistake popularity for leadership.* If you observe young people at work or at play, you'll notice that some individuals are popular and admired. Their peers cluster around them. This is

not necessarily an indicator of authentic leadership ability. Sometimes, the most popular kid in class is actually spoiled, arrogant, disrespectful, lazy, unmotivated, and lacking in good character traits and values. In fact, such kids may be popular and admired by a number of their peers precisely because they have a "bad boy" or "bad girl" reputation.

John Dasburg, chairman and CEO of ASTAR Air Cargo, recalled, "Most of the young so-called leaders I knew when I was growing up were not really leaders at all. They were very popular, but popularity is not leadership, though it is often mistaken for such."

Lawrence Frank, head coach of the New Jersey Nets, told me he "would rather be respected than liked. It is nice to be liked, but you can't please everyone." Former NBA coach Bill Fitch agreed. "I didn't want my players to love me," he said, "just respect me."

25. *Look for spiritual strengths when training spiritual leaders.* Jim Henry, senior pastor of the First Baptist Church in Orlando, said, "Look for young people who have a sincere love for God and for others; a grateful attitude; a servant's heart; a respect for authority; a sense of self-discipline and self-control, coupled with an ability to discern right from wrong; a desire to make right choices; a humble and teachable spirit; a determination to do things well and to persevere in all that they do; a respect for others; a respect for the opposite sex; respect and honor toward parents; and active involvement in the church. If you find a young person who has most or all of these qualities, you have someone who can be mentored and trained to be an effective spiritual leader."

These, then, are the twenty-five key traits to look for or to be aware of when you seek to identify young leaders. No young leader will have all of them. Only a few will have most of them. But if you find a young person with as few as one or two of them, you have something to build on. So affirm these positive traits and encourage that young person to improve his or her existing skills and to learn new ones. Train and mentor that person. Begin building a leader.

■ The Danger of Natural Leadership Ability

All leaders need to be taught, mentored, nurtured, guided, and disciplined. That includes so-called natural leaders. Many young people have a seemingly "natural" gift for taking charge, attracting followers, and achieving goals—but they lack the wisdom, maturity, and judgment to pursue the right goals. Instead of leading, they *mis*lead. They take their followers right off the edge of the cliff because they know how to get people to follow them, but they don't know where they should walk.

Kevin Renckens is CEO of Lockheed Martin Financial Services in Orlando. He told me, "When I was a boy, we lived next door to the public library, a two-story building with a ledge that went all the way around. I thought it would be fun to get up on that ledge and walk around the entire building, so I climbed up there with one of the other boys. Unfortunately, when we got about halfway around, we decided we couldn't go any further, so one of the boys who was down on the ground went to get help. Sometime later, we were brought safely to the ground, but I didn't receive any leadership encouragement that day from any of the adults who were involved in our rescue."

Bill Fay, a sportswriter in Orlando and a father of three boys, told me, "I coach my boys' teams, so I have the opportunity to study young athletes and this whole issue of leadership. One time, our team was playing for the flag football championship. On the very first play of the game, the other team intercepted a pass and ran it in for a touchdown!

"At that moment, our best player and team captain said, 'That's it! We're toast! We can't win!' Immediately, all the other players said the same thing. The attitude of the whole team had soured just because of this one boy's statement of despair. I knew we had to turn that around—

and fast. I said, 'Wait a minute! The game just started! You can win this game! Now get out there and play!' We went on and we beat them big-time.

"What this story says to me is that one kid can have a powerful influence on the entire team—for good or for ill. The attitude of one leader can instantly infect the entire team—all the other kids just fall in line with whatever that leader says. So we need to teach young leaders to use their influence wisely. We need young leaders who inspire confidence, courage, and hope—not defeat."

This lesson was brought home to me when I was seventeen, growing up in Wilmington, Delaware, with my friend and classmate Ruly Carpenter. His father owned the Philadelphia Phillies, and Ruly was a young man with a forceful and charismatic personality. Everybody, including me, looked up to Ruly.

One summer, I spent the weekend with Ruly at Rehoboth Beach, Delaware. We took a couple of rafts out on the ocean, and we got out pretty far. Soon, we noticed that the lifeguards were waving us in. Ruly didn't respond—so I didn't either. Next thing we knew, the lifeguards were coming out after us in rowboats. Ruly saw them coming, so what did he do? He started heading the other way, paddling toward Europe! For the life of me, I don't know why I did it, but I followed Ruly out to sea.

Finally, the lifeguards overtook us and hauled us to the police station, where they called our parents. I drove home and pulled into the driveway. My mother was waiting, and she asked one question: "How far are you going to follow Ruly Carpenter?"

Now, Ruly wasn't a bad guy at all. He was a straight-A student, an All-State athlete, and in general, a law-abiding citizen. But in this one instance, he proved to be too strong a leader for me. I couldn't answer my mom's question. I just hung my head.

The ability to lead others is an awesome power. Young leaders need to learn to wield it responsibly. Blessed with an abundance of leadership ability—such as the ability to make plans, communicate persuasively, and motivate people—young natural leaders often have to be taught how to lead people in the right direction and how to become servant leaders rather than dictators and bosses.

Marianne Horinko, acting administrator of the Environmental Protection Agency, said, "Natural leaders sometimes need to learn humility. They have to be taught to rein themselves in so that they don't run roughshod over other people. If you have a strong natural leader on your hands who is elementary school age, I recommend you have that child read the Junie B. Jones series by Barbara Park. The books have such titles as *Junie B. Jones and Her Big Fat Mouth* and *Junie B. Jones and the Stupid Smelly Bus*. Junie is a very smart little girl who tends to be bossy and self-important. The books are fun to read aloud, and kids can often learn from Junie's mistakes."

Vince Dooley, former athletics director at the University of Georgia, was another young natural leader. He told me, "I recall at an early age reading about being a leader, and I was intrigued. While I didn't know exactly what it was all about, I liked the idea of being a leader. To me, being a leader meant taking charge, especially at recess, when we would go out to participate in a physical activity.

"I was always the first one out of class when the bell rang, and since they separated boys and girls during recess, we had to run to the school yard across the street to play in the boys' section. One day, I led the boys down the driveway, but the tall, metal gate which was always open was closed. We all stopped, and no one knew what to do. I said, 'Let's go over the top!' So we did.

"Unfortunately, we piled fifteen kids on top of the gate at the same time, and the gate came crashing down. I led the group to the boys' yard, and we played ball. Well, the nuns investigated, and the evidence pointed to me! So I was called to the principal's office, and the nun took me out and walked me around the yard so that we could talk about it.

"It was not the first time I had led my peer group in the wrong direction. She balanced firmness with understanding, and as we walked around the yard, I admitted my responsibility for wrecking the gate. I told her that the reason I had led the boys over the gate was that I had read about being a leader and I enjoyed assuming that role.

"She said, 'Leadership is a wonderful ability to have. It's a fine ambition to be a leader. But it's extremely important that you learn to lead in the right direction and not the wrong one.' That made a big impression on me. From that day forward, I always tried to be a positive leader. That was probably the first time I was ever taught or mentored as a leader. I have been learning and developing my leadership skills every day since then, and I'm still learning today."

■ Don't Overlook the Quiet Young Leaders

I owe my career as an NBA executive to Dr. Jack Ramsay. On July 8, 1968, Jack—who was then the general manager of the Philadelphia 76ers—placed a telephone call to my office at the baseball park in Spartanburg, South Carolina. He offered me a job as the business manager for the 76ers. Thanks to Jack Ramsay, I left minor-league baseball for major league basketball, and I've been in the NBA ever since.

Jack coached basketball at Saint Joseph's College in Philadelphia for eleven seasons, then coached four pro teams over a span of twenty-one years and 906 games. He is the author of two books on coaching, *Pressure Basketball* and *The Coach's Art*, and has spent the last decade as a radio and television broadcaster. I asked Jack about his early experiences as a young leader, and he described his evolution from a quiet and rather reluctant kid who just liked to play ball to a confident and vocal leader.

"I was shy as a youngster," Jack said, "and I was reluctant to take leadership roles. I did what I was told and followed the group. But when I was about eleven or twelve years old, in an effort to assure myself of a chance to play baseball, I laid out a baseball diamond in a vacant lot across from my house. I measured the distances from home plate to the bases and pitcher's mound. I used discarded pieces of wood as crude replicas of home plate and the pitcher's rubber. For the bases, I filled empty chicken feed sacks with dirt, and I built a backstop out of old flooring lumber.

"Then I told my friends at school about the ball field I had made, and I drummed up interest for playing games there on weekends. Well, the saying is true: If you build it, they will come. My friends came and we played ball. When I marked off that baseball diamond, I wasn't making a leadership statement. I just wanted to play baseball—but it turned out to be a big step in my education as a leader.

"My family moved to the Philadelphia area when I was in tenth grade. I attended Upper Darby High School, where I played basketball and soccer, and was captain of the baseball team. I still wasn't a vocal leader. I just played hard and hoped my teammates would do the same. In those days, basketball players didn't go to the bench to talk to the coach during a time-out. They stayed out on the floor. I wasn't the team captain, but since no one else assumed leadership, I took it on myself to organize plays and strategies when they were needed because I wanted to win."

Throughout his youth, Jack Ramsay remained the quiet, shy young athlete who simply wanted to play ball. He led only by default because if he didn't lead, either he couldn't play ball or his team wouldn't win. At no time in his boyhood did young Jack Ramsay demonstrate the kind of vocal, take-charge, natural leadership ability that would enable you to pick him out as the leader in a crowd of kids. Yet his early experiences prepared him for the day when he would become one of the most commanding and vocal leaders in the sport of basketball.

"Real leadership was thrust upon me," Jack recalled, "when I became an ensign in the Navy in World War II. I was a platoon leader in Underwater Demolition Team No. 30. The leader of the team, Commander Murray Fowler, showed confidence in his platoon officers to do the tasks we were assigned. His confidence in me raised my confidence in myself. By the time I was twenty, I was made captain of an interisland cargo ship in the South Pacific. I had to make decisions and give orders, so I became what I had never been before—a vocal leader. I carried that leadership ability with me throughout my adult life, especially in coaching."

In the Old Testament, we see that God looked at leadership a bit differently from the way that most of us do. When picking out young leaders, we tend to look for the obvious traits. We tend to seek out the talkers, the skilled, the kids with the swagger and the confidence. But God had a different set of criteria in His mind when He was looking for a young leader to be the king of Israel in Old Testament times.

In 1 Samuel 16, God rejected Saul as king of Israel and spoke to the prophet Samuel, saying, "I am sending you to Jesse of Bethlehem. I have chosen one of his sons to be king. . . . You are to anoint for me the one I indicate." So Samuel did as God told him to do. He went to Bethlehem and visited a man named Jesse, the father of several sons.

The first son Samuel met was a strong, athletic young man named Eliab. Seeing Eliab, Samuel thought that he had found the one God had chosen to be king. But God told Samuel, "Do not consider his appearance or his height, for I have rejected him. The LORD does not look at the things man looks at. Man looks at the outward appearance, but the LORD looks at the heart."

In all, Jesse brought seven of his sons before Samuel, and they were fine boys, brimming with leadership potential. But as Jesse's sons were brought to Samuel, one by one, the old prophet listened to God's voice—and rejected each one. Finally, Samuel told Jesse, "The LORD has not chosen these . . . Are these all the sons you have?"

"There is still the youngest," Jesse answered, "but he is tending the sheep." So Samuel said, "Send for him."

Jesse's youngest son was brought in from the fields. He was the quiet one, the sensitive one, the poet—but when Samuel saw him, he heard the Lord say, "Rise and anoint him; he is the one." And this young shepherd became one of the most famous kings in human history—David, king of Israel.

We easily fall into the trap of stereotyping young leaders, saying, "He can't be a leader—he's not a confident communicator," or, "She's not leadership material—she doesn't take charge and tell the other kids what to do." As parents and mentors, we should avoid confining our mental picture of a leader to just a few strong-willed or charismatic personality types. Leaders come in all shapes, sizes, and personality configurations. Authentic leadership takes many forms—and some of those forms don't fit the common stereotype of a leader. Don't put young leaders in a box; think outside the box.

Dan Wood, executive director of the National Christian College Athletic Association, stated, "A vibrant, vocal, outgoing personality should not be mistaken for leadership. Being outgoing does not make a leader, nor does being quiet and reserved disqualify a person. Leadership demands skills and character qualities, not just personality traits. I have found that the real makings of a good leader are found in those who persevere, who are willing to learn the lessons of adversity, who have integrity and strong moral character, and who are willing to work hard. You often find these traits in the shy ones, the quiet ones—and they are often your best candidates for leadership."

Ron Polk, baseball coach at Mississippi State University, offered a similar perspective: "I have had outgoing kids as leaders and quiet kids as leaders. Leadership is a trait that one cannot pinpoint with exact certainty. The common denominator among all the young leaders I have coached is not personality, but character. The true leaders are always kids with great moral character and a strong work ethic. True leaders lead by example."

Edward J. Barks is president of Barks Communications. He trains people to achieve peak performance when speaking in public and dealing with the media. Based in the Washington, D.C., area, Ed has trained more than a thousand government leaders, business leaders, physicians, nonprofit leaders, athletes, entertainers, and other leaders to communicate effectively in public settings. Ed Barks is a leader—but he didn't always see himself that way.

"Call me a late bloomer," Ed told me. "As a painfully shy kid, I was never much of a joiner, let alone a leader. I would have been among the last ones tagged as having leadership qualities in my youth. I was a bright kid with terrific grades, but I lacked confidence. I'm living proof that if you give young people opportunities to lead—even shy, quiet young people—they will often rise to the occasion. Radio broadcasting proved to be my ticket to leadership. As I sharpened my communication skills, new doors opened for me.

"Young people never really know what their capabilities are until they stretch themselves. They learn about themselves and their abilities by jumping in and doing things they never knew they could do. As we give young people opportunities to lead and to serve, they will gain confidence, build on those abilities, and stretch themselves in new ways. Every young person has a unique set of leadership skills. Our job, as their parents, mentors, teachers, and coaches, is to identify those abilities and create opportunities so that young people can discover strengths they never imagined they had.

"My fourteen-year-old daughter, Polly, is a straight-A student who loves to write. She has never been interested in traditional forms of leadership, such as running for class president. Yet she is a leader. She has decided to create leadership opportunities for herself that don't always fit the conventional notion of leadership. For instance, she was invited to participate in the People to People Ambassadors Program, traveling to Australia and New Zealand to expand her horizons while representing the United States. She met with New Zealand's ambassador to the U.S., the Honorable John Wood, when he visited our area. While my daughter didn't exchange diplomatic credentials, she was able to talk to a world leader—ambassador to ambassador, as it were. No matter how you define leadership, Polly was being a fourteen-year-old leader."

Exactly so. If we want to identify and encourage young people to become young leaders, we need to focus more on character traits than on personality traits. We need to recognize that all young people, not just a few, have leadership potential. We need to be careful not to overlook the less obvious leadership qualities that are often found among young people who are quiet and reserved, and who don't fit the obvious leadership stereotype.

Once we have identified some young leaders, we need to build them up, inspire them with vision and confidence, and hold up a mirror to them so that they can see in themselves what we already see in them. So let's keep our eyes open for those less-than-obvious leadership traits, then let's begin training and mentoring those young people to lead.

■ Give Them Opportunities to Lead

"Many young people are willing and ready to serve as leaders," said Bud Selig, the commissioner of Major League Baseball. "But they need opportunities and encouragement from adults. After I finished college and my time in the service, my dad, a businessman in Milwaukee, said to me, 'Think about joining me in the business. You know how to get along with people and get the best out of them.' I had just been thinking about getting a job and making a living. But when Dad said that, I started thinking about a career in leadership."

Young people will step up and lead—and succeed—if they are given leadership opportunities. Former twelve-term Colorado congresswoman Patricia Schroeder (now president and CEO of the Association of American Publishers) told me, "When I grew up, opportunities for girls to learn leadership, especially through sports, were limited. Thank goodness for Title IX [federal legislation that banned sex discrimination in both academics and athletics in schools]. My daughters' generation has grown up under new rules, with new opportunities to lead.

"It's important for kids to get praise, encouragement, and leadership opportunities from their parents. But it means even more to a young person to receive these affirmations and opportunities from adults outside of their families—from coaches, teachers, Scout leaders, and mentors. As a young person, I was given opportunities to lead in debate clubs, theater clubs, glee clubs, and Spanish clubs. I worry today that too few adults are taking the time to coach kids, sponsor youth clubs, and provide leadership opportunities to young people. That's the way to be leaderless tomorrow! Young people will inherit this country and they need to learn to lead it."

John Weisbrod is chief operating officer and general manager of the Orlando Magic. A Harvard English major who played hockey in the NHL, John took over as general manager of our organization even though he had no background in basketball. He told me how a leadership opportunity he was given as a young adult changed the course of his life—and the fortunes of a pro hockey team.

"I was twenty-three," he said, "when the New Jersey Devils offered me a job as the general manager of their AHL team in Albany, New York. The team was on the verge of folding, so the plan was to play one more year then dismantle the franchise. They offered me the job because I was the only one dumb enough to take it. No one expected a green kid like me to do anything other than preside over the demise of the team. I got there and found that the whole organization was a dysfunctional mess. Our last-place team attracted six hundred fans a night to a fifteen-thousand-seat stadium.

"I had a decision to make: Ride it out or try to fix it? I took up the challenge of trying to fix it. Within two years, we were first in attendance, our team won the title, and instead of losing ten million dollars, we made ten million. I was given an opportunity to lead, and I took it. That job launched my career."

I've seen this principle again and again in the lives of my own children: Give a kid an opportunity and there's no telling how far and how high he or she will go. My son Bobby, in order to graduate from Rollins College, needed to write a major term paper on the subject of leadership. I read it and was so impressed with Bobby's insights that I photocopied it and mailed it to a number of Major League Baseball executives. I didn't hear back from any of them, and I assumed that they were all too busy to look at the paper.

I didn't know that one baseball executive—Jim Bowden, then general manager of the Cincinnati Reds—read it, was impressed with it, and copied it for all the top execs in his organization. Not long afterward, Bobby was attending grad school at Georgia Southern and needed an internship to get his degree. So Bobby wrote to Jim Bowden and asked if he could intern with the Reds, completely unaware that Bowden had read his paper.

Bowden gave Bobby the internship sight unseen, making him a coach in uniform with the Reds rookie team in Billings, Montana. So here was twenty-two-year-old Bobby Williams, possibly the youngest coach in the history of pro baseball. He did such a good job that the Reds hired him as a fulltime coach in their minor league system. When this book is released, Bobby will be finishing his fifth year in uniform with the Reds organization. Why? Because Jim Bowden took the time to read Bobby's paper, and he decided to give an ambitious young leader a shot.

Another Bowden, Bobby, the legendary Florida State football coach, also believes in giving young leaders a chance. One year he had just dismissed his freshman players from their first practice after a brief talk. "The next thing I knew," he told me, "an eighteen-year-old tailback, Leon Washington, said to the players, 'Okay, everyone over here.' He had all the players around him and was giving them a pep talk, then he led them in a Florida State cheer. I told my coaches, 'Now we know who the leader of this group is.' I have never seen anything like that in all the years I've been coaching. And Leon has been leading ever since."

Our job as adult leaders is to open doors for the next generation. Let's give them the opportunities they need to prove themselves, to discover their hidden talents and abilities, and to step up and lead.

In the next part, we will consider the seven dimensions of effective leadership—the seven keys to building good leaders for today and tomorrow.

PART II

■ ■ ■

The Seven Keys to Effective Leadership

| 5 |

First Key:
See a Vision

It was a Saturday in the early summer, and my wife, Ruth, and I were jogging along in the ninety-degree heat and 100 percent humidity. We reached the corner of Lee Road and Highway 17-92, a corner where a Hardee's hamburger place once stood. The Hardee's was gone, and a new building was going up. However, there was no sign to indicate what sort of establishment this new building would house.

We noticed some workers on the site. I told Ruth, "Let's find out what they're building. These guys will have the inside word."

So I went up to one guy who had a cinder block in his hand. I said, "Excuse me, but what are you building?"

He said, "A wall, man."

I said, "Let me rephrase that. When this entire project is finished, what will it be?"

He shrugged and said, "I dunno."

Three other men were working on the wall, so I decided to ask them. Surely, one of them had to know what was going on. So I said, "Guys, what are you building?"

"A wall," they answered.

"But when it's finished, what will it be?"

"We dunno," they chorused.

As Ruth and I left that work site and finished our run, I thought, *Gee, these guys haven't any vision of what they are building. Imagine starting work on a construction project without any idea if you are building an outhouse or the Taj Mahal!*

I later found out that those workers were engaged in constructing a Fleming's Prime Steakhouse—an upscale steak restaurant. I expect to enjoy some fine meals there once it's built. I have a vision of that experience—and it makes my mouth water just to think of it.

But when I asked those workers what they were building, all they could answer was, "A wall, man." How sad. And how typical of the way too many organizations are run these days. People are told to do a job, but they are never shown the big picture. All they know is their tiny little piece of the puzzle: "A wall, man."

In order for a team to be enthused, inspired, fired up, and energized to achieve great things, that team must have a leader with a vision—and the leader must communicate that vision to everyone on the team. Leaders—even very young leaders—must be people of vision.

■ Imagine the Possibilities

Jerry West is literally a living symbol of the National Basketball Association. The silhouetted basketball player on the NBA's logo is taken from a photo of Jerry West. Prior to embarking on a fourteen-year career with the Los Angeles Lakers, he won a gold medal with the U.S. Olympic team in the 1960 games in Rome. Jerry attributes much of his success to his ability to envision a bright and successful future.

"I have always lived in a fantasy world," Jerry told me, "a world that I visualized as a boy and which came true as I grew up. My mind is my best friend.

"As a kid growing up in Cabin Creek, West Virginia, I loved basketball. I'd practice alone, and in my 'games,' I'd be the coach, the announcer, and the star player. I practiced making last-second shots millions of times as a boy. Later, in the NBA, I gained a reputation for making those clutch shots because I already had all of that mental preparation. In my mind, I always made those shots.

"Sometimes, in those boyhood practice 'games,' I'd mentally let the other team win a game—just to motivate me so I would come back and crush 'em in the next game.

"Coming from where I started in West Virginia to where I've gone in life, I sometimes can't believe it myself. My whole life has been a fairy tale, and I think a lot of it has to do with the fact that I had this vision of my future when I was practicing basketball as a boy."

Dick Vermeil, head coach of the Kansas City Chiefs, told me that he owes his career in the NFL to a high school coach who gave him a vision of a future in football. "When I was at Calistoga High School in northern California," he said, "I had a young football coach and teacher, Bill Wood. It was a small school, so we all played four sports or there'd be no teams. Coach Wood had a tremendous impact on me. He made me the quarterback and kept telling me I could go to college and play football. I never even considered playing in college until he said that. I just assumed I would work in the garage with my dad. Bill Wood gave me a vision of a future I never imagined for myself. He's the biggest reason I'm coaching in the NFL today."

Bill Giles, chairman of the Philadelphia Phillies baseball organization, has spent his life around baseball and leadership. His dad, Warren G. Giles, was president and general manager of the Cincinnati Reds and president of the National League. Bill started his baseball career as an errand boy with the Reds, and except for a three-year hitch in the Air Force, Bill has never held a job outside baseball.

"I first realized I had leadership ability," Bill told me, "during my senior year at Winthrow High in Cincinnati. I was in charge of planning our senior prom. Traditionally, the school would hire a small local band

and hold a party in a local hotel ballroom with about three hundred people. I had a vision for something special, something really big.

"So I rented a huge dance hall called Castle Farms—the place could handle up to three thousand people. Then I hired a famous big band, the Stan Kenton Orchestra." (I should add, for those too young to recognize the name, that the Stan Kenton Orchestra was, at one time, the biggest of all the big bands—no less a figure than Frank Sinatra called Kenton "the most significant figure of the modern jazz age." Clearly, as a young high school senior, Bill Giles was thinking *way* outside the box!)

"In order to break even on the prom," Bill continued, "I had to sell two thousand tickets at twenty dollars each, so it was a big gamble. I had some huge posters made, and I plastered them in all of the high schools in that part of town. I sold twenty-five hundred tickets—five hundred more than my break-even number—and it was the best high school party ever. That experience opened my eyes to what leadership is all about, and I learned that one of the most important aspects of leadership is to be a person with a vision. You should never be afraid to dream too big. Your only fear should be, 'Am I dreaming too small?'"

Former U.S. congressman Newt Gingrich told me, "I was a ten-year-old kid in Harrisburg [PA]. One day I watched two movies about animals and was so moved, I walked right to City Hall. I asked the receptionist, 'Who do I see about building a zoo in Harrisburg?' She sent me up to the Parks Department, where I spoke with a nice old man. He pulled out his files and tried to explain to me what it costs to feed a lion. He told me to come back to the City Council meeting on Tuesday. I showed up on a slow August afternoon and made my pitch. It ended up in the newspaper, and later my dad, a military man stationed in Korea, saw the article. He wrote back, 'Keep the kid out of the newspapers.' That hasn't exactly happened."

Leadership begins with vision. Every leader, young or old, must have a vision to define what *success* looks like. A vision is what the leader and the entire team compete for, struggle for, and sacrifice for. So every young leader must be, first and foremost, a young visionary.

■ What Is Vision?

"Vision is the essence of leadership," observed Theodore M. Hesburgh, president emeritus of the University of Notre Dame. "Knowing where you want to go requires three things: having a clear vision, articulating it well, and getting your team enthusiastic about sharing it. Above all, any leader must be consistent. As the Bible says, no one follows an uncertain trumpet."

A vision is a glowing word-picture of a desirable and optimistic future. Great leaders are always great visionaries. They dream big dreams, then they share those dreams with their followers. In the process of communicating their vision, that private dream becomes a shared dream. It becomes a dream that is owned and pursued by everyone in that organization. When the team or organization buys into the leader's vision, that leader's effectiveness is magnified a hundred-fold.

Bryant Lancaster is the former basketball coach at Hillcrest High School in Tuscaloosa, Alabama. "Leaders," he said, "are people who have a vision. They not only see the parts, but they have the ability to piece the parts together in order to form the whole picture. That whole picture should ignite, excite, unite, inspire, and motivate the team to perform at a higher level. That's what a vision does for a team."

■ Uncorking the Imagination

Visionary leaders believe in limitless possibilities. They refuse to accept any limits on the imagination. Andrea Myers is director of athletics at Indiana State University. Andi told me about an early incident that gave her a vision of limitless leadership possibilities. "In 1956," she said, "our school had a mock presidential election. I was nominated to run for president on the Democratic Party ticket. Some boys said I couldn't run for president because I was a girl. Our civics teacher made it clear that women could be president. So I ran and won. I was fourteen years old at the time, and I have been breaking barriers ever since."

Andi Myers was fortunate to have a teacher who was dedicated to un-corking the imagination of her students and opening their minds to limitless possibilities. So what if a woman had never been elected president before? Why shouldn't it happen? The idea that "a girl can't be president" is only a mental barrier, not a physical wall. Andi's teacher taught her—and her fellow students—that mental barriers were made to be broken. A teacher like that one deserves a statue in the park and a library named in her honor!

Unfortunately, not every teacher is so inspired and inspiring. Some teachers seem to set a goal of programming a roomful of little robots—thirty little minds slotted into nice, neat little pigeonholes. In the process of establishing order, such teachers punish creativity and squelch vision.

Now, I don't for a moment advocate anarchy in the classroom. A certain amount of orderliness is necessary for an environment of learning. But there has to be some allowance for the messy spontaneity and unbridled enthusiasm of an imaginative, visionary child.

A fourth grade teacher once set a bowl of flowers in front of the classroom and told her students to sketch the flowers. Most students produced drawings that slavishly imitated the contours and colors of that bowl of flowers. One student, however, put his visionary imagination in high gear. He interpreted those flowers in a new way, changing the proportions and dimensions, then added an extra dollop of imagination by drawing faces on the flowers!

When the teacher saw the boy's interpretation of the flowers, she scolded him and said, "Flowers do *not* have faces!" Fortunately, that boy paid no attention to the admonition. He went on to produce animated cartoons featuring flowers with faces, a talking mouse, a flying elephant, and more. That boy's name, of course, was Walt Disney.

This world needs young people with limitless, unbridled imagination—kids who will dream big dreams, then inspire people to turn those dreams into reality. I worry about those imaginative, excited, enthusiastic kids—the ones who run wind sprints on the ceiling, talk when they should listen, and run afoul of the rules now and then. I worry that instead of helping these potential visionaries uncork their imaginations, their teachers and parents are squeezing them into a mold, forcing them to be quiet and sit still, and even drugging them into submission with Ritalin. I worry that a kid who might have become the next Sally Ride or Neil Armstrong, the next Maya Angelou or James Michener, the next Condoleeza Rice or Martin Luther King, Jr., is going to end up marking time in the back of the class until graduation.

As parents, we should become involved in our children's schools, encouraging and supporting the teachers who draw out the dreams and creativity of our kids. We should make sure our kids are being mentored and inspired by such teachers.

At the same time, we as parents need to make sure we enhance the optimism, creativity, and imagination of our kids. There are so many ways that we thoughtlessly suppress their imaginative and visionary potential. We are so quick to resort to harsh, critical words: "Can't you do anything right?" We are often too busy or too inattentive to encourage their ideas and imagination: "Not now! Can't you see I'm busy?" We are quick to ignore the positive and focus on the negative: "Six A's and a C minus in math, eh? How come you're doing so lousy in math?" Sometimes we make our kids feel clumsy and incompetent: "Here, let me do that. You're doing it all wrong."

One concept that has meant a lot to me as a parent is the "red thread" metaphor. A "red thread" is a talent, interest, or passion that stands out in a child's life. The child who spends all his before- and after-school time running a paper route or a lemonade stand may grow up to become a Fortune 500 CEO. The child who tinkers with CO_2-propelled toy rockets may become a NASA administrator. The child who spends hours banging away at the piano could end up being an accomplished performer or composer. These early interests and abilities are a child's red threads. They are the richly colorful aspects of a child's soul that stand out against the bland background of ordinary life.

My red thread was sports. My whole boyhood was about athletics; I played baseball, basketball, football, every kind of ball I could get my hands on. Going into my twenties, I tried my hand at pro baseball for a couple of years—and my red thread still showed its true color. As a boy, I pictured a career in Major League Baseball, but I ultimately found that I had a talent for sports management and promotion. You never know where a child's red threads will lead.

When we discover and encourage the red threads in our kids, we accentuate the positive interests and talents in their lives. We reinforce healthy self-esteem and confidence. The child who has no red threads, who sees his life as a pattern of dull grays, is a prime candidate for mediocrity and failure in life. As parents, we can't let that happen to our kids. We have a duty to our kids to challenge them and encourage them to uncork their imaginations, envision a grand future for their lives, and live the adventure of leadership.

In November 1988, our family adopted four Filipino brothers, ages four through nine. We gave these four boys a whole day to adjust to their new situation—then we threw them right into American life. We exposed them to one new experience after another, and with each new experience they exclaimed, "We can't do that!" Coming from an orphanage in Mindanao, the southernmost island of the Philippines, they hadn't had many opportunities or new experiences. They had never competed in athletics, and they didn't want to be challenged. They simply couldn't imagine themselves doing the kinds of things that most American kids take for granted.

One of the first experiences we shoved the boys into was youth swimming, which is very popular in central Florida. We took them to the Rollins College pool and handed them over to veteran coach Harry

Meisel and his son, Kevin. Those four boys went into the water, kicking and screaming, and as they were going down for the third time, we could hear them glub-glub-glubbing, "We can't swim!" And they were right. They couldn't swim to save their lives—but they learned, and they learned fast!

Harry and Kevin challenged my four new sons to attempt the impossible—at least, those four boys thought it was impossible. In a few days, all four of them discovered that they were equipped with something they never knew they had: gills and fins! The same boys who had been wailing, "We can't swim!" were soon swimming every day. Suddenly, my biggest challenge was trying to get those boys out of the pool! They didn't want to leave! Within a few years, three of the four boys had qualified for the Junior Olympics in Florida—they had become three of the top youth swimmers in the state!

But before that could happen, we had to uncork their imaginations and give them a new vision of themselves. They had to learn to stop saying, "We can't do that," and start saying, "Anything is possible!" One of our biggest challenges as parents, teachers, coaches, pastors, and youth workers is to pop the corks off those youthful imaginations and get the young people to see that there are truly no limits in life and no ceilings to their leadership aspirations.

■ How to Build a Vision

Dr. Vincent Mumford is director of the Sports Leadership Graduate Program at the University of Central Florida. He told me, "We adults have tremendous opportunities to help develop the leadership potential in youngsters. We have the ability to make a student's experience a positive one and to help shape his or her outlook on school, sports, leadership, and life. The ability to construct a vision for the future is essential to that young person's outlook. Here, then, are some key strategies we should focus on as we encourage and develop young leaders:

"First, *help students dream big dreams*. Don't let them settle for anything less than a grand vision of the future. Teach them how to remove the limits from their thinking and to dare to envision the impossible.

"Second, *help them develop a game plan based on their dreams*. Teach them how to think practically and constructively about their vision for the future. A vision is worthless unless we have a plan for turning that vision into reality.

"Third, *encourage them (push them, if need be) to get up and take action*. Challenge them to work for their vision. Encourage them to apply shoe leather and elbow grease to their dreams. This is where a strong work ethic comes in. If a person is not willing to work hard to make a dream happen, then the dream isn't worth very much.

"Fourth, *show them how to keep score by being accountable*. Teach them how to break down their grand vision into a series of smaller, achievable steps and goals. As they reach each of these milestones, show them that they are making measurable progress toward their dreams. Teach them that real success is measured not by how they compare to someone else, but how much they improve from where they started.

"Fifth, *encourage them to celebrate small victories and to recharge themselves by becoming lifelong learners*. Young people are impatient. They sometimes get down on themselves if they don't achieve their big dream instantly and all at once. Teach them the value of patience and steady, measurable progress. Teach them the importance of continually reading, learning, educating themselves, and sharpening their skills. Affirm their successes along the way. Encourage them when they fail. Keep telling them that they are on the right track, and if they persevere, they will reach their goal and realize their vision."

The idea of constructing a vision for the future may seem a bit vague and somewhat forbidding. It needn't be. I believe that envisioning the future can be simple, practical, and even fun—if we go about it the right way. Here, then, is my ten-step plan for building a vision. When you talk to kids—whether as their parent, teacher, pastor, mentor, whatever your role in their lives—you can use this ten-step plan as a guide:

1. *A vision should be clear and simple.* A vision of the future must be simple enough to be grasped by everyone on the team. It should be so simple that anyone on the team can explain it to the next person without distortion or ambiguity. It should be simple enough to be easily understood and remembered. Habakkuk 2:2 (Amplified Version) urges us, "Write the vision and engrave it so plainly upon tablets that everyone who passes may [be able to] read [it easily and quickly] as he hastens by."

2. *A vision should be powerful, visual, and easy to imagine.* Every member of the team or organization should be able to picture what the vision will look like when it's achieved. A vision should be "drawn" for the listener in the form of word pictures, metaphors, and stories.

3. *A vision should be focused on change.* The purpose of a vision is to take a team or organization to a new and better place. A vision is a picture of a brighter future. This implies positive change, progress, growth, expansion, and improvement. It focuses everyone's attention on completing today's tasks in order to achieve tomorrow's promise.

4. *A vision should demand sacrifice.* "If your vision doesn't cost you something," said John C. Maxwell, "it's only a daydream." We need to teach young leaders that they must be willing to pay the price to achieve their vision—and they must be willing to ask their teammates to pay a price. When the people see their leader is sacrificially committed to a vision, they are inspired to commit themselves as well.

Todd Lickliter, head basketball coach at Butler University in Indianapolis, told me, "Making sacrifices is often the price of being a leader. You pay the price now in order to reap the benefits of your future vision. Leaders know that the price they pay today will be well worth it when the future goal is met and the vision becomes a reality."

5. *A vision should be communicated with contagious optimism.* A vision is a word picture of a coming celebration. People should associate your vision with confetti, noisemakers, whoops, and hollers. The mental image your vision creates should fill the entire team with a sense of excitement, expectation, and exhilaration. "You have to be so excited about your vision that people can't wait to come and try to achieve it with you," explained Carol Bartz, CEO of AutoDesk. "You have to have people excited about what you are doing."

6. *A team's vision should connect with the personal vision of each individual.* The achievement of the leader's vision should make everyone's life better—not just the leader's. The shared accomplishment should produce individual benefits for every member of the team. Each person's desire for a better life should be bound up in the organization's dream of a brighter future. When everyone on the team has a personal stake in the success of that vision, then the collective desire and effort to achieve that vision will be increased and intensified.

7. *A vision should be stated and restated relentlessly.* "A vision of the future is not offered once and for all by the leader, then allowed to fade away," asserted management expert Warren Bennis. Young leaders should never tire of restating their vision for the future. They should celebrate it, underscore it, and put it up in lights for everyone to see. People quickly forget; it's the leader's job continually to remind and reinspire the team.

8. *A vision should be personified by the leader.* People should not be able to see the leader without being reminded of his or her vision. And when people hear about the vision, they should auto-

matically picture the leader. The vision and the leader should be inseparable, and the leader should be the walking embodiment of the vision.

9. *A vision should be a broad vista, not a detailed plan.* Detailed plans tend to be rigid and confining. A genuine vision is boundless and liberating. A vision is flexible enough to withstand changing conditions within the organization and in the marketplace. Jack Welch, former CEO of General Electric, put it this way: "Trying to define what will happen three to five years out, in specific, qualitative terms, is a futile exercise. The world is moving too fast for that. What should a company do instead? [It should] define its vision and its destiny in broad but clear terms."

10. *A vision should be difficult—even seemingly impossible—to achieve.* A vision that is easily within an organization's grasp is not a vision. It's just a goal. It doesn't take much visionary leadership to say, "We're going to climb that hill over there." A true visionary leader says, "We're going to climb Mount Everest, and when we've done it, we're going to have a big party at the top of the world!" A true vision should be daunting in its scope and breathtaking in its audacity.

■ Don't Forget to Celebrate!

This all-important word *vision* has become watered down in recent years due to overuse and misunderstanding. Some people think that *vision* is merely another word for *perception, comprehension,* or *foresight*—but to me, this word is much more powerful than that. A true vision is a daring, daunting, startling word picture of a possible future. When people encounter a leader's vision, they should experience a moment of so-called shock and awe.

The most effective and powerful vision engages not just our visual imagination, but *all* the senses. For example, we don't just *see* our team holding up a trophy, but we *hear* the cheers and the applause, we *feel* the warm glow of triumph, we *smell* the sweet fragrance of the playing field. When every member of the team has that vision planted in his or her mind, that vision becomes an irresistible force, drawing the team toward a successful future the same way a magnet draws iron filings to itself. Like those iron filings, people will unite and align themselves when they are drawn together by the vision of a high calling and an elevated sense of purpose, expressed in visual, emotionally powerful terms.

A vision gives the entire team something grand and exciting to look forward to and celebrate. All members of the team look forward to the day that they can throw a party, hug each other, and say, "We did it!" I mean that literally—the leader should throw a party, a real wingding, once the vision has been achieved. And the crowning moment of that party should include the unveiling of the *next* and even *grander* vision! Don't forget to celebrate!

America witnessed a profound example of visionary leadership on May 25, 1961. On that day, President John F. Kennedy spoke before Congress and unveiled a bold, audacious, seemingly impossible vision: "I believe that this nation should commit itself to achieving the goal, before this decade is out, of landing a man on the moon and returning him safely to the earth. No single space project in this period will be more impressive to mankind, or more important for the long-range exploration of space; and none will be so difficult or expensive to accomplish. . . . But in a very real sense, it will not be one man going to the moon. If we make this judgment affirmatively, it will be an entire nation. For all of us must work to put him there."

Notice the elements of President Kennedy's vision. It has a powerful visual component; in his simple words, we can actually *see* a space-suited man standing on the airless, hostile surface of the moon, then returning safely to earth. It is a challenging and difficult vision; President Kennedy plainly states, "No single space project . . . will be so difficult or expensive to accomplish." It will be a vision that requires the sacrifice and commitment of the entire nation, not just a few individuals: "All of us must work to put him there."

Leaders sometimes fear to issue too great a challenge; they fear to ask too much of their followers. But the truth is that people *want* to be challenged; they are *eager* to sacrifice and work hard to achieve lofty goals. When President Kennedy articulated his vision of a man on the moon, the nation responded. Though President Kennedy didn't live to see his dream fulfilled, his bold vision became a reality on July 20, 1969—six months before his deadline of "before this decade is out."

John Whitehead, president of the Rutherford Institute, vividly recalled how he was inspired as a young man by the visionary leadership of President Kennedy: "I clearly remember President Kennedy's inauguration speech in January 1961. He said, 'The torch has been passed to a new generation of Americans.' He was calling for idealistic sacrifices, and he demanded of Americans, 'Ask not what your country can do for you; ask what you can do for your country.' We who were young then answered that call, drawing our inspiration for civic and social involvement from Kennedy's vision of America. That hope for a better America continues to motivate me in my own life and work. I think of that vision today whenever I encourage young people to take a stand for the things they believe in."

■ Where There Is No Vision, the People Perish

As we parent, train, coach, and mentor young leaders, the issue of vision is doubly important. We need to teach and encourage young leaders to become visionaries—and we need to model visionary leadership. One of the most important dreams we must instill in these young leaders is a vision of themselves as leaders. We must help these young people to envision what they can become—and what they can accomplish.

A. J. Smith, the general manager of the San Diego Chargers NFL franchise, told me, "My father, Raymond Smith, instilled in me at an early age the vision that I could be a front-runner, a leader. He often told me to always be up front, never to hang back. 'If you are on a team,' he said, 'then be a leader, be a captain.' Again and again, he told me, 'Work hard and be confident!' He said that people respected and admired someone who works hard, displays confidence in his abilities, and can get along with people in a working environment. The older I got, the more I realized that everything he tried to teach me was true."

As an NFL player, A. J. was coached and mentored by the great Buffalo Bills coach, Marv Levy, who led the Bills to four consecutive Super Bowls. "I had the good fortune of working for Coach Levy for fourteen wonderful years," A. J. told me. "Professionally, Marv Levy is the man I admire and respect the most in the twenty-five years I've been involved in pro football. Coach Levy was a visionary leader—and he was not just the leader of the team, but of the entire Bills organization."

A. J. isn't the only person who sees Marv Levy as a visionary leader. Indianapolis Colts president Bill Polian, who once worked alongside Levy as the Buffalo Bills general manager, said, "Marv Levy is one of the greatest leaders this game has ever known. He has an incredible vision for what his teams and players could become and a magnificent ability to articulate that vision." Levy himself once stated, "A great football coach has the vision to see, the faith to believe, the courage to do—and Brett Favre to play quarterback."

"Watching, listening, and learning from Coach Levy," A. J. Smith recalled, "gave me a firsthand look at what it takes to be a leader and how to act like a leader. He instilled in all of us a respect for being part of a team. He gave us a vision, he told us what victory would look like and feel like, and he told us that if we worked hard and pulled together, we would be successful; we would be hard to beat. We all believed in him, respected him, and followed him. I am proud to say that I was a part of his team during the glory years of the Buffalo Bills."

I believe that there are essentially two ways of motivating people to reach a goal. One is positive; the other is negative. The positive way of motivating people is with a vision. The negative way is with fear and punishment. Dictators motivate people through fear and punishment. Leaders motivate people with a bright and optimistic vision of the future.

Jack Canfield, coauthor of the *Chicken Soup for the Soul* books, learned the importance of visionary leadership at an early age. He was a patrol leader in the Boy Scouts in his early teens. He held leadership positions at the military school he attended. He was the president of the youth fellowship in his church in Martin's Ferry, Ohio. There, his pastor once took him aside and gave him a vision of his future, telling young Jack Canfield, "You are an extraordinary young man, and you have great leadership potential."

"My football coach," Jack told me, "was Eugene Lamone, who used to play at the University of West Virginia. Coach Lamone taught me the importance of visionary leadership. He believed that a team performs better when the players are having fun. He didn't want us to be out on the field feeling scared or pressured. He wanted us to have fun and to have a vision of winning. He said, 'If you lead people by being a visionary, you don't have to rule them with fear.' I never forgot that."

"The Bible tells us, 'Where there is no vision, the people perish,'" said Rev. Bruce Chesser, pastor of Geyer Springs First Baptist Church in Little Rock. "The word for 'perish' can also be translated 'lose control.' People need visionary leadership at every level—in the home, in the church, in the nation. An organization or society without a vision—and without a leader to articulate that vision—is in big trouble. A lack of visionary leadership produces chaos. That is why young people need to step up, dream their dreams for a brighter future, and become leaders and proponents for those dreams. Without a vision, without leadership, our organizations and our society will be out of control; they will perish.

"That's what happened when Moses went up on the mountain to receive the Ten Commandments from God. While Moses was up on the mountain, there was no leadership among the people camped below. The Bible tells us that when Moses returned, he found that the people were 'out of control.' The Bible used the very same word for 'out of control' that Proverbs used for 'perish' in the statement, 'Where there is no vision, the people perish.' In other words, where there is no visionary leadership, the people are out of control.

"So we need to train young people to think about the future in visionary terms. We need to encourage them to dream grand dreams of a better tomorrow. We need to raise up young visionary leaders. What's in it for them? Everything! If God has wired them for leadership, if God has placed them in a situation that cries out for leadership, then they can have the satisfaction of knowing that they are fulfilling God's plan for their lives. There is no greater satisfaction in life than doing the work God created you to do."

A final word of caution about vision came from Rev. Mike Schirle, senior pastor of the Orlando Baptist Church. He reminded us that, as adult leaders, our tendency is to *inflict our vision* on young people rather than allow and encourage them to dream their own dreams and pursue their own visions.

"We should never forget," Mike told me, "that we are all gifted differently and wired differently, and God has a unique plan and vision for every individual life. We should never try to fulfill our unmet dreams through our kids. They have their own lives to lead, their own dreams to fulfill. If we want to raise visionary young leaders, then we need to step back, take our hands off the steering wheel, and let them drive the vision. If we're going to train young leaders, we have to let them lead. We have to allow them to dream their own dreams, even if they are not our dreams."

This world desperately needs change, and only leaders with a vision can truly change the world. With an optimistic, creative vision as their blueprint for change, young leaders can inspire their generation to build a brighter tomorrow out of the raw materials of today.

Next, we will examine the second crucial dimension of great leadership—the ability to communicate effectively and persuasively.

| 6 |

Second Key:
Be a Communicator

According to *The Book of Lists* by David Wallechinsky and Amy Wallace, the number one fear is the fear of public speaking. Amazingly, the fear of death ranks seventh on that list. From my early classroom experiences with public speaking, I can believe it. As a boy, I was scared to death of public speaking. I vividly recall the sweaty palms, rapid pulse, nausea, and shortness of breath. I tell you, getting up in front of my classmates and giving a speech literally made me sick!

Today, I give more than a hundred speeches a year, and I've given literally thousands of speeches in my lifetime. So it amazes me to recall how my knees knocked and my voice quavered as I stammered my way through a little three-minute speech in Miss Barbara Bullard's ninth grade English class. Miss Bullard would allow us only a single 3 X 5" card for our notes. Well, I wrote my entire speech, word for word, in lettering so small a gnat would need reading glasses. I stood up in front of the class, looked down at my little index card—and I couldn't read a word of it. Needless to say, my first speech was a total disaster. It's a wonder I ever got up the nerve to give another!

I came out of my shell in the fall of my junior year at Wake Forest University. To this day, I don't know what happened to bring about such a change. I always admired radio sports announcers, and I secretly wished I could do what they did. Finally, I walked over to the campus radio station and asked the station manager, Dr. Julian Burroughs, if I could give it a try. He agreed to give me a shot, and he assigned me to broadcast the freshman basketball games and conduct a sports interview show. Suddenly, the kid who couldn't even read a speech off a 3 X 5" card was communicating with thousands of radio listeners (okay, it was probably only a few dozen—but at the time I *believed* it was thousands).

Dr. Burroughs gave me a lot of freedom to run my interview show the way I wanted. I designed the format, lined up the guests, selected the theme music—I put my heart and soul into that radio show. Sometimes I'd bring guests into the studio for interviews, and sometimes I'd go out and tape an interview on location. My guests ranged from Wake Forest coaches and players to such famous names as Ted Williams (my baseball idol!), golfing great Arnold Palmer, baseball legends Harmon Killebrew, Jim Gentile, and Roger Maris (that was the year Maris set a record of sixty-one home runs—what a show *that* was!), and evangelist Billy Graham, our chapel speaker that week (Dr. Graham is an avid sports fan and gave me one of my best interviews ever).

I learned a lot about myself in the course of doing that radio show. I discovered that if I tackled a challenge that scared me (and, yes, I was still uncomfortable with the idea of public speaking), my confidence level went up—and I had fun! But I also learned something that wasn't much fun—I discovered that whenever you try to accomplish something, there will be people who will try to tear you down.

After my very first broadcast, I came back to my room and found a note on my bed. The note, which was placed there by my roommate, read: "I'm not a broadcaster, but I tried." Ouch!

Maybe he was trying to give me some friendly advice: "Don't delude yourself, Pat. You're terrible, so save yourself a lot of embarrassment and quit now." Or maybe the guy was a little jealous that I had accomplished something on that radio show. Whatever his motivation for writing that note, it hurt. After all these years, I still remember what that hurt felt like.

But let me tell you—that note was a powerful motivator in my life! I remember thinking, *So he says I'm not a broadcaster? Well, I'll show him!* I learned a lesson that is important to impress upon the young leaders we are teaching and mentoring: Whenever you set out to accomplish anything, expect people to try to belittle you, discourage you, and minimize your accomplishments. Don't let them stop you. Just ignore them, and keep moving forward. That's what leaders do.

The radio show made me something of a campus celebrity, and it elevated my confidence as a public speaker. I studied speech in my junior and senior years, and the skills I learned from my professor, James Walton, still serve me well. Learning to communicate before groups was probably the number one factor in my transformation into a leader.

■ Communication: Trigger for Transformation

George McGovern was born in 1922, the son of a Methodist minister. As a college student, he served as class president and won a statewide oratory competition with a speech titled "My Brother's Keeper" about his belief in our responsibility to our neighbors and to humankind. World War II interrupted his college education and took him to Europe, where he flew thirty-five combat missions as the pilot of a B-24 bomber, earning the Distinguished Flying Cross.

He lost his first bid for the U.S. Senate in 1956. In 1960, President John F. Kennedy appointed him the first director of the Food for Peace Program. He was elected to the Senate in 1962, and reelected in 1968 and 1974. In 1972, Senator McGovern ran unsuccessfully as the Democratic nominee for president.

"My high school English teacher told me that I had a talent, both in literary expression and in speaking," Senator McGovern explained to me. "She introduced me to the high school debate coach, who transformed me from a somewhat shy and reticent student into a more confident and persuasive public speaker.

"The great ancient Roman orator Marcus Fabius Quintilian once defined an orator as 'a good man speaking well.' You must first become a good man or a good woman before you are worth listening to as a good speaker. So it is with other activities: a good teacher is a good person teaching well. A good coach is a good person coaching well. A good parent is a good person parenting well. Become a good person and a good speaker, and use your ability to help others be better people. The good life is its own reward."

If the first task of a leader is to dream big dreams, then the very next task a leader faces is the challenge of communicating that vision to the team or organization. It's not enough to simply lay out a vision. A leader must sell the vision, forcefully and persuasively, so that "my vision" becomes "our vision." The leader must be able to excite, inspire, and motivate the entire team to buy into his or her vision. To become an effective speaker, a leader must learn a number of techniques for holding the attention of the audience and persuading them to take action—such techniques as storytelling, employing metaphors and analogies, using gestures and vocal variation, and combining speaking with visual aids, such as video or PowerPoint.

In the hundreds of interviews I conducted for this book, I was amazed at how many people reported that becoming a public speaker triggered their transformation into a leader. For example, Dr. Richard E. Lapchick, director of the DeVos Sport Business Management Program at the University of Central Florida, told me, "I realized that, as a returning tenth grade student, I had the ability to lead. I left home that summer thinking I was going to play basketball, but I ended up traveling in Europe instead. I was a different person when I came back. I told my fellow students about my experiences going to Dachau, the Nazi concentration camp, and the tremendous impact it had on my life.

"I noticed that other students paid much more attention to me when

I talked to them about serious issues and values than when I simply made jump shots. It was the first time I realized that I could discuss serious events and people would listen.

"At the same time, I saw the influence that speakers and leaders in the civil rights movement were having on the world. I was especially impacted by such leaders as Martin Luther King, Malcolm X, Cesar Chavez, Nelson Mandela, and Robert Kennedy.

"As a senior in high school, I was asked to give the salutatorian address at commencement. I was expected to greet the graduates and their families, then sit down. Having been to previous commencements, I knew it was usually the least notable moment on those occasions. But I decided to do something a bit more memorable. I decided to talk about racism and the civil rights movement.

"The impending March on Washington was several months away, scheduled for the summer of 1963. There was a great deal of apprehension nationwide about what would happen. I talked about how the races could work together using the model of sports. My dad coached basketball, and my friend, Leroy Ellis, played for him. Leroy was an All-American center, and he attended the commencement.

"I gave my talk, and the audience wasn't sure how to react until this big six-foot eleven-inch center rose up above the crowd, giving me a standing ovation. Seconds later, the rest of the audience joined him on their feet, clapping. At that moment I understood that the power to speak is the power to influence—and the power to lead."

Bobby Cox is the winningest manager in the history of the Atlanta Braves. Since 1990, he has led the Braves to twelve straight division titles. "You must have good verbal skills in order to lead," he told me. "Leaders are persuaders, and that means leaders need to be able to communicate enthusiasm to an audience. Every student should be required to take classes in public speaking."

Vini Jacquery, founder of International Reach, became a public speaker at a very early age. "From my earliest childhood," he told me, "I was surrounded by adults who were willing to share their world and their ideas with me. They provided opportunities for me to practice and test my speaking skills.

"When I was twelve, we lived in São Paulo, Brazil, and my parents took me to a weeklong conference led by an American speaker. I was the youngest attendee—the sold-out conference was aimed at adults. The conference was focused on personal development and healthy relationships, and it ignited my interest in psychology and teaching.

"My mother taught religion in the public school system, so I asked her to help me learn how to teach. By the time I was fifteen, I was practicing my public speaking skills by giving talks to my family members while using our living room television as a lectern. By age seventeen, I was speaking every Friday to high school students throughout the city of São Paulo about the Bible and spirituality. By age nineteen, I was speaking in large cities and military installations across Brazil and appearing on TV talk shows. By twenty-one, I had spoken in over four hundred churches throughout the United States, and later in such countries as Spain, Portugal, Cyprus, Greece, Italy, and Holland.

"I believe one of the best ways to encourage young people to lead is by exposing them to events, ideas, and people. Take your children with you—take them everywhere! Expose them to what you do at work; answer their questions; encourage them to listen—and to speak up and contribute! We tend to segregate children off with other children—but what can a ten-year-old learn from another ten-year-old? At dinners and gatherings, instead of putting children at the 'little table' away from the adults, we should bring the children to the grown-ups' table and involve them in the conversation. We must encourage young people to listen, learn, communicate, and lead."

Adam D. Witty is the founder and self-styled "big kahuna" at Ticket-Advantage.com, an innovative company that matches season ticket holders who have tickets to sell with single-game ticket buyers for events such as pro and college sports events, racing events, concerts, and more. "Early on in my journey as an entrepreneur," Adam told me (and he's a very young man, so that wasn't long ago!), "I met with the CEO of a large construction company in South Carolina. Before I left his office, I asked if he had any words of wisdom to impart. He said something very profound, and I never forgot it: 'The world belongs to a salesman with leadership ability.' To this day, those words hang above my desk.

"Your ability to lead is dependent on your ability to sell yourself, to communicate your vision, and to get results through people. So if we want to encourage young people to become young leaders, we need to help them become confident communicators, so they can effectively sell their vision and their ideas. If you're a parent, you need to ask yourself, 'Does my child enjoy speaking or performing in public? Does my child enjoy the challenge of convincing others to follow his or her lead? Is my child willing to go above and beyond what is expected?' If the answer is yes, then you have a child who is demonstrating the fundamentals of leadership. If the answer is no, then it's time to start encouraging and training for those qualities.

"Encourage kids to speak in public, everything from the blessing at the dinner table to the debate team at school. Help them discover the pleasure of seeing smiles on the faces in an audience and the confidence that comes with realizing, 'They're smiling because of the words I just said!' The ability to speak before an audience is basic to leadership."

Syndicated columnist Kathleen Parker has praised the public speaking skills of General Colin Powell. "Can he talk!" she wrote. "Anyone who has heard him speak knows that Powell can talk for an hour straight, with fluency and polish, without ever glancing at a note."

Author Mark Kurlansky writes that "Martin Luther King, Jr., was a small, unimpressive-looking man until he began to speak. From the beginning he was picked for leadership roles because of his speaking abilities and because he seemed to the press to be much older and more mature than he was. Dr. King's communication skills changed the course of American history."

Clyde McCoy, Ph.D., is chairman of the Department of Epidemiology and Public Health at the University of Miami, and he is a leading researcher in the field of adolescent drug abuse and HIV/AIDS risk reduction among chronic drug abusers and criminal offenders. Dr. McCoy pastored two churches in Ohio, earned five degrees in Cincinnati, taught at the University of Kentucky and the University of Cincinnati, and then enjoyed a thirty-year career at the University of Miami. He is not only a professor at U.M., but is also the faculty athletic representative and works with student-athletes and coaches in one of the top university athletic programs in the nation. Clearly, he has had quite a career as a leader—and he owes his career to the fact that he discovered and developed a gift for public speaking at an early age.

"I grew up in Appalachia," he told me, "and began working at age nine—which was also the age when I was baptized and gave up smoking. My father was a coal miner, and he and my family also ran a grocery store. I collected orders in the morning before I went to school, then delivered groceries evenings and Saturdays. Sundays and Wednesday nights were reserved for church.

"Growing up in church, I began to preach at age thirteen or fourteen, and I was an active leader in our youth meetings and at school, where I was usually elected chairman of this or president of that. I was chosen for leadership roles because I love people, I was a good communicator, and I could build a consensus around the needs of the group.

"Growing up in the mountains, you really only have two role models—ministers and teachers, people who preach and teach. So the leadership model I saw every day was a model of communication, of public speaking. I aspired to emulate these role models, which explains why I have been both a minister and a teacher in my career.

"The person who was most influential in encouraging my speaking ability was the wife of the minister of a church I attended. She was an adult leader for our youth group, and very early on she tapped me to be a young leader. I had just moved to the city from the mountains, and this minister's wife was able to see beyond the stereotypical image I presented of a hillbilly kid who was having trouble fitting in. She would encourage me to speak in front of groups and actually had me preach at our church. I remember that she coached me on my first sermon and wrote on my sermon notes, 'Breathe deeply, talk slowly, and pick out one person who is listening.' Her advice really worked well for me, and I soon became comfortable speaking in public. Young people need mentors like this minister's wife to encourage them, to give them opportunities, and to build their confidence so that they can lead."

Pastor David Self of Houston's First Baptist Church credits his minister-father for affirming his leadership talent. David first realized the importance of public speaking as a leadership ability when he gave a speech during a campaign for a student government office. "When I was twelve," he recalled, "Dad preached a sermon on using our talents. I wasn't musically inclined, so I didn't think I had any talents. Dad explained to me that there were all kinds of talents, and he told me the kind of talent he saw in me. 'David,' he said, 'you are a leader. I see kids following you wherever you lead them. God's given you a great responsibility. Make sure you use your gifts for God.' From then on, I began to understand that God expected me to lead people to him.

"During my senior year, I ran for class president. On the first day of the campaign, the halls were plastered with professional-looking campaign posters and banners. I was busy leading my church youth group and carrying out other leadership roles, and I had no time, talent, or organization to produce posters of my own.

"The day of the assembly where the candidates gave their speeches, I got up and said, 'You probably noticed that I haven't displayed a single poster or banner. I haven't handed out one piece of campaign literature. That's because we are seniors and we know each other. You know who I am and that I stand for Christian principles. So as you go to the ballot box, you must ask yourself: "Will I vote for a poster—or a person?" ' The class of over eight hundred students voted me into office without a runoff. I never forgot the lesson of that day: The ability to communicate is fundamental to the ability to lead."

■ The Confidence to Communicate

The teen years are tough for most kids. They are dealing with profound changes in their lives. Their schoolwork is harder (how many of us adults have to face a challenge as hard as learning calculus or chemistry?). Their hormones are raging, and their relationships are getting more complex. They are trying to cope with braces and a bad complexion. Their self-esteem suffers setbacks on a daily basis—and we come along and want them to become leaders! We want them to stand up and speak in front of audiences! Aren't we asking too much of them?

No. Because, in the process of building them up as leaders, we will also be building their confidence to tackle the many challenges that life throws at them. When they gain confidence and poise in one area of life, it carries over into every other area. The confidence to communicate becomes the confidence to lead—and the confidence to face the many challenges and character tests that inevitably come their way.

Mark Atteberry, pastor of the Poinciana Christian Church in Kissimmee, Florida, told me about a public speaking experience early in his life that nearly destroyed his confidence forever: "I was nineteen years old and preaching only the second sermon of my life. It was the first sermon I'd ever preached away from my home church, so needless to say, I was a nervous wreck. Admittedly, my sermon was short on theology (at nineteen, I didn't know much theology) and long on stories (I had several good books of sermon illustrations).

"The theme was simple enough: 'The world will always be at odds with Christian values.' Not very profound, but at nineteen, it was the best I could do. At one point in the sermon, I started comparing my experience at a secular college to my experience at Bible college, and I described how an atheist science teacher I had in college would make fun of me for believing the creation account in the Bible.

"While I was telling this story, a man stood up in the audience. He raised his arms and stopped me in midsentence, saying, 'Hold it right there!' I stopped, dumbfounded. I had never seen anyone protest a sermon before, and I had no idea who this man was. I later learned that he was the superintendent of schools in that area and a lifetime educator. He said, 'I'm sorry, but I can't sit here and listen to anybody bash public education!' And then he started lecturing me like I was seven years old. I absolutely wanted to die.

"Fortunately, the pastor of the church stood up from his seat in the front row and intervened on my behalf. After some cross words, the two men sat down, and I was given the signal to continue. I ended the sermon as quickly as possible, then sat down, completely humiliated.

"That night, I decided I wasn't cut out to preach, and I made up my mind to look at other career options. I couldn't imagine ever stepping into a pulpit again for the rest of my life. I'm grateful for a few close friends and Bible college professors who came alongside me, talked to me and prayed with me, and rebuilt my confidence to a point where I could work up the nerve to try again. The next time I stepped into a pulpit, I was absolutely terrified. But I got through it, nobody stood up to protest my sermon, and I went on from there. I'm forty-seven today and have been preaching every Sunday for the last twenty-eight years.

"Here's the lesson: One thoughtless, impulsive comment to a young potential leader might be all it takes to destroy that young person's confidence—and that young person's leadership potential would be lost to us forever. Confidence is a fragile commodity—especially among the young. One of our most important jobs as parents, teachers, and mentors is to nurture confidence so that young people can stand up and boldly lead. My life as a minister was saved by those people in my life who lovingly and patiently treated my emotional wounds and gave me the courage to get back into the pulpit and try again."

■ Helping Young Leaders Overcome Their Communication Fears

What do young people fear most about communicating in public? For some, it is the fear of embarrassment. They are afraid they will do or say something foolish and be laughed at. For others, it is the fear of failure. They are afraid they will lose their place or forget what they wanted to say. For others, it is the fear of rejection: "Everybody's going to hate me," or "What if people hate what I have to say?" Couple these fears with the fact that most young people are facing self-esteem problems and simply don't like to be center stage, and you can see why it is hard to motivate them to get up and speak in public.

Here, then, are twelve tips on public speaking that you can share with the young person you are coaching and mentoring. I have applied these principles in my experience as a public speaker, and I guarantee that they can help build the confidence and competence of a young leader:

1. *Be organized and prepared.* Half the battle of speaking confidently is knowing that you will never be at a loss for words. Your presentation is organized, you have good stories to tell, you know your material so well that you don't worry about getting lost or derailed, and you have good notes.

2. *Keep it simple.* Limit your outline to three main points. After your opening story, tell your audience those three points, so they know where you're going. At the conclusion, recap those three points, so they know where you've been. Keeping it simple and making the outline of your talk clear will make it more memorable, understandable, and persuasive.

3. *Prepare simple notes, not a written script.* Don't write out a speech word for word—never read from a script. Instead, when you make your notes, use short phrases, trigger words, symbols, and little pictures to jog your memory about each point. Instead of delivering an overrehearsed oration, simply have a conversation with the audience.

4. *Relax.* When you get up to speak, use a relaxed, informal, extemporaneous style. You put your audience at ease when you are at ease. Don't lock yourself in place behind the lectern—pick up the microphone and walk around the stage, or step down onto the floor with the audience.

5. *Become a storyteller.* Stories rivet the attention, create mental pictures, illustrate principles in a dramatic way, and make your message unforgettable. "The best way to learn is through stories," said leadership guru Ken Blanchard. "I know that because of the way people respond to my stories in my lectures. Stories permit the audience and readers to identify and get into the characters and learn right along with the characters. It makes learning effortless and enjoyable." When I speak before groups, I keep an eye on the audience. If I see people begin to yawn or check their watches, I always use a phrase that captures their attention: "Now, let me tell you a story . . ." Business consultant John Eldred told me, "We are hard-wired to retain stories, not PowerPoints, thank goodness."

6. *Practice your talk.* Don't memorize, but know the outline of your material—your main points, analogies, stories. Become so familiar with your talk that you can deliver it at a moment's notice—not word for word from memory, but enthusiastically and conversationally. Time your talk in advance, allowing for questions and answers, and cut out material if it seems too long. (But don't cut out your best stories!)

7. *Be aware of the nonverbal component of your talk.* We tend to focus so much on the *words* we speak that we forget that the way we deliver those words is just as important, if not more! Avoid a monotonous tone of voice—vary tone and volume of your voice. Make sure everyone can hear you; project your voice to the back of the room. Use big gestures—the bigger the room, the more expansive your gestures should be. Avoid plac-

ing your hands in front of you in the fig-leaf position; this makes you look nervous and conveys that you have something to hide. Don't speak too fast or too slowly. Move around; avoid locking yourself in one place. Make eye contact with your listeners—don't look down at your notes or over their heads. Remember, you are having a conversation with your audience, so look them in the eye. Above all, be energetic and smile!

8. *Arrive early.* Check out the room; familiarize yourself with the sound system and the layout. Stand at the lectern, talk into the microphone, sit in a few audience seats, and picture how you will come across to different parts of the room. Then meet and greet people as they come in. Mingle with the audience before your talk, and establish rapport.

9. *Never apologize for being nervous.* Your stomach might feel as if it's filled with butterflies, but your nervousness rarely shows to the audience. If you don't mention being nervous, they will never know—so why call attention to it? Just put on a confident smile, and soon it won't be a put-on at all. You'll genuinely *feel* confident—and that confidence will carry over to your next speaking engagement.

10. *Don't worry about a few mistakes.* If you lose your place, don't call attention to it. Pause, take a deep breath, take a drink of water, back up, tell a story, pick up and move on—and *no one will ever know* you were momentarily lost. If you get tongue-tied or you stumble over a word, make a joke about it, keep it light, and move on. Your audience will love that little human touch. If you handle flubs with a relaxed manner and a sense of humor, you will actually put your audience at ease and get them on your side. People don't judge you for mistakes—they appreciate you and relate to you all the more when you show a little human imperfection. An occasional goof or gaffe tells the audience, "I'm not perfect. I'm not an

Audio-Animatronic robot. I'm just like you—a real, likable human being."

11. *Be aware of your audience's attention span.* Don't overstay your welcome. Keep the length of your talk appropriate to your audience and setting. Remember, less is sometimes more.

12. *Take questions.* If you are comfortable being interrupted, tell your audience to put up a hand if they have a question about something you just said. Taking questions in the middle of your talk gives your presentation an air of relaxed, conversational informality—this can be a good approach in small, intimate settings. If you don't want to be interrupted during your talk, and particularly if you are speaking to a very large group, allow time for a Q and A session at the end of your prepared talk. Keep answers brief and to the point. Avoid getting into a debate with someone who disagrees (offer to talk privately with that person after your talk).

These twelve principles have served me well as a public speaker, and I believe they will help to build the confidence of young leaders. Encourage young people to accept speaking opportunities whenever they are offered, and to make their own opportunities by volunteering to speak at school, church, youth groups, clubs, organizations, and events. Confidence comes with experience.

■ Words Have Power!

Stan Morrison is director of athletics at the University of California, Riverside. "My parents encouraged my development as a leader," he told me, "by continually reinforcing the message, 'You can do anything you set your mind to,' and by giving me positive reinforcement for my achievements. My high school coach, John Caine, also helped me to discover and develop my leadership potential. He and my other teammates convinced me to run for student body president.

"Though my own informal polling told me I was running behind, I went into the assembly and gave a speech to the student body that really knocked 'em dead—and I won. That day, I learned that public speaking is a crucial aspect of leadership. You must be able to communicate and persuade in order to lead.

"Words have power. The wrong words can tear down and destroy; the right words can build up and heal. I decided early on that I wanted to use the power of words in a constructive and healing way.

"I was involved in Youth for Christ when I attended U.C. Berkeley. I once had an opportunity to speak at an exchange involving a fraternity and a sorority. It was a Friday afternoon, and not the ideal time and setting for a presentation about the Christian faith. There was a lot of beer drinking going on, it was noisy, and nobody wanted to listen to a speaker. I really wasn't enthused about being there.

"But I sucked it up and began to speak. I suddenly realized that everyone was listening—and I mean, people were paying rapt attention! I presumed they listened because they couldn't believe that someone would have the audacity to make a religious presentation under these adverse circumstances. When I finished, several people came forward and wanted to talk seriously about faith and life issues. There was a strange and quiet pall over the room—everyone seemed incredibly subdued.

"That experience actually frightened me. I wasn't afraid of the people in the room. I was afraid of the power of my own words and the amazing impact they had on people. I wasn't sure if I could handle that much power. It was an overwhelming experience to see how I could affect people's thinking and feelings just by getting up and talking. To this day, I am awed by that enormous power, and I believe in using it with great care and a deep sense of responsibility. But that experience taught me something about myself: I could speak, and I could lead!"

I asked Stan Morrison what abilities adults should look for in potential young leaders—abilities that could be developed and encouraged in order to make those young people more effective as speakers and as leaders. "The first key in recognizing leadership potential in youngsters," Stan said, "is to ascertain their capacity to listen. Next, do they fully comprehend what they hear? Finally, do they have the capacity to paint pictures with words that come to them as a result of what they have learned from their listening and observations? If they do, they are off to the races in the leadership arena.

"Can the youngster tell a story and keep people's interest? Does he or she include details without losing the context or rhythm of the story? If so, then that young person knows the difference between giving speeches and having a conversation with a crowd. It's important that young speakers become comfortable in front of an audience and know how to read the audience, whether that audience is one person or a thousand.

"Adults must learn to influence the degree of moderation or embellishment a youngster attaches to any story. That young person needs to learn the consequences of not telling everything (which creates a false impression) or of telling things that are not true just to enhance the story. Young people need to be impressed with the fact that honesty is as essential as speaking ability. They need to understand the importance of modeling values, truth, and appropriate behavior. Role modeling is the strongest form of leadership, and when it is coupled with an effective speaking ability, you have a champion on your hands."

In the process of working with young people and developing young leaders, we will probably find a few young people who are natural talkers. Bob Seddon, baseball coach at the University of Pennsylvania, recalled being very comfortable as a public speaker during his high school years: "I spoke at a year-end sports banquet at my high school. A player from each sport was supposed to speak that evening. I was so enthusiastic that I got up and spoke for a full hour. There should have been a trapdoor under my feet! I still hear about that speech to this day."

With these born communicators, our challenge is not to motivate them or build their confidence. They're already revved up and ready to talk at a moment's notice. With these young people, our challenge is to help them use their gift of gab in a constructive way—not as a means of feeding their egos, but as a tool for serving God, others, and the team.

With most young people, however, we will have the opposite challenge: How do we motivate them to speak? Dal Shealy is the president and CEO of the Fellowship of Christian Athletes, and he is an excellent speaker. But speaking before groups didn't come naturally for him.

"As a sophomore in high school," Dal recalled, "I was running for a position in the high school council. I was to make a speech in front of the student body and teachers. I really didn't want to stand up on stage and make this speech. Mrs. Sara Hite, my Latin teacher, knew that I had a problem with stuttering and that I lacked confidence as a speaker.

"In those days, I went by my given name, Dalumuth. Mrs. Hite told me my name compelled me to take this opportunity and become a public speaker. 'Dalumuth,' she said, 'your name says, "Dal-You-Muth get up and speak."' So I did, and I have been speaking before groups ever since.

"Most kids are reluctant to get up and speak to groups. It's easier to simply stay in their comfort zone than to get up and take that kind of risk. So it's important that we, as parents and teachers and coaches, find positive ways to encourage and motivate young people to step up to these challenges that come their way. Sometimes all it takes is a pat on the back or an encouraging word to move young persons into action. We need to help them believe in themselves so that they will be willing to take that risk.

"Don't let them get by with half an effort—push and prod, gently but firmly. Always be positive and encouraging, never harsh or sarcastic. If they fail, then we need to be the ones who pick them up, dust them off, and put them back in the game.

"Young people need to learn at an early age that they are special, they are created in God's image, and God wants them to succeed in life. We need to set a positive example and influence kids in a positive way. We should help them set high goals, and we should hold them accountable to learn and grow on a daily basis."

Dale Brown was head basketball coach at Louisiana State University for twenty-five years. Dale recruited Shaquille O'Neal to LSU, turned around a failing LSU basketball program, and became the winningest coach in LSU basketball history. He told me a story that underscores the importance of communication in the leadership role.

"In a close game with only seconds left," Dale recalled, "I told a freshman to foul the man wherever he went and don't let him break free. With only eleven seconds left, this young player followed his man all around the court. He didn't let the other player break free—but he didn't foul him like I told him to! I was irate after the game. I jumped all over him for not following my instructions. He said, 'But I did follow your instructions, Coach! You told me to follow him, and I did!'

"Of course! *Foul* and *follow* sound almost exactly alike—especially in a noisy arena, in a pressure situation. It wasn't the player's fault. It was poor communication on my part. I've never forgotten the lesson of that disaster. It's a leader's job to communicate clearly. That's a lesson every leader needs to learn."

Words have power. The ability to communicate is the power to lead—or to mislead. Our challenge as parents, teachers, coaches, and mentors is to encourage young leaders to get up and speak—and to use their words wisely and well.

Next, we will examine the third crucial dimension of great leadership—the ability to work effectively and harmoniously with people.

| 7 |

Third Key:
Build Good People Skills

After graduating from Wake Forest University in 1962, I got in my car and drove to Florida to play for the Miami Marlins, a Phillies farm club. Arriving in Miami, I reported to Andy Seminick, one of my boyhood heroes. Andy was a powerfully built guy, standing five feet eleven inches, with a chest like an oaken barrel. He caught for thirteen years in the big leagues in the 1940s and 1950s. I had gotten to know him while I was a teenager, hanging around Shibe Park in Philadelphia. Andy was one of the Whiz Kids, the National League pennant-winning Phillies of 1950. So it was a thrill to have Andy as my first manager in the pros.

I can still see him on the top step of the dugout—no dugout bench for Andy! With that ever-present plug of tobacco in his cheek, Andy stared intently at every pitch, every play. He left a profound impression on everyone who knew him, including yours truly.

A while back, I started getting letters from a fellow named Joe Short, who was a minor-league pitcher in the Phillies farm system. Purely on his own, Joe had put together an Andy Seminick reunion, scheduled for August 2003. Joe Short managed to get many players who had played for

Andy in the minors to come back to Philadelphia to honor their old skipper. More than fifty ballplayers came for that weekend at their own expense just to pay tribute to their minor-league manager—a guy they had played for as much as forty years earlier and hadn't seen since.

Joe Short asked me to emcee the Saturday luncheon, introduce the ballplayers, and ask them to share a memory of Andy Seminick. The players had all been eighteen to twenty-four years old when they played for Andy; now they were in their late fifties or early sixties. After everyone had spoken, it occurred to me that each of their remarks and stories would fit into one of four categories:

Category 1: "Andy was the best teacher—in some cases, the only teacher—I ever had in my early baseball career."

Category 2: "Andy taught me what a strong work ethic is all about."

Category 3: "I've never been around anyone who competed as hard as Andy or wanted to win as much as Andy."

Category 4: "Andy cared about me as a person, not just as a ballplayer. After every game he came to my locker to congratulate me if I played well or encourage me if I had a bad night."

The comments and stories in Category 4 were the most impressive to me. Those guys would not have given up their weekends and flown to Philly from all around the country at their own expense if not for the fact that Andy Seminick had truly cared for them as individuals.

Take Joe Short, for example. He organized that whole event because he had a special regard for Andy Seminick. Who was Joe Short? In 1959, Andy Seminick was managing the Phillies farm club in Elmira, New York, and Joe was a pitcher Andy had to release from the team. Now, how many ballplayers do you think would be released by a manager, yet hold that manager in such high esteem that they would throw a reunion in his honor more than forty years later?

Clearly, there was something special about Andy Seminick. I'm not sure how many of those guys Andy specifically remembered—he had known so many players and it was so long ago. But, boy, they remembered him! And they remembered him fondly. Andy thought he had just been doing his job, but in reality, he had deeply affected every one of the guys who was there that day—including a former minor-league catcher named Pat Williams. I am so glad that Joe Short arranged that reunion when he did because in February 2004 Andy died of cancer at his home in Florida. He will never be forgotten by anyone who knew him.

How was Andy able to have such an impact on so many lives? Because he cared about people as *people*, not just as ballplayers. Andy was a leader with great people skills.

A leader is someone who achieves results and reaches goals through other people. That's why the third key to becoming an effective leader is build good people skills.

■ A List of People Skills

General Richard B. Myers, USAF, serves as the chief military advisor to the president, the secretary of defense, and the National Security Council. "Everyone has leadership potential," he told me. "The secret is to identify each individual's unique strong suits and interests, then encourage active involvement in those activities—be it sports, clubs, Scouting, music, or the arts. There are leadership opportunities in all of these endeavors. The three most important leadership attributes are confidence, accepting responsibility, and interpersonal or people skills.

"First, *confidence*. Now, there are many ways to build confidence in young leaders. The best way I know to build confidence is to help them develop an area of expertise and work hard to help them become the very best. As their confidence grows, other people will soon recognize their expertise and look up to them. The more confidence a young leader has, the more willing he or she becomes to accept new challenges and additional responsibilities.

"Second, *responsibility*. Everyone who has ever served in the military knows that leaders accept many serious responsibilities, including the responsibility for the safety of human lives. Learning to take responsibility for the success of any organization requires dedication and self-sacrifice. The personal and professional satisfaction of successfully leading your organization is what makes these challenges worthwhile. Since leadership responsibilities vary greatly, it should not be difficult for any person to find a leadership niche where he or she feels comfortable.

"Third, *people skills*. There are many ways to lead. Not everyone should feel the need to be the team captain. Successful leaders can also be found using such leadership abilities as public speaking or administration skills or interpersonal skills (people skills). In fact, mastering people skills is one of the most challenging leadership tasks of all. People have strong desires to contribute. Leaders must learn to value everyone's contributions and understand everyone's concerns. Expressing appreciation for the efforts of all will foster mutual respect and develop a strong sense of loyalty within the organization."

A people skill is an ability that can be applied in a wide variety of activities and settings. Our job is to look for those abilities in the young leader we are parenting or mentoring, affirm those abilities, and encourage the young leader to exercise them while seeking to learn new ones. Here is a list of people skills from my leadership experiences and study (you may think of others that I haven't listed):

1. *Affirmation*: The ability to give realistic acknowledgment and praise to team members. Genuine affirmation is focused on singling out strong character and personality traits, not merely praising people for achievements.
2. *Authority*: The ability to determine procedures, assign duties, promote efficiency, oversee activities, take responsibility, and hold people accountable for their progress in meeting the objectives of the team or organization.
3. *Coaching*: The ability to think strategically, to oversee a team activity, to motivate the team, and to teach the team members how to improve their performance, both individually and collectively.

4. *Conflict resolution*: The ability to intervene in personality clashes and to mediate disagreements between factions or individuals; the ability to solve interpersonal problems and unify the team.

5. *Counseling*: The ability to listen with empathy and help people with their career concerns, educational goals, personal problems, and family issues.

6. *Delegating*: The ability to entrust responsibility and authority to others on the team. Delegating is the essence of achieving results through other people.

7. *Facilitating*: The ability to manage the interaction and dialogue in a group in such a way that everyone in the group feels free to express ideas and no one feels intimidated or inhibited.

8. *Fairness*: The ability to hear complaints and resolve them courteously, tactfully, justly, and impartially.

9. *Hospitality*: The ability to entertain guests and give parties and social events that further the goals of the team by enhancing team unity and spirit.

10. *Motivation*: The ability to encourage and inspire people to reach within themselves and achieve their best performance—usually a much better performance than they imagined they were capable of achieving.

11. *Negotiating*: The ability to exchange information, opinions, ideas, and things of value in order to reach a mutually beneficial conclusion or decision.

12. *Organization*: The ability to plan and arrange events, meetings, and social functions that involve people in a team effort.

13. *Persuasion*: The ability to influence others—fairly, honestly, and sincerely—to one's own point of view.

14. *Recruitment*: The ability to attract and acquire the best and most effective people for a team or organization.

15. *Sociability*: The capacity to meet and converse with strangers in a relaxed, friendly, outgoing way.

16. *Teaching*: The ability to impart knowledge to others and train others in the skills they need to perform their tasks in the team environment.

Every one of these skills is a learnable skill. That means that young leaders-in-training have a responsibility to learn and develop these skills within themselves—and it means that we, as parents, teachers, coaches, and mentors, have a responsibility to encourage and teach these skills to the young leaders we are training.

■ Affirm the Best in People

Phil Frye was a Chicago-based attorney and part of the ownership group of the Chicago Bulls. He was a good friend of my mentor, baseball owner Bill Veeck. Unbeknownst to me, Phil had been following my career while I was with the Philadelphia 76ers, and he was one of the key people who invited me to interview for the general manager position with the Chicago Bulls. I got the job and worked with the Bulls for four years, beginning in 1969 when I was twenty-nine years old.

Every month, from my first month on the job, Phil and I met for lunch at his club, The Chicago Club. It was an elegant place with an oak-paneled dining room. Phil would always arrive after his mid-day squash game, his hair still wet from the shower. We never met for less than an hour and a half. We'd discuss matters affecting the Bulls organization, or we'd discuss the issues of the day, or we'd talk about our families, our beliefs, and our values.

No matter what subjects we would talk about, there was one thing Phil always did: He affirmed and praised the work I was doing. He always found something good to say, something positive to underscore, even during times when I had made mistakes or the organization wasn't performing well. Phil Frye was my boss, and he was not obligated to invest so much time in me, yet he went out of his way to be my encourager, my cheerleader, my life coach, and my friend.

I didn't realize at the time what a rare privilege I had. Few young leaders ever get the chance to have that kind of relationship with their boss. Looking back, I deeply appreciate what that relationship meant in my life and I have tried to be that kind of encourager and mentor to the young people around me. All young leaders need a Phil Frye in their lives—someone who will build their confidence by affirming their positive traits and accomplishments.

The ability to realistically affirm others is a crucial people skill that we need to practice in our dealings with young leaders. It is a crucial skill that we should encourage young people to build into their own lives.

David Brandon, CEO of Domino's Pizza, told me, "My father never went to college and was an electrician in a factory for the majority of his work life. He never had the benefit of management classes or training. Nor did he ever have those kind of responsibilities during his career. The day I received my first promotion into management at Procter and Gamble, I called my proud dad to tell him his oldest son had just gotten promoted into a management position within two years of being out of college. During our very fun conversation, I decided to ask him for some advice. I had sought his advice on virtually every other important matter affecting my life to that point, so why not now? I asked, 'Dad, what advice can you give me so I can be a great boss in my new job?' With only a slight pause, he responded, 'Dave, I would just suggest you find out how people want to be treated . . . and treat them that way!' It was the best management training I have ever received."

Longtime NBA coach Mike Dunleavy spoke of working with his son: "Throughout his school years, my son Michael was always the best player on his teams. He was intensely competitive, very driven—and he got upset whenever his teams lost. Michael would get on the guys who made mistakes and really be rough on them. One day, I took him aside and told him, 'The other kids on your team look up to you. Try being more positive with them. Praise them when they do something great, and encourage them when they mess up. Try a little more sugar and a little less vinegar. Things will go a whole lot better.'

"It wasn't easy for him—old habits die hard, and people skills take time to learn. But Michael eventually figured out how to become a positive motivator while still keeping a tough competitive edge."

Basketball great Bill Russell paid tribute to Red Auerbach, his coach with the great Boston Celtics teams of the 1950s and 1960s: "Red never gave us orders. He always consulted with us, and he'd make coaching decisions based on that information. So we were part of the process, and that's why it worked so well."

Indianapolis Colts president Bill Polian learned the importance of people skills during his early days as a coach at the U.S. Merchant Marine Academy. "My first boss in coaching was George Paterno, Joe Paterno's brother," Bill told me. "George helped me greatly by showing me, both by instruction and by example, how to deal with leadership challenges presented by different personality types on a team. I was the head baseball coach and the defensive line coach in football.

"We had this one player who was an immensely talented but emotionally fragile defensive end. I rode the young man in an honest but misguided attempt to get the best from him. As you might imagine, things between us went from bad to worse, and he was ready to quit.

"Coach Paterno called me in and explained that it was my responsibility to find the correct way to get the most out of this player. 'Every player is different,' he said, 'and one coaching approach doesn't fit all. This player has a lot of talent, and you need to find an approach that will work with his temperament.'

"At this juncture, Coach Paterno's true genius showed through. He said, 'Now, I'm not going to tell you how to do it. I want you to think about it. I want you to talk with the player about it, and I want you to work together and find a way to make this work.' Just to make sure I got the point he added, 'I can always find another defensive line coach—but All-American–caliber defensive ends are hard to come by.'

"Well, Coach Paterno had motivated me! So I sat down with this player, and we talked. I told him I wanted him to maximize his great talent. He told me he would do anything I asked so long as I didn't scream at him. Well, that was a reasonable request. So I developed a low-key, positive approach with him. As a result of his own great effort, he became the best defensive end in academy history and an All-American.

"Coach Paterno taught me that leaders must understand how to get the best out of people—and that means leaders need to have good people skills. Every individual is unique, but as a general rule, a positive approach is better than a negative approach. I have never forgotten this lesson and have applied it throughout my career."

Former Detroit Tigers executive Don Miers related an incident from his experience as a Little League baseball coach: "At the start of the season, I made it clear to all the parents that they were not to come near our dugout during practices or games. My coaches and I were the only ones who were going to talk to the players during our activity. Having others around would be a distraction. I said that parents could talk to their kids or ask our staff any questions that they wanted to *after* our practice or game was over.

"I also demanded that only words of encouragement be yelled from the stands. If I heard a parent saying anything negative to our team or the opposing team, I would let that parent know that it was unacceptable and that parent's child would be benched.

"During my first year coaching, one parent started screaming because I took his son out of the game. I asked him to be quiet, and he demanded to see me after the game. I acknowledged his request, and we met after the game. He told me that I wasn't committed to winning because I took his son, our most talented player, out of the game. I said, 'That's absolutely correct. I'm not here to win every game. I'm here to teach twelve young people how to play baseball, how to work as a team, and how to have fun doing it.'

"I explained to him, as I had explained to all the parents, that the players would get equal playing time, regardless of ability, if they came to practice and worked hard. He thought this applied to everyone other than his son. 'I'm going to the Little League board,' he said, 'because I've never heard of a coach who didn't care about winning.' I said, 'I'm all for winning, but winning is secondary to teaching at this level. But you need to do what you think is best. If you're not happy with this situation, then you should go ahead and talk to the board.'

"As he left, his final comment was, 'I'm going to ask them to put my son on another team!' Again, I advised him to do what he thought was best for his son—but I also suggested that he check with his son first. So he talked to his son, and the boy said that he really liked the way our team did things by rotating all the players. He told his dad that I had made the rules clear since the beginning of the season and he wanted to stay on our team. The father and I shook hands, and we have been friends ever since."

That is an excellent example of several people skills working together to solve a problem. Don Miers displayed the people skill of *authority*; he determined the rules, stated them clearly, assigned duties, and took responsibility for the results. He exemplified the people skill of *coaching* by overseeing the team activity and teaching the boys how to improve their performance. He exemplified *conflict resolution* by dealing squarely but calmly with the disgruntled parent so that in the end, he had turned an angry critic into a lasting friend. He displayed *fairness* by hearing the man's complaint and resolving it with tact, courtesy, and impartiality. And there were a few other skills I could name that Don demonstrated in this encounter. By handling this tense situation with such cool-headed skill, he not only kept his best player, but he also modeled leadership to the kids he was coaching.

One of the most important people skills that we should model to young people is *affirmation*. Many leaders, unfortunately, tend to focus only on goals and performance. When a team member fails to meet a goal or makes a mistake, the leader sees only the failed performance and proceeds to attack that performance and criticize the individual. Obviously, leaders sometimes have to criticize and confront, but constant, unrelenting criticism can break a person's spirit. That's why leaders need to learn the people skill of affirmation.

Affirmers focus on what people can become in the future, not how they failed in the past. When affirmers see failure, they encourage people to learn from the failure and do better next time. Affirmers discover previously unknown strengths and abilities in the people they lead.

Leaders sometimes have to be tough. They have to confront, and confrontation hurts. But the goal of leadership is to build people up, not tear them down. So if a leader spends 98 percent of the time affirming, encouraging, reinforcing, and building people up, then that leader will earn the right to confront, honestly and bluntly, during the 2 percent of the time when toughness is needed. Positive affirmation lends credibility to confrontation.

■ Leadership Without Bossiness

People skills are problem-solving skills. Daniel Boggan, Jr., is senior vice president of the National Collegiate Athletic Association (NCAA). He recalled an incident from his high school years when he discovered that he had the people skills of a leader: "I was a senior in high school when I became aware of the fact that people would follow me. This was partly a result of the respect I received for being a good student and a fair person, partly due to my ability as an athlete, a baseball player, and partly due to my organizational abilities (I was president of our high school club, and we put on dances for the community and we actually made a profit).

"On one occasion, we had a school assembly. We were getting ready to begin the program, and the principal went out and tried to get the attention of the audience—but the room wouldn't quiet down. Nobody paid attention. The principal struggled for fifteen minutes to get the room quiet, without success. Finally, I took the microphone, and I said a few words that got everyone focused on our program. The principal thanked me for rescuing her."

Daniel Boggan demonstrated *authority* in a situation that was out of control. He demonstrated the people skill of *facilitating*—of managing group interaction. And he demonstrated the people skill of *persuasion* by influencing the audience to be quiet and pay attention. As a high school student, he exemplified an important leadership strength: the ability to bring resolution out of confusion, order out of chaos.

Steve Gilbert, head football coach at Jacksonville University, was a natural at the people skill of *authority*. "I'm the oldest of six kids," Steve told me. "My parents said I have been guiding (or ordering around) my brothers and sisters since the age of six. My leadership ability was recognized in high school where I was elected captain of the football, basketball, and baseball teams. I was also selected captain of the triathlon team while I was coaching football at the University of San Diego.

"My youngest brother, Brian, is an excellent athlete who played quarterback for Michigan State (he was also an outstanding basketball and baseball player). When we were kids, I practiced coaching him in the backyard. I pretended I was Bud Grant and Brian was Joe Namath. We played out entire games in the backyard. The players would come out of the tunnel—that is, Brian would come out of the basement. We'd stand for the national anthem; we'd have the coin toss. I coached Brian to a lot of big wins in our backyard in New Jersey. That was the beginning of my love of leadership.

"What may initially seem like bossiness in kids could actually be an inclination for leadership. My mom would see me coaching and giving orders to my brothers and sisters as part of our childhood play, and she thought I was being bossy. I call it taking charge of the situation—and I'm serious about that. I don't think I was being bossy at all; I think I was practicing being a leader. I believe that adults can cultivate leadership in youngsters by simply encouraging them to organize their own activities in their neighborhood or the backyard.

"Of course, leadership must be tempered by people skills. A leader without people skills is just a boss, a dictator. My first and best model as a leader with people skills was my dad. He is a retired vice president of Johnson and Johnson. When I was a boy, I really watched him and emulated his example. I soaked up his work ethic. I saw how he dealt with people in his sales force. I observed how he handled challenges and problems—and watching him in his leadership role was crucial to my personal development.

"My dad's people skills are second to none. He was a motivator and a persuader, and he was positive and fair to all. He treated the cafeteria worker and the janitor exactly as he treated the CEO and chairman of the board. He is my biggest role model and hero!"

Leaders need people skills so that they will be effective as leaders, and so that their people will be effective as team players. Don't make the mistake of assuming that leaders need people skills to make them likable as leaders. Obviously, a leader who is affirming is going to be more likable than a boss who is critical and abusive—but that's not the point. Leadership is not a popularity contest. The ultimate purpose of leadership is to accomplish goals, produce change, and make the world a better place. No leader, regardless of how good his or her people skills may be, will be universally liked.

Young leaders-in-training must understand this principle, and they must give up the notion that if they do all the right things, everyone will like them. The truth is that when leaders do the right things, they usually end up making at least a few enemies.

Danny Litwhiler was an outfielder who played for the Philadelphia Phillies, the St. Louis Cardinals, the Boston Braves, and the Cincinnati Reds. An intense ballplayer with a strong work ethic, Danny enjoyed a twelve-season career. The five-foot ten-inch 190-pounder had a .281 lifetime batting average with 107 home runs and 451 runs batted in. He later went on to a successful college baseball coaching career and was inducted into the American Baseball Coaches' Hall of Fame

When Jackie Robinson and the Brooklyn Dodgers went to Cincinnati for the first series of the '48 season, Warren Giles, president of the Reds organization, took Danny aside and asked him, "Would you agree that Jackie Robinson should be allowed to play Major League Baseball?" Robinson, of course, was the courageous African-American infielder who broke baseball's color barrier.

"Yeah," Danny said. "If he can play baseball, that's fine. I wouldn't want to see anyone come in just for reasons of race, but if he can play, let him play."

Giles said, "That's what I thought you'd say. Danny, Jackie's coming to town a day early, and I'd like you to pose for a picture with him. That will let the people know that the Cincinnati Reds welcome Jackie Robinson."

Danny readily agreed, and the photo ran in the newspapers the day before the game. Danny and Jackie Robinson became friends after that. The act of having that picture taken showed leadership on Danny's part. It showed a willingness to affirm Jackie Robinson, a willingness to oppose bigotry and seek resolution of a long-standing national conflict, a basic sense of fairness and hospitality, and a desire to persuade people to a tolerant and accepting point of view.

Danny took a lot of flack from players and Reds fans for having his picture taken with Jackie Robinson. But he never doubted that he had done the right thing.

I asked Danny Litwhiler about his philosophy of leadership, and he explained, "A good leader tries to find the good things about a player and work on those, then gradually work into the problem areas. Players must feel good about themselves, and coaches should try to get their players to feel this way, to have confidence in their own abilities. However, it's not necessary that players feel good about their coach. Fact is, a coach will never be successful if he attempts to have all his players like him. He must have their respect, even if they don't like him. Respect will win games and develop players. A coach who tries to get all his players to like him often neglects to teach all fundamentals."

■ Scouts' Honor

"I was raised without a father," said former Detroit Tigers executive Don Miers. "The first and foremost person who helped me become a leader is my mother, Stella. She did it by example. She had an incredible work ethic that I have not seen in any other human being. We lived in the northern New Jersey suburbs of New York City. We didn't own a car until I was in high school. My mother commuted via bus, train, and subway to work—a two-hour commute to New York. She was never late for work. She never called in sick. She never took a day off. She worked in the international banking business on Wall Street, beginning as a bank teller and working her way up to a vice president.

"Because I was an only child without an adult male influence, my mother and I thought the Boy Scouts of America would be good for me. It certainly was, largely because of the influence of my scoutmaster, Mr. John Collins. He was a true leader, and he taught and trained his Scouts to be leaders as well. He got involved with his Scouts, showing us, hands-on, how to do things. As a leader with authority, he was firm, yet fair. If there was a problem or disagreement, he would listen to both sides before making a decision.

"Mr. Collins was a great role model—not only a leadership example but a great model of people skills. During the four years that he was such a big part of my life, he was always available to talk when I needed advice or someone to talk to. When I was sixteen, Mr. Collins died of cancer while only in his midforties. I miss him to this day."

Don Miers is just one of dozens of people who spoke glowingly of the role that Scouting had played in their development as young leaders and in the development of their people skills.

Winston Churchill was undeniably one of the most inspiring leaders in human history, and he was an enthusiastic admirer of the Boy Scouts. In his 1937 book *Great Contemporaries*, Churchill wrote that the Boy Scout movement "speaks to every heart its message of duty and honour: 'Be Prepared' to stand up faithfully for Right and Truth, however the winds may blow."

In Scouting, young people make a commitment to live lives that are "trustworthy, loyal, helpful, friendly, courteous, kind, obedient, cheerful, thrifty, brave, clean, and reverent." Traditionally, not everyone can be a Scout, but only those young people who are willing to make this pledge:

> On my honor, I will do my best
> To do my duty to God and my country
> And to obey the Scout Law;
> To help other people at all times;
> To keep myself physically strong,
> Mentally awake and morally straight.

The Boy Scouts have recently come under attack for being "politically incorrect" and even "intolerant." Well, the Boy Scouts are, in fact, intolerant of several things that our society unfortunately has begun to embrace: dishonor and dishonesty, disloyalty and disrespect, impurity and irreligiousness, indifference and ignorance. The Boy Scouts (and related Scouting organizations) teach respect for God and country, moral virtue, good citizenship, a love for learning, and the principles of leadership. The attacks on Scouting have only hurt our nation's ability to develop and train the next generation of young leaders.

In the name of so-called "tolerance," a number of government agencies and private organizations have been actively intolerant of a movement that has always been associated with everything that is good and moral in America. A few examples:

In August 2000, the Clinton White House began investigating the

Scouts with the intention of denying Scouts the right to use our national parks for Boy Scout jamborees. Since then, scores of United Way chapters have denied funding to the Scouts, and the Pew Charitable Trust has cut off $100,000 in funding.

The city of Philadelphia has threatened to evict the Scouts from their Philly headquarters at Twenty-second and Winter Streets—a site that the city had given the Scouts "in perpetuity" back in 1929. In June 2003, the Philadelphia *Daily News* ran an outrageous editorial that compared the Boy Scouts to the terror-supporting Taliban.

The Los Angeles City Council has also voted to ban the Boy Scouts from city facilities. Florida's Broward County school board voted to ban Boy Scout troops and Cub Scout packs from school property. The list of "politically correct" attacks on Scouting goes on and on—and very few people are willing to stand up and defend the Scouts.

Well, I'm going to go out on a limb here and suggest that we all ought to get behind the Scouting movement. (I still find it hard to believe that I even have to write a sentence like that!)

How have things gotten so backward in America that the Boy Scouts have become a hated, demonized, and criminalized organization? How have things gotten so absurd that one feels that it is an act of risky, daring moral courage to say, "I support the Boy Scouts of America"? Whatever happened to the America I grew up in, where the Boy Scouts were one of the most admired and Norman Rockwellesque organizations in the country? Let's face it, the Boy Scouts haven't changed. But something in America has—and not for the better.

We desperately need the Boy Scouts and the leadership training that they provide for thousands of young people. The Scouts help young people to develop the people skills they need to be well-rounded leaders. Scouts respect authority; they are coachable and teachable; they respect principles of fairness; they learn how to resolve conflict, how to delegate, how to serve others, how to motivate others, how to be organized, and on and on. If we lose Scouting, we lose one of the most important institutions for training young people in the principles of leadership.

Scouting produces young leaders, and wonderful memories, like this one that Todd Shaw shared with me: "I was the bugler in our Scout troop. On our third day at the state park, a very tired-looking man from the neighboring campsite came over to where our troop was eating lunch. 'I'd like to know who the bugler is,' he said. I proudly and eagerly spoke up: 'That would be me, sir!' He said, 'Boy, if you blow that #@%* bugle again tomorrow morning, I'm gonna—' And he described the consequences in terms that are not fit to print. Then he peacefully made his way back to his campsite. And my bugle made its way into my backpack, where it remained for the duration of the trip.

"When I was moving out of Cub Scouts and into Webelos (the transition level between Cub Scouts and Boy Scouts), we needed an adult leader. So I appointed my dad without his knowledge—and he accepted the job (with a little coaxing). Twenty years later, he's still very involved in Scouting, and he loves every moment. The key to a great Scout troop is a great Scout leader. My dad knew nothing about Scouting, but that didn't stop him. He took courses, recruited great help, and the end result was a great troop.

"Of all the memorable things we did in Scouting, the most meaningful were the service projects our troop did. Every Christmas, we delivered fruit and care baskets to the needy. My father made sure we didn't just drop off the baskets and say, 'God Bless' and 'Good-bye' in the same breath. He showed us how to talk to people and truly listen to them. That was a big factor in the development of my people skills—my ability to strike up a conversation with people I didn't know, and my ability to really reach out and care about people and their needs.

"We also worked with Mr. Don Capps of the Columbia Federation of the Blind in Columbia, South Carolina, on their annual barbecue fund-raiser. For two months we would be guides for the blind as we went door to door selling tickets. During that time I got close to a man named Marshall Tucker. Mr. Tucker was a piano tuner by trade and a man who loved a good conversation. If his name sounds familiar, it's because a country-rock band from Spartanburg, South Carolina, admired him so much that they named their band 'The Marshall Tucker Band.'

"Those experiences helped turn a bunch of young boys into leaders. I'm reminded of the quote by the great Dallas Cowboys coach, Tom Landry: 'Leadership is getting people to do what they don't want to do, to achieve what they want to achieve.' That's what Scouting is all about— building moral character, faith in God, loyalty to country, and leadership skills, including people skills."

■ It Doesn't Take Much

Gene Conley was a longtime major league pitcher in the 1950s and 1960s. The six-foot nine-inch Conley played for the Phillies, Braves, and Red Sox, and he also played several seasons with the NBA Boston Celtics as a backup center for the great Bill Russell. Gene had a remarkable career and now lives in the Orlando area.

As this book was being written, I had a two-hour lunch with Gene. I asked him who was the most memorable baseball manager he ever played for in his long career.

"Eddie Sawyer," he said without a moment's hesitation. Eddie Sawyer managed the Phillies in 1948–52 and 1958–60, and led the Whiz Kids to a pennant in 1950.

"Eddie was the kindest man I ever pitched for," Gene said.

"Do you have an Eddie Sawyer story you can tell me?" I asked.

"Yeah," Gene said, "but I still get kind of emotional when I tell this."

I thought, *Wow! This is going to be a great story for the book!* "Gene," I said, "I'd love to hear it if you can do it."

"Sure," he said. "One day, back in 1959, the Phillies are playing a doubleheader with the Cardinals. I'm in the bullpen, it's the bottom of the ninth, and the Cardinals have two on, two out, and Stan Musial comes to the plate. So Eddie goes out to the mound, removes the pitcher, and waves me in from the bullpen."

At that point, I was on the edge of my chair. "Then what happened?"

"I strike Stan Musial out and win the game," Gene replied. "As I'm walking off the field, Eddie's standing alone in the dugout. He puts his hand out and shakes my hand. And he says, 'Thanks a lot, Gene. I appreciate that.' "

Sure enough, Gene got a little choked up.

I sat there, waiting for the rest of the story, the punch line, the moral—but there was none. I thought, *That's it? Eddie said, 'Thanks a lot, Gene. I appreciate that.'? That's what got Gene Conley all choked up?*

And then it hit me: That is a *powerful* story! Why? Because all Eddie Sawyer did was give Gene Conley a few little words of appreciation, a handshake, and a thank-you. Forty-five seconds later, Eddie probably forgot he even said it—but Gene Conley remembered those words *forty-five years* later! Not only did he remember, but he got emotional just talking about it!

That little story spoke volumes to me. It taught me something profound: It doesn't take much for a leader to reach a person's heart. Just a few affirming words is all it takes—and affirmation is one of the essential people skills of a great leader. That's a lesson we need to remember as leaders, and it's a lesson we need to drive home with the young leaders we are training and mentoring: As leaders, what we say to others is never forgotten. That goes for the good things we say—and the bad.

A positive word, a handshake, or an arm around the shoulder is such a small thing to do, yet it can change a life forever. So as we train young leaders, let's demonstrate and exemplify good people skills, and let's teach them the people skills they need to be effective leaders.

Next, we will examine the fourth crucial dimension of great leadership—the elusive but essential ingredient called good character.

| 8 |

Fourth Key:
Build Good Character

John Wooden began playing basketball in 1918, when he was eight years old. He stuffed one of his mother's stockings with rags and rolled it up—that was his "basketball." His father knocked the bottom out of a tomato basket and nailed it to the wall of the barn; that was John's "hoop." He played basketball practically every day as a boy, and he had an All-State career at Martinsville High School. When he played at Purdue University for Hall of Fame coach Ward "Piggy" Lambert, he quickly gained fame as the Indiana Rubber Man. Wooden was named College Player of the Year in 1932, the year he led Purdue to a national championship.

After a few years playing semipro basketball, he turned to coaching. The UCLA basketball teams of the John Wooden era became legendary. Under Coach Wooden's guidance, the UCLA Bruins set unparalleled records with 4 perfect 30-0 seasons, an 88-game winning streak, 38 straight NCAA tournament victories, and 10 national championships (including 7 in a row).

So John Wooden has long been a hero to me. In recent years, I have gotten to know Coach Wooden as a friend, and I'm currently in the process of researching and writing a book about his life, his character qualities, and his coaching philosophy. I make it a point to visit Coach whenever I'm in Los Angeles. Every time I visit him, I come away challenged, inspired, and motivated to be a better human being. He recently shared a story with me that illustrates what it means to have the character of a great leader.

"In my third year of teaching," Coach told me, "the cocaptains and best two players on my team failed to show up for a game. The next day, they told me they had both been sick in bed. I showed them a picture that had been taken the night of the game—a picture of these two young men having a good time at a dance. I said, 'It looks to me like that dance was more important to you than the game or the team.' Then I dismissed them from the team for the entire year.

"One of those boys, whose father was the vice principal of the school, said that his dad would have me fired. I later talked to the boy's father. He was disappointed when I told him that his son would be off the team for the whole year. But he later thanked me for taking the action I did. He said, 'That was the best thing that had ever happened to that headstrong son of mine.' The incident gave me confidence in standing up for my beliefs. I was trying to do more than build a winning team; I was trying to build character. And building character is always the right thing to do.

"When I was in the service during World War II, I received letters from young men who had been under my supervision in high school. That is when I realized that my coaching had made an impact. Everyone who wrote to me expressed appreciation for times that I had helped them learn some life lesson through basketball. Many of these young men were going through very trying and frightening situations in the war, but they said that my influence in their lives had helped them to accept their situation and persevere through it. They expressed a desire to stay in contact. That meant a lot to me."

Coach John Wooden is the all-time-winningest college basketball coach in history—but there was always one thing more important to Coach than winning games, and that was building character. If you look at all the advice he gave his players, you find that it is almost exclusively focused on building good character.

For example, Coach often said, "There are two sets of threes. The first three is, 'Never lie, cheat, or steal.' The second three is, 'Don't whine, complain, or make excuses.'" Coach also had what he called his Seven-Point Creed for building the character qualities of a leader:

1. Be true to yourself.
2. Help others.
3. Make each day your masterpiece.
4. Drink deeply from good books—especially the Bible.
5. Make friendship a fine art.
6. Build a shelter against a rainy day (have faith in God).
7. Pray for guidance and counsel, and give thanks for your blessings each day.

By focusing on character building, John Wooden became a legendary coach. As parents, teachers, coaches, pastors, and mentors, we should have the same focus: Great leadership begins with good character.

■ Why Character Matters

General Matthew B. Ridgway (1895–1993) commanded the Eighty-second Airborne Division in World War II and oversaw the return of Japan to full sovereignty after the war. He also succeeded General Douglas MacArthur in the Far East Command in 1951, and replaced Dwight Eisenhower as supreme allied commander in Europe (NATO) in 1952.

"During a critical phase of the Battle of the Bulge," General Ridgway once recalled, "when I commanded the 18th Airborne Corps, another corps commander just entering the fight next to me remarked: 'I'm glad to have you on my flank. It's character that counts.' I had long known him, and I knew what he meant. I replied: 'That goes for me too.' There was no amplification. None was necessary. Each knew the other would stick however great the pressure; would extend help before it was asked, if he could; and would tell the truth, seek no self-glory, and everlastingly keep his word. Such trust breeds confidence and success."

Character is a moral quality; it stands completely apart from such leadership traits as talent, intelligence, personality, experience, or competence. *Character* may be defined as "a commitment to do what is right, regardless of circumstances, temptation, hardship, or need." A person of good character does not steal even if his need and temptation are great. He perseveres when exhausted, is honest when the truth is costly, and is courageous when there is no hope of victory.

A person of good character never says, "It wasn't my fault that I cheated or lied or stole because the temptation was just too much for me." People of genuine character have programmed themselves to always do what is right and to take personal responsibility.

"Character is the will to do what is right, as defined by God, regardless of personal cost," says Pastor Andy Stanley. "It involves doing what's right because it's the right thing to do, and there is a standard that is permanent . . . an unwavering benchmark by which we can measure our choices."

As a leader who works primarily with youth, Todd Shaw, president of On-Track Ministry, understands the need to build strong character into young leaders. "One thing I often encounter as a youth pastor," Todd told me, "is the question of what is—and is not—a leader. On one occasion, I had a kid in the group who was nothing but trouble. The other kids would follow his lead, and he would have a strong influence on the group as a whole—on attitudes and behavior.

"With a kid like that in the group, I would actually find myself fighting and competing for leadership of the group! He was a leader, but his leadership was negative in nature.

"Other adults became aware of this kid and the situation he created, and they said to me, 'What a waste! He could be such a good leader.'

"I would respond, 'I hate to tell you this, but he *is* a good leader—good at leading the group in the wrong direction.'

"It's like comparing Hitler and Jesus Christ. It's an offensive comparison, and forgive me for making it, but there's a valid point here. You see, both Hitler and Christ were effective, influential leaders. They knew how to persuade people and get results through people. Both men had a dramatic impact on history and humanity. Obviously, the outcome of Hitler's leadership was very different from the outcome of Jesus Christ's leadership. Hitler's leadership produced the worst evil the human race has ever seen. Jesus' leadership produced the greatest good the world has ever seen.

"What was the defining difference between the leadership of Jesus and that of Hitler? I would say it was a difference in character. Jesus was a man of unparalleled good character, and He was committed to doing what is right, serving God the Father and serving humanity, even at the cost of His own suffering and His own life. Hitler was a man of incredible evil and selfish ambition; he was committed to elevating and deifying himself, even at the cost of millions of innocent lives.

"That's why it's not enough to teach young people *how* to lead. We also have to teach them *what kind of people they should be.* If we fail to teach character, then we run the risk of waking up one day to discover that all of our wonderful leadership training has only helped to create another Hitler. That's why character matters."

■ The Qualities That Make Up Good Character

My friend Jay Strack, president of Student Leadership University, told me, "Good character is crucial to good leadership. In my own life, I battled drugs and alcohol as a teenager. First I was a victim, then a villain, and finally a victor. I had an experience with God that was good for me because it gave purpose to my life. If God was for me, who could be against me? Without alcohol and drugs, my awareness improved, and I quit making horrible choices.

"When I was nineteen, I met Zig Ziglar, one of the great motivators of our time. He saw potential in me, and he started to invest in my life. The secret he shared with me was, 'Use the experiences you've gone through to help others get on the right path and make their dreams come true.' That concept changed my life. Soon Zig helped me to start speaking in schools, and those speaking appearances launched my career."

Jay Strack was talking about the transformation he experienced, from victim to victor, from a person of low character to one of the best role models I have ever met. My wife and I think so much of Jay as a person of character that we had him perform our marriage ceremony.

I have assembled a list of character qualities that are essential to good leadership. As we develop young leaders, we need to impress these qualities upon them through our instruction and our example. At every teaching opportunity, we need to hammer home these qualities. If a young leader demonstrates a failing in one of these areas, we can use that failure as a teaching opportunity. We can encourage the young person to learn and grow in character from that experience.

Here is my list of character qualities (you may think of others that I haven't listed):

• *Integrity*: This should be first on any list of character qualities. In his book *Answers to Satisfy the Soul*, my writing partner, Jim Denney, explained integrity this way: "Integrity is the quality of being whole and uncompartmentalized. A person of integrity is exactly the same at home, at work, and at church or synagogue. He or she is the same person, behaving the same way, whether in public or in private, whether being watched by a crowd of thousands or totally alone and unobserved."

My friend Pat Croce, former president of the Philadelphia 76ers, told me, "My dad was a man of integrity. His toes were always pointing in the same direction as his tongue." In other words, Mr. Croce walked the walk.

Integrity is essential to building trust, and trust is essential to leadership. People only follow a leader they can trust. People need to know that their leader is a person of integrity, a person who will not say one thing and do another, a person who is exactly who he seems to be and claims to be. If people find out that their leader lacks integrity, they will cease to trust him—and they will refuse to follow him.

General Richard B. Myers told me, "One of the many leadership lessons I learned early in my Air Force career was that you must have high credibility in your primary field of expertise first before anyone will want to follow you. Credibility comes from character—and especially from the character trait called *integrity*.

"I grew up in America's heartland, in Kansas. My teachers and coaches were part of the greatest generation. Many of them served in World War II and Korea. They were not boastful about their service; they were simply men and women of quiet integrity. By their actions and through their words, they taught us all that integrity means being true to one's values and standards. It means saying what we mean, and meaning what we say. It means holding fast to our honor so that we are trustworthy and incorruptible. To be a leader and a role model, you must be a person of integrity."

My son Michael recently said to me, "Dad, integrity is honesty with a little *oomph*." Couldn't have said it better myself.

• *Honesty*: This may be defined as "total sincerity and uncompromising commitment to truth." An honest person tells the truth, owns up to mistakes, and doesn't fudge or cheat on taxes. If an honest person finds a wallet with five hundred dollars in it, she will find the owner, not consider it a lucky windfall. If an honest person gets back too much change at the grocery store, he will correct the mistake, not say, "Aw, the store can afford it." Honest people do not download music from a Web site to avoid buying a CD—that is stealing. Leaders must be uncompromisingly honest, or they can't be trusted.

- *Diligence*: The character quality of diligence is also called a work ethic. A diligent person is a self-starter, a hard worker, and a person with a dedication to excellence. "Good enough" is never good enough. Diligence is important because a leader can't inspire the team to work hard if he or she is not willing to set an example. A hardworking leader inspires the entire team to work hard and produce excellence.

People with a strong work ethic do not merely believe that work is a means to success; they truly believe that work is a moral good, and that laziness and sloppiness are morally wrong. It's important to teach a strong work ethic to people when they are young; it's very difficult to take a lazy, indifferent, unmotivated adult and teach him or her to be diligent. An attitude of diligence tends to take hold when it is taught at an early age.

- *Patience*: This is the willingness to defer immediate gratification in order to achieve a better future. It is the willingness to be at peace while waiting. Patience seems to be a lost virtue in today's world. In this Internet-speed age of fast food, microwave ovens, automated tellers, and e-mail, we no longer have the patience to wait, to endure, to hope, to expect. But great leaders are always people of great patience. This is a crucial character quality to develop in young leaders.

- *Humility*: The character quality of humility involves having a sober view of oneself and others. It does not mean degrading oneself or having a low opinion of oneself, nor does it mean being soft, wimpy, or passive. Genuine humility is a form of strength, not weakness. A humble person can be confident without being arrogant, and can have a respect for others while still maintaining self-respect. A humble person recognizes that his or her self-worth is not determined by what others think. The person's ego cannot be inflated by praise or deflated by criticism. Both praise and criticism roll off him like water off a duck's back because his self-esteem isn't tied to what other people say about him. As Mother Teresa once said, "If you are humble nothing can touch you, neither praise nor disgrace, because you know who you are."

Bestselling author Ken Blanchard told me about the author Jim Collins, who believes that "the two main ingredients of successful leaders are will and humility. Humility is the main thing God uses to qualify you to lead. Leaders can be made if they possess a humble spirit."

Brooks Robinson was a legendary third baseman who played twenty-three seasons for the Baltimore Orioles, hit 268 career home runs, and earned the league MVP Award (1964) and World Series MVP Award (1970). "In my first big-league game," Brooks told me, "I went two for four and knocked in a big run. I was eighteen years old. After that game, I ran back to the hotel to call my dad. I was thinking, *Man! I should have been in the majors all along!* Well, on my next eighteen times at bat, I went 0 for eighteen, including ten strikeouts. Being humbled like that was just about the best thing that could happen to me. There's nothing worse than a ballplayer with a swelled head. That dose of humility definitely gave me a more realistic perspective, and it made me a better baseball player and a better person."

Andy Dolich is president in charge of business operations for the NBA Memphis Grizzlies. He told me about a lesson in humble leadership he learned from legendary sports owner Sonny Werblin, the man who purchased the floundering New York Titans and transformed them into the Super Bowl–winning New York Jets. When Andy was general manager of the Washington Diplomats (North American Soccer League), Werblin was CEO of Madison Square Garden.

"The Diplomats were playing the New York Cosmos at RFK Stadium in Washington, D.C.," Andy recalled. "I was with Sonny Werblin in a car coming into the VIP parking entrance. The game was a complete sellout at fifty-eight thousand. The security guard wouldn't let us in because we didn't have the proper VIP parking credentials. A lot of owners and big shots would have thrown a fit and called for the guy's head. But as we were driving to another entrance, Sonny turned to me and said, 'I want you to make sure that guard gets a bonus for sending us away. He was doing exactly what we pay him to do.' That example has stuck with me ever since. A leader should never place himself or herself on a higher plane of entitlement than anyone else in the organization."

• *Responsibility*: The quality of responsibility is a willingness to act productively and decisively without having to be told what to do, without having to be monitored, without having to be guided or goaded into action. It is the capacity to admit and correct one's mistakes without making excuses or shifting blame. Fred Claire, former GM of the Los Angeles Dodgers, told me, "You can't possibly take a leadership position unless you are ready to take responsibility for your own actions. Leadership starts with taking responsibility and being accountable."

How do we build the quality of responsibility in young people? Assign them appropriate goals and tasks, then allow them to either rise to the occasion or incur the consequences of failure. Set performance expectations, and let them take responsibility for meeting those expectations—no reminding or nagging! If the young person seems intimidated by a project that is too large, help him or her break it down into a series of smaller, more manageable, bite-size tasks.

Young people develop a sense of responsibility when they are allowed to suffer the consequences of their actions and inaction. If they are continually rescued from the consequences, they will eventually feel entitled to be rescued all the time.

Above all, affirm responsible behavior. When the young person performs responsibly or accepts blame for a mistake, say, "I'm proud of you—this shows that you are becoming a responsible leader."

Phil Roof spent eleven consecutive seasons as a catcher in Major League Baseball, and now manages the AAA Rochester (Minnesota) Red Wings. "I grew up on a farm in a big family," Phil told me. "We had horses, mules, cows, pigs, chickens, and ducks, and we ran a dairy. I had older and younger brothers, and we all had to take turns feeding the animals on a daily basis. When my dad was sick or away, he would always tell my mom, 'When I leave the chores to Phil, I always know he'll do it the way I want it.' It made me feel good to know that he trusted me and thought that I was dependable and responsible."

Billy Knight, general manager of the Atlanta Hawks, grew up in Pittsburgh one of eleven children. "When I was twelve," he told me, "my mother gave me the grocery list and the money and sent me to the store to do the shopping. She saw that I was dependable, responsible, and trustworthy, and I would get exactly what she wrote. If it was Campbell's chicken noodle soup, that is what I got. It was the first time I realized I was being depended on to be a leader."

Jim Henry, senior pastor of the First Baptist Church in Orlando, said to me, "I was president of my high school Student Council, and our school was one of the largest in the state of Tennessee. One day, prior to a big football game, the school held a pep rally. In the bleachers, some students lifted up a hapless little underclassman and started passing him around on their hands. The poor guy moved up and down the rows like he was a beach ball. I was one of the ones laughing and participating and passing the boy around.

"The principal saw this activity and didn't like it. He called off the pep rally and sent us to our rooms. Then he called me into his office and eyed me coldly. 'Mr. Henry,' he said, 'were you a part of these shenanigans?'

" 'Yes, sir,' I said, acknowledging my guilt.

"He said, 'In that case, you, as president of the Student Council, will speak to the student body. You will apologize to the teachers and your fellow classmen for your participation, and you will challenge the student body never to engage in such an activity again.' He then assembled the students, more than a thousand of them, and had me get up and speak.

"I got up, took responsibility for my part in the activity, and issued the challenge to the student body as he had instructed me. When I had finished, he dismissed us. It was a powerful lesson on the importance of responsibility, accountability, and the influence we wield as leaders. The experience stung me at the time, but it was an important lesson and I never forgot it."

• *Self-discipline*: Self-discipline involves mastering one's behavior and impulses so that time and energy can be used to achieve one's goals. A self-disciplined person is not a slave to bad habits (smoking, drinking, chemical addictions, sexual compulsions, gambling, overeating, and so forth). A self-disciplined person builds good time-management habits and is not lazy. A self-disciplined person maintains a healthy and balanced lifestyle, allowing adequate time for sleep, rest, exercise, and devotional periods with God.

Eric Musselman is the former head coach of the NBA's Golden State Warriors. "My mother and father had a huge influence on me," Eric told me. "They were very big on self-discipline and self-control. I was not allowed to drink alcohol or be out past midnight all the way through high school. My friends didn't have the restrictions I did, and there was a lot of pressure for me to go along. But my father taught me to fight peer pressure, to stand up and be my own person.

"When you are the one person who doesn't go along with the crowd, you kind of stand out—and no high school kid likes to stand out that way. No one likes to be the one who's 'not cool.' But my dad told me to continue standing against peer pressure and to continue being a leader. I did—and eventually others followed. Soon, many of my fellow athletes at Brecksville High in Ohio decided it was actually cool *not* to drink. I learned that when leaders demonstrate self-discipline, it gives them a surprising amount of influence among their peers."

Phil Jackson, head coach of the L.A. Lakers, told me, "When I was a senior at the University of North Dakota, my coach was Bill Fitch. I was captain of the team, but at one point I had the job taken away from me. We were playing a game in Chicago, and I went out with some friends to Rush Street. I got back to the hotel after curfew, so Bill took away my captaincy. He said, 'You won't be captain again until you prove to me you deserve it.' Bill made me prove to him that I had the self-discipline to be captain. He gave me a lesson in discipline that has helped me throughout my life."

• *Courage*: The character quality of courage involves a willingness to take risks, withstand opposition and attack, and struggle against opponents and obstacles in the pursuit of a worthwhile goal or the defense of a just cause. Courage does not mean fearlessness. Courageous people do the very thing that they are afraid of, and they do it because it is the right thing to do. We should always affirm young people when they demonstrate courage. In an increasingly dangerous world, courage becomes a crucially important leadership trait.

As a player and then the head women's basketball coach at Mount St. Mary's College, Vanessa Blair has racked up an armload of awards, including two Northeast Conference (NEC) Player of the Year Awards, NEC Player of the Decade, and NEC Coach of the Year. "I was given a tremendous opportunity at age twenty-seven," she explained. "I was given the job as the head women's basketball coach at a Division I program. I was nervous about following the most successful coach the program had ever had, Bill Sheahan.

"So I built myself up on Scripture in order to stay strong and courageous, no matter what might come my way, whether good or bad. What carried me was a passage from Jeremiah 1. God calls Jeremiah and says, 'Before you were born I set you apart; I appointed you as a prophet to the nations.' But Jeremiah says, 'I do not know how to speak; I am only a child.' And God answers, 'Do not say, "I am only a child." . . . Do not be afraid . . . for I am with you.'

"That empowered me because I knew that there were great people in the Bible who were also young, but God gave them a great task to carry out. My very first season, we went twenty-one and seven, and I was named Coach of the Year."

• *Perseverance*: It is not easy to turn a vision into reality. That is why perseverance is so critical to effective leadership. Young people need to learn that nothing worthwhile ever comes quickly or easily. No great goal is ever achieved without opposition, obstacles, and setbacks. In order to achieve anything lasting and worthwhile, young leaders must have a quality that is variously known as perseverance, determination, persistence, or (as Walt Disney called it) "stick-to-it-ivity."

The best way to build perseverance in young leaders is to assign them projects or tasks that require a long-term commitment of time and effort. When they encounter difficulties and become discouraged and want to quit, cheer them on! Motivate them to keep going. When the young leader finally completes that project or task, make sure he or she is rewarded for persevering to the end. As young people discover the rewards of perseverance, they will gradually build a strength of purpose and determination into their lives.

• *Fairness*: People of good character are evenhanded and fair-minded, treating all people equally and without regard to such superficial distinctions as class, gender, race, and so forth. To build fair-minded leaders, always model fairness in our words and actions.

• *Tolerance*: The character trait of tolerance is a willingness to put up with people and ideas even if we don't like or agree with them. True tolerance is a "live and let live" attitude. We don't have to agree with this religion or that political perspective, but we can be respectful and tolerant around people of that persuasion. Tolerance is an important character trait for leaders because leaders are often called upon to facilitate, mediate, and unite people with widely contrasting viewpoints and beliefs.

Bob Johnson, founder and CEO of Black Entertainment Television (BET), told me, "One skill that all leaders must learn today is the ability to tolerate and embrace diversity. The world is a multicultural experience, and our society is becoming more multicultural every day. A leader must be willing to understand other people and other cultures in order to lead effectively in the twenty-first century."

• *Compassion*: The character quality of compassion involves a willingness to listen to people with needs, offer encouragement, and help them carry their burdens. It means demonstrating unselfish kindness toward others and willingly sacrificing some of our own comfort and convenience in order to comfort someone else. It means giving altruistically and generously, out of authentic love for people, not out of a desire for recognition and ego gratification. An effective way to encourage compassion among young leaders is to place them in situations where they can reach out and help people who are less fortunate than they.

• *Self-sacrifice*: The character quality of self-sacrifice involves the willingness to subordinate our own will, interests, desires, and benefits to a higher purpose. That higher purpose may be God, country, other people, or an organizational or team goal. It may mean that we are willing to sacrifice money, possessions, comfort, reputation, or the right to have our own way. At its most extreme, self-sacrifice may motivate us to lay down our very lives for a higher purpose—for the sake of a noble ideal, for our faith in God, or for the life of another human being. Few people want to follow a selfish or self-centered leader; a truly self-sacrificing leader, on the other hand, always inspires followers to emulate his or her example.

• *Faith*: The character quality of faith involves a willingness to live and act in accordance with the nature and promises of God. The word *faith* is often misunderstood and misdefined to mean "blind belief in an idea for which there is no evidence." But I see authentic faith in God as rational; it is based on reliable evidence.

In my experience, people of faith make the best leaders because they regard themselves as accountable before God for their actions and decisions. In the Judeo-Christian Scriptures, God calls us to be people of character—that is, to be people of integrity, honesty, diligence, patience, humility, responsibility, self-discipline, courage, perseverance, fairness, tolerance, compassion, self-sacrifice, and faith. So, in a very real sense, the character quality of faith embraces and embodies all of the other character qualities. People of authentic faith should always be people of good character.

I asked New York Yankees broadcaster Charlie Steiner about Tony Clark, the team's first baseman. "Tony Clark is a man," Charlie told me, "a real man. He has a calm within him, and he's smart. Tony doesn't proclaim that he's a leader, but the players go to him to seek advice and guidance." Tony Clark is a man of character because of his Christian faith.

■ Character Under Construction

One of my favorite biblical personalities is Joseph, whose story is found in the book of Genesis. Back in the early 1980s, I heard Bible teacher Ron Hutchcraft speak at the NBA All-Star Chapel in New York. His topic was Joseph and the four "life-preserver principles" that allowed Joseph to be unsinkable. I was so inspired by the message that twenty years later, I wrote a book about Joseph titled *Unsinkable*. I gave a copy of that book to Grant Hill of the Orlando Magic. A few days later, Grant took me aside and said, "I like this book! In fact, Joseph may be the best guy in the Bible—next to Jesus, of course."

I think Grant Hill is exactly right. Joseph truly is one of the "best guys" in the Bible. The story of Joseph and Potiphar's wife (Gen. 39) is the story of a young leader and his good character. Joseph was the second youngest among the twelve sons of Jacob. When Joseph's father sent him out to find his ten older brothers in the fields, they jealously pounced on him and sold him into slavery in Egypt. An Egyptian army captain named Potiphar purchased Joseph at a slave auction.

Joseph's good character, particularly his integrity, diligence, and responsibility, quickly became apparent to Potiphar. The Egyptian military leader trusted Joseph and placed the youth in charge of everything he owned. Imagine being somewhere between sixteen and nineteen (Joseph's approximate age) and having your boss trust you with his checkbook, his cash, his possessions, and even the keys to his new chariot! Potiphar invested that level of trust in young Joseph.

One day, while Joseph was in charge of Potiphar's house, the boss's wife tried to entice him into her bed. Her husband was away. No one would know. Joseph refused.

"My master hasn't withheld anything in his house from me except you, his wife," he said. "How could I do such an evil thing to him and sin against God?" That's integrity talking. That's faith talking. Joseph knew that having sex with the woman would mean betraying the man who had trusted him—and more to the point, it would mean betraying his values and his relationship with God.

There's an important principle in the story of Joseph—a principle that we need to impress on the young people under our mentorship and leadership. That principle is this: You must prepare yourself ahead of time in order to maintain your character and integrity when temptation comes. If you have not determined beforehand to conduct yourself as a person of character, you will fall and you will fail when temptation comes your way. Joseph had already determined that he was going to live in accordance with his character and his faith. So when Potiphar's wife invited him to sin with her, he stood firm against her pressure and temptation.

And how was Joseph rewarded when he demonstrated his faith and integrity? The woman became enraged, and she attempted to destroy Joseph. When her husband returned, she lied about Joseph and claimed that he had tried to rape her. Potiphar believed his lying wife and had Joseph tossed into prison. So Joseph's integrity was rewarded with slander, injustice, and imprisonment.

Young leaders need to understand that *character is its own reward.* There is enormous value in being able to look back on one's choices without guilt and regret, regardless of whether those choices resulted in advancement or abuse. We need to make the point (and exemplify it in our own lives) that the right thing to do is always the best thing to do. That is what character is all about.

Ultimately, Joseph—again due to his character, faith, and integrity— became known to Pharaoh, the ruler over all of Egypt. Pharaoh took Joseph out of prison and elevated him to be the second most powerful leader in the land. By his flawless moral character, Joseph proved himself worthy of Pharaoh's complete trust.

Joseph's character was tested by temptation and adversity. These tests come to every leader, sooner or later. The only way a leader can stand firm in such times is to strengthen his or her character.

How, then, do we teach and motivate young people to build strong character so that they can stand, as Joseph stood, when trials of temptation and adversity come their way? Here are some suggestions for constructing character in young leaders:

1. *Be a person of absolute integrity and character.* You can't lead a young person to a place you will not go. If you expect a young person to have integrity, you must model integrity—especially at times when you think no one is watching. You can't take a break from being a person of character—either you have good character all the time, or you don't. And if you don't have it, you can't teach it. Whenever and wherever you are tempted to compromise on character—on the job, in your car, at the store, or in the privacy of your home—remember that young people are watching and learning from your example.

2. *Give your children regular religious instruction.* Regularly attend your house of worship along with your children—don't just drop them off at Sunday school and drive away. Exemplify faith in the home. Read the Scriptures and pray with your children. Discuss your faith and values with your children on a daily basis, especially at mealtimes and at times when situations arise that become object lessons for teaching good character. Make practicing your faith a daily part of your family life.

Among the rules in our house is this: If you live under our roof, you're going to church and Sunday school every week—it's that simple. Are the kids eager to go every Sunday? No. We have to roust them out of bed and cross-check to make sure they're not asleep. But everyone knows that church is what we do on Sunday mornings.

3. *Serve others.* Model service to others in your life, and find ways to involve your children in volunteering and service, especially toward people less fortunate than yourselves. Encourage your kids to get involved in volunteering at a homeless shelter or ministering to needy people through

service projects or visiting elderly people or sick children at a hospital. If you need ideas for service projects, talk to your pastor.

4. *Involve your children in sports.* There is nothing about athletic activity that automatically builds character. Kids learn nothing about good character from parents and coaches who have a "win at any cost" mentality. However, sports can have a *powerful* character-building influence if parents and coaches are people of good character who set an example of honesty, fairness, and respect for others.

Yes, winning is important because leaders and their teams must be competitive. But those who cheat to win have betrayed their character. Yes, competition is important—but opponents are to be respected, not hated. So involve your children in sports, and use sports to teach lessons in good sportsmanship and good character.

After receiving more than seven hundred responses to my request for interviews and information, I was amazed at how many of these leaders, both men and women, received their very first leadership lessons in some athletic endeavor as small children. Most important of all, those lessons in leadership have never left them.

5. *Praise and correct kids on the basis of character.* When a child does something right, affirm the child and say, "Do you realize what this means? You just demonstrated good character! You just showed the character quality of honesty or integrity or responsibility. I'm really proud of the way you are growing and maturing in your character!"

When a child does wrong, don't just punish that action. Say, "When you do this kind of thing, you hurt your character. You want to build good character so that people can trust you and be proud of you. The way to build good character is to make good decisions when you face this kind of temptation. The next time you find yourself facing this kind of decision, think about how the choice you make will affect the character you are trying to build."

Joel Glass, publicity director of the Orlando Magic, has a nightly drill with his two children, ages seven and three. "What do we do with drugs?" he'll ask. "Just say no," his children reply. "Do we treat other people equally?" "Yes." "Do we get into a car with strangers?" "No." What a powerful idea for instilling strong character and decision-making skills in young leaders!

6. *Allow your children to experience the consequences of poor choices.* Make sure that your children understand that there is a price to pay for poor character and poor decisions. When other people are hurt by their poor choices, make sure they understand the hurt and harm they have caused. Don't defend, shield, or rescue your young people from consequences. Make sure they learn that there is a cause-and-effect relationship between bad choices and unpleasant consequences.

7. *Talk to your children about heroes.* Read with them or watch films with them about heroic people who exemplify outstanding character. Tell them stories about heroes of the Bible or heroes of American history or contemporary heroes. After your children hear the story of that person's life, ask what character qualities they see in that story.

8. *Post inspirational quotations in your home.* Put them on the fridge or in another visible place, and change them once a week or once a month. Recite the quotation together at the dinner table every night, and memorize it together. Discuss the meaning of the quotation, and make sure everyone understands it and can apply its meaning to everyday life. Here are some examples:

Do not be misled: "Bad company corrupts good character."

(1 Cor. 15:33)

Character is manifested in the great moments, but it is made in the small ones.

(Phillip Brooks)

Character is simply habit long continued.

(Plutarch)

When wealth is lost, nothing is lost; when health is lost, something is lost; when character is lost, all is lost.

Anonymous

Bill Walton was an NCAA superstar when he played for Coach John Wooden's UCLA Bruins in the early 1970s. Bill's son, L.A. Lakers strong forward Luke Walton, said that Bill has always been a John Wooden disciple and a big believer in motivational quotes. "As kids growing up," Luke recalled, "all four of us Walton boys had John Wooden motivational quotes posted everywhere—on our refrigerator, on the bathroom mirror, in the car. Dad would even tape Wooden sayings on our lunch pails."

We never stop building character. What's true for children is true for us adults: Our character is always under construction. Every decision we make is a decision to construct a stronger character for our lives—or to chip away at the foundation of our character. This thing we call character is built day by day, decision by decision, trial by trial. And our most potent influence on the character construction of our children is the character we construct for ourselves.

■ Character for Adversity

Sooner or later, all leaders face adversity. Responding to adversity is the ultimate test of a leader, and only leaders with strong character can stand the test. Leaders who lack integrity will crumble in the face of temptation. Leaders who lack courage will panic in the face of danger, criticism, and opposition. Leaders who lack perseverance will fail the test when they encounter obstacle after obstacle. Leaders who pass the test of adversity invariably find that the testing of their character has made it grow deeper, stronger, and more durable.

Jim Tooley, executive director of USA Basketball, recalled, "I first became aware that I had leadership ability when I began organizing pickup basketball, baseball, and football games as a youngster growing up in Yonkers, New York. My involvement on the sports field was important in teaching me not only the skills of leadership but the importance of character in leadership.

"Early in my career in sports leadership, I had an experience that profoundly affected my perspective on life. I was promoted to director of operations for the Continental Basketball Association at the age of twenty-three by then commissioner Jay Ramsdell. Jay was only twenty-five and one of the youngest to reach his position at the time. I plunged into the job—it was a tremendous opportunity for me to grow professionally, yet it was also hectic and all-consuming. I was very busy preparing league schedules and also dealing with the players and coaches on transactions, fines, suspensions, and so forth.

"On July 19, 1989, less than one year after I was promoted, my boss and friend, Jay Ramsdell, was killed aboard United Flight 232, which crashed in Sioux City, Iowa. It was a shock and my first real dose of 'perspective.' Living our lives is serious business, and the things that seem so important to us one moment can all disappear in an instant. There are more important things in life than schedules and transactions. There are issues like relationships and spending time on things that matter and making sure we are becoming the right kind of people. After Jay was killed, my job became less consuming. I focused more on keeping balance in my life."

Tragedy and adversity have a sobering effect on young people. Painful experiences often promote character growth in young lives. Dr. Peter Likins, president of the University of Arizona, told me, "There was never a time in memory when I did not expect to lead. In my youth I was always the team captain and the group president. I came to think of these roles as my normal duties. It probably goes back to when I was seven years old and my father abandoned his family—his wife and four kids, aged eight, seven, two, and one. Thanks to his irresponsibility, I grew up with an overwhelming sense of responsibility. When he abandoned us, I felt a responsibility to stay the course and see things through to completion. That was my father's gift to me.

"In my youth, I confused winning with leadership. I thought that leading was about a successful performance. But the rewards of winning are transitory. Later in life, I discovered that leading is about serving. Service to others brings a deeper kind of satisfaction."

Dr. Jordan Cohen, president of the Association of American Medical Colleges, discussed his experience in Boys State, a learning-by-doing leadership training program that teaches young people how government functions (there is also a Girls State program). It's a seven-day program in which young people participate in moot-governmental activities, such as selecting mayors and representatives. There are also musical and athletic activities for the young people.

"I was a delegate to Missouri Boys State between my junior and senior year," Dr. Cohen told me, "and I was encouraged by my Boys State 'town' to run for governor. Being elected would have meant a trip to Washington, D.C., along with the governors of all the other Boys States in the country. After a vigorous campaign, I 'lost' to another boy.

"After the result was announced, a counselor who had befriended me took me aside and told me that I had actually won the election but that the powers that be thought that it would be unseemly to have a Jewish boy represent the state in Washington, so they gave the election to the other candidate. It was a sobering experience, and it taught me that there are people who are supposed to be leaders, and who are supposedly in the business of training leaders, who failed the character test of leadership— they failed to demonstrate integrity and basic fairness. That experience also taught me something about the character quality of perseverance because it fueled my determination to succeed."

Lynn Bria, head women's basketball coach at the University of Ohio, was tossed into a leadership crisis by a double tragedy in her life. She said, "My first job as a head coach was at a Division II school in Texas. While

I was there, I received word that one of my brothers was killed in a car accident. I felt that I needed to be closer to my family in Orlando. As much as I loved being a head coach and running my own show, I decided I needed to move back to Florida, even if it meant going back to being an assistant.

"At that same time, Jerry Richardson, head coach at the University of Central Florida (UCF), offered me an assistant's position. I was grateful to Jerry and thankful for the opportunity to be closer to my family during a difficult time, so I accepted the position. I packed up, got in my car, and left Texas, headed for Orlando. Stopping in Mobile, Alabama, I called my parents, and they informed me of a second tragedy that would change my life: Jerry Richardson had been killed in a car wreck.

"I was stunned. In fact, I was in such a state of shock that I can't even remember the drive from Mobile to the Florida coast. When I reached Orlando, UCF offered me the job of interim head coach. As much as I had loved being a head coach in Texas, I certainly didn't want a head coaching job under such tragic circumstances.

"Yet I knew that God was calling me to be closer to my family. It's a good thing we can't see the future because I never would have taken the interim job at UCF if I could have looked ahead. Being overwhelmed is a natural feeling when you are a leader, and especially in times of adversity. In fact, I believe that if you aren't feeling overwhelmed, you aren't taking on a big enough leadership challenge. I don't think I have ever felt totally prepared or adequate for any leadership position I've held.

"My first year at UCF, we had a thirteen and fifteen season. We improved to seventeen and eleven the following year. Throughout my time at UCF, I had to be totally dependent upon God. Only my faith could get me through it because the challenge was so far beyond me. I believe that when God chooses us, leadership isn't a choice; it's a calling. All I know is that coaching, especially in times of adversity, doesn't just reveal your character strengths, but it brings out every weakness you have as well. But God chooses us for those challenges whether we want them or not."

I asked Lynn what strengths and qualities she looks for in evaluating young people for leadership roles. "I watch them to see how they respond to adversity, conflict, or challenges," she replied. "That's a real key to becoming a great leader. I pay close attention to how players respond when things aren't going their way or when they are having a bad game.

"I also watch how they treat other people. I'm convinced that whatever players do to others, they'll do to me, their coach. If I see them cheating, lying, loafing, or being disloyal toward their teammates and others, I know it's just a matter of time before they do it to me. That's not the kind of leadership I want on my team. So in my book, good character is definitely an essential component of a good leader.

"People with great leadership potential tend to have strong convictions. They are people who just can't help feeling strongly about certain things—which, of course, doesn't always endear them to the people around them. People with strong convictions take a stand for something bigger than themselves, whether it's God or some sort of Higher Power. They're secure in their convictions, and they aren't hungry for the approval of others. They tend to live on the edge a bit and keep things stirred up.

"When I spot young people with leadership potential, I give them a lot of encouragement, especially when they are battling adversity. I encourage them to read great books, especially the Bible, and to attend workshops that focus on building leadership skills. I give them the freedom to step out and make their own decisions, and even make some mistakes. I affirm them and cheer them on, but I don't fix everything for them. They need to figure it out and fight their own battles."

Character is not like a talent or a skill. With talents and skills, you can always compensate for weaknesses by running with your strengths. But there's no way to compensate for a weakness in your character. Weaknesses in your character eventually eat away at your strengths. You can have all the courage and persistence in the world, but if you lack integrity and honesty, those weaknesses in your character will be your undoing. Bad character is eventually exposed.

The good news about character is that you can strengthen and improve your character by your choices every day. You can't choose to be gifted and talented. You can't choose to have a high IQ. But we all choose the character we will have. We choose it every day by the decisions we make.

When tested by adversity, we can choose to respond with character—or with compromise. The leader who compromises has failed the test. The person who chooses to maintain good character has earned the right to be called a leader.

■ Knowing What Is Right—and Doing It

The city of Fort Worth calls him "Mr. Baseball," and with good reason. Bobby Bragan has served in just about every baseball capacity you can think of: Shortstop for the Phillies. Catcher for the Brooklyn Dodgers. Scout and coach. Minor-league manager. Major league manager for the Pirates, Indians, and Braves. President of both the Texas League and the National Association of Professional Baseball Leagues. Now in his eighties, Bobby continues to make public appearances and also leads the Bobby Bragan Youth Foundation, which has awarded almost $700,000 in scholarships since it was founded in 1991.

"Playing for the Brooklyn Dodgers in the 1940s," Bobby told me, "I got to watch and learn from two of the best managers in the game, Leo Durocher and Burt Shotten. I also got to learn from Mr. Branch Rickey—a great baseball executive who easily could have had a career as a great psychologist. Mr. Rickey knew how to get his point across.

"I'll never forget the welcome home luncheon for the team after we returned from spring training. It was held at the St. George Hotel in Brooklyn, April 1947. Mr. Rickey made two announcements at the luncheon. First, Leo Durocher had been suspended by Commissioner Happy Chandler for the entire season for consorting with gamblers. Second, Jackie Robinson would officially join the team and open the season at first base the next day.

"I was born and raised in Birmingham, Alabama, and like my teammate, Dixie Walker, I wasn't exactly elated about Jackie joining the team. But we watched the way Jackie handled the pressure of being the first player to cross the color line in Major League Baseball. We saw the way Ben Chapman, the Phillies manager, baited him, but Jackie kept his cool.

"By the end of the first road trip, about twelve days, Jackie had turned us all around. We traveled by train in those days, and on our first trip, nobody would sit with Jackie in the diner. On the second trip, Dixie, Eddie Stanky, and I were all fighting to get to sit with Jackie Robinson. What won us over? Jackie's character, his courage and his sheer determination and will in the face of so much opposition. He was a real leader on the team, and that brought all of the players to his side.

"This world needs more young people like Jackie Robinson—young people with character and courage and a sense of fair play. That means that the grown-ups in this world need to set a better example about how to treat other people. Parents need to illustrate character by their own example. If you promise to take a boy or girl to the ballpark, don't come later and say you were too busy. Kids are watching us grown-ups to see how we handle ourselves in different situations. If we don't teach our kids what character is all about, who will?"

When Reginald Jones, long-time CEO of General Electric, died recently, his wife of sixty years, Grace, wrote down his last words: "Leadership requires ethics, morals, and values."

Young leaders need to know what is right, care about what is right, and do what is right. If we teach them the principles of good character—and if we show them good character through the example of our lives—then we will empower them to be great leaders and good human beings. Good character is the essential foundation for great leadership.

Next, we will examine the fifth crucial dimension of great leadership—a key ingredient called competence.

| 9 |

Fifth Key:
Build Competence

Late in the 1998–99 season, Coach Ken Carter's high school basketball team was undefeated, a perfect 13-0. But Coach Carter wasn't happy with his team. He believed there was something more important in life than winning basketball games. So in early 1999, he made a decision that placed him squarely in the middle of a national media ruckus. Soon, the actions of this high school coach had made front-page headlines from coast to coast. He received interview requests from such diverse outlets as the *Los Angeles Times*, NBC's *Today* show, and Rush Limbaugh's radio show.

What was Ken Carter's controversial decision? And why did it prompt such a firestorm of publicity and controversy?

The story begins in the fall of 1998 when Carter, the owner of a local sporting goods store, accepted a part-time coaching position at Richmond High School. Richmond is a poor, crime-plagued, gang-infested city across the bay from San Francisco. Coach Carter had grown up in Richmond, and in the 1970s, he was the highest-scoring basketball player in the history of the Richmond High Oilers—that is, until his son, Damien Carter, broke his records for scoring, assists, and steals.

When Ken Carter took the coaching job, he sat down with his players, and together they hammered out a nineteen-point academic contract. Among other things, players agreed to maintain a 2.3 grade point average (the state required only a 2.0 GPA for sports participation), study ten hours a week, achieve perfect attendance, and sit in the front row in class. All the players agreed to the contract and signed it.

As the season progressed, however, the thirty-nine-year-old Coach Carter received troubling reports from teachers. About a third of his forty-five players were showing up late for class—or not showing up at all. They had quit turning in homework and were performing poorly on tests. Coach Carter responded by making the youths perform push-ups and run laps, but the academic problem didn't improve.

Finally, Coach Carter took drastic action. When the Richmond players showed up at the gym to practice for the big game against rival Fremont High, they found the doors chained and padlocked. A sign read, "No Practice Today—All Basketball Players Report to the Library." The stunned athletes—all forty-five players on the varsity, junior varsity, and freshman squads—trudged to the library.

Coach Carter held a team meeting in the library. There he informed his players that fifteen of them were not living up to their signed agreement. As a result, the entire team would be locked out of the gym and kept out of competition until every player was in compliance.

The lockout decision could not have been an easy one for Coach Carter to make. After all, one of those most affected was his own son, Damien, a star point guard with a sterling 3.7 GPA. Damien hated to forfeit games as much as the next guy, but he understood what his coach—his father—was trying to accomplish. "Education comes first," Damien said—then, speaking for his team, he added, "We haven't been handling our business in the classroom."

The response to Coach Carter's action was immediate—and furious. Players and their parents were angry, school officials were angry, and someone even egged Carter's car. "I got calls at home, at school, at my job, and they were all negative," he told one reporter. "People wanted a state championship, and I know we sacrificed that. But my goal was to get these boys into college, where they could learn to become leaders and come back to this community as productive citizens."

■ Competent to Lead

Coach Carter had an objective in mind when he benched his undefeated team: "My goal was to get these boys into college, where they could learn to become leaders." He wanted his players to become educated so that they could become *competent to lead*.

One key ingredient of leadership is competence. And what is competence? I see competence as a combination of five components:

1. *Knowledge.* A competent leader is educated and is committed to lifelong learning.

2. *Experience.* A competent leader has the know-how that only hands-on, practical experience can bring.

3. *Confidence.* A competent leader exhibits a sense of assurance and calm, even under pressure. Confidence is contagious. A confident leader inspires confidence in his or her players, employees, or troops.

4. *Commitment to excellence.* A competent leader demonstrates a zeal for being the best and doing the best. Competent leadership never tolerates a shoddy or second-rate effort.

5. *Competitiveness.* A competent leader is a fierce competitor. Competent people hate to lose, and they play to win.

These five qualities make up the quality called competence. Why is competence crucial to leadership? Because competence qualifies a leader to lead. Competence enables a leader to make good decisions. Followers look for competence in a leader before they will give their trust to that leader. Competent leaders produce competent teams and organizations.

All of this is foundational to what Ken Carter meant when he said, "My goal was to get these boys into college, where they could learn to become leaders." Coach Carter wasn't just trying to win basketball games.

He was trying to build leaders, and he was doing so by building their competence through education and academic achievement. To achieve that goal, he was perfectly willing to padlock the gym, sacrifice a championship, and accept the insults and scorn of an angry community.

■ "We Rise as a Team, and We Fall as a Team"

So let's get back to the story of Coach Ken Carter and the Richmond Oilers. After Coach Carter benched the entire team and locked them out of the gym, the players pulled together and got down to business. The academic achievers tutored the players who struggled in math or science. The lagging students pulled up their on-time attendance and began improving their grades.

Day by day, Coach Carter monitored the academic progress of his team. On January 11, after the Oilers had forfeited two games, the coach allowed them to resume practice. The following day, January 12, the Oilers played in a big game against Oakland's St. Elizabeth High.

Among those who attended the game was California governor Gray Davis, who came to show support for Coach Carter. As the governor and the coach sat together and chatted, Governor Davis asked, "Coach, could some of these young men play at a professional level one day?"

"Governor," the coach replied, "now that they've seen you here, maybe one of them will even become governor. Some of them might have great careers in politics or business. It's fine to be like Michael Jordan—but why shouldn't they be like the person who *pays* Michael Jordan?"

The Oilers finished the season with a record of 19-5 and lost in the second round of the district play-offs. Even after the season was over, even after it was clear that Coach Carter had gotten his players to bring up their grades and improve their study habits, some parents and school officials continued to criticize his decision. Some said it was unfair for Coach Carter to penalize the entire team for the failure of a few.

To these criticisms, Coach Carter responded, "We rise as a team, and we fall as a team. Some kids are doing extremely well in school. And so they said, 'Well, you're punishing me, and I didn't do anything wrong.' I tell them, 'Well, we've won thirteen basketball games. Did you score every point?'" In other words, not every player on a team makes baskets, yet all share in the thrill of the win. If a few players break their contract, then all must share in the pain and disappointment. From a teamwork point of view, the lockout was totally fair.

What were the results of the lockout? Damien Carter received a basketball scholarship to West Point. Another player, Courtney Anderson, spent two years at a junior college, then received a football scholarship from the University of Nevada at Las Vegas. Another, Wayne Oliver, attended West Hills College in Coalinga, California, for two years, and is going to Cameron University in Oklahoma on a basketball scholarship. And the list goes on and on. In fact, every senior player coached by Ken Carter has gone on to a junior college or four-year school.

Coach Ken Carter wants his players to succeed—not just on the basketball court, but in life. He wants them to be leaders. And to lead, they must build their competence, including their academic competence.

"I show these boys the facts," he said, "how fifty-five percent of all inner-city school kids think they're good enough to play professional sports. But in all pro sports—from baseball to basketball—there are only 2,400 jobs total." Coach Carter added that in the Microsoft corporation alone there are 15,000 millionaire employees. Obviously, if a young person wants to succeed in life, the odds are a lot better in the corporate world than in the sports world—*if* that young person has an education.

Coach Ken Carter understands that leaders must be competent to lead. As parents, teachers, coaches, mentors, pastors, and leaders of all kinds, we need to do whatever it takes to make sure our young people are building their competence to lead and succeed in the real world.

■ Sacrificing for Experience

Charley Casserly, general manager of the Houston Texans, learned how to be a coach and a leader from some of the top leaders in the game of football. "I broke into the NFL under Hall of Fame coach George Allen of the Washington Redskins," Charley said. "During my career, I have been mentored by Bobby Beathard, the longtime NFL general manager; Joe Gibbs, the greatest coach in NFL history in my opinion; the fiercely competitive Redskins owner, Jack Kent Cooke; and Bob McNair, owner of the Texans, who combines the best traits of all of these leaders.

"In 1977, I wrote to all twenty-eight teams in the NFL, seeking a coaching job at some level. Out of those twenty-eight letters, I got twenty-two responses, only two of which invited me to interview for a position. From those two interviews, I received two offers: Both Washington and New England offered me unpaid internships. When I met with George Allen, I told him that he didn't invent the idea of working for nothing—New England had the same idea. The deal George Allen offered me was that I would work for a year for nothing—then, if they liked me, they would hire me for ten thousand a year.

"I had very little money saved. My car was a clunker with a hundred twenty thousand miles on it. I owned three pieces of furniture—one of which was a bed that had collapsed. So, with all of that going for me, I moved to Washington and started my unpaid internship for the Skins. I lived at the local YMCA for eight dollars a night. My first day there, I brought my own lunch, a jar of peanut butter and jelly—the kind where the peanut butter and jelly were swirled together in one jar. I figured PB and J was the cheapest and most complete nutrition I could get in a single jar.

"My second day with the Skins, I opened up the fridge and the jar was gone. Someone had stolen my PB and J! Not only was I working without pay, but someone was stealing my food! I was off to a terrible start.

"That summer, my work as an intern involved just about everything.

I got the job of telling players they had been cut. I worked in the public relations office. I ran errands. After the summer was over, they sent me out as a college scout—and that's what saved my life. Working as a college scout was the only way I could survive financially because while I was on the road, the team paid my expenses. Otherwise, I was paid absolutely nothing.

"Was I crazy to work a whole year at no pay? No, I was just paying my dues. The following February, I was hired as a scout for seventeen thousand a year, and football has been my career ever since. When you're starting out, and when you want it bad enough, you do what you have to in order to get the job and get the experience."

Unfortunately, many young people today lack the patience and desire that Charley Casserly showed as a young man at the beginning of his NFL career. Some young people come roaring out of college, diploma in hand, and they're ready to interview for the CEO's position! Our job is to help these young wanna-be leaders see that they need to slow down, be patient, and put in the time to gain experience.

Gaining experience is one of the five keys to gaining competence as a leader—and there is no shortcut to experience. Charley Casserly sacrificed everything, even his last jar of PB and J, to gain the all-important experience that would open the door to a career in the NFL. That's a lesson all young leaders need to learn.

Ian McCaw, athletics director at Baylor University, recalled how he first acquired the experience that made him a competent leader: "I was named athletics director at Northeastern University in Boston in 1997. I was twenty-four and one of the youngest NCAA athletics directors in the nation. I arrived at work feeling excited and enthused about assuming leadership of the department.

"My first day at work, I learned that somebody had taken over the office of the previous athletics director. I was shown to a little utility room furnished with thrift shop furniture. The climate in the room was controlled by a thermostat that kept the temperature in the low nineties.

"At ten A.M., I received my first correspondence—notice that a lawsuit had been filed against Northeastern for failing to comply with Title IX. After that, I met with each head coach. After exchanging pleasantries, each coach read his or her list of complaints, grievances, and problems to me. Clearly, I was going to get a lot of on-the-job experience in a big hurry. It was a tough challenge, but it also became one of the most valuable learning experiences a young leader could have."

Ian McCaw knows: For building competence, tough experience is the best experience. While gaining knowledge is a good first step in building the competence to lead, nothing beats hard-won, dirt-under-the-fingernails, hands-on experience.

George Barna, president of Barna Research Group, Ltd., of Ventura, California, told me, "As much as anything else, young leaders need to be encouraged, held accountable, prayed for, and given a variety of experiences to help them determine their abilities and limitations. There is no substitute for experience; the more opportunities they have to try their hand at various aspects of leadership, the better they will become."

Everybody starts out with a set of God-given talents—raw, undeveloped, diamond-in-the-rough talents. Some people have a talent for speaking, some for singing, some for taking charge of a group situation, some for throwing and catching a ball. But raw talent is of little use unless it is developed—and practical experience transforms a raw talent into a polished skill. To be competent and skilled, leaders must gain this all-important commodity called experience.

■ Build Confidence to Build Competence

When a young leader gains experience, he or she becomes more competent in the leadership role. The more competent this young leader becomes, the more successes he or she experiences. With each new success, the young leader's confidence grows—and that confidence leads the young leader to attempt greater challenges and gain more experience. Or, to put it more succinctly:

Experience → Competence → Success → Confidence → More Experience

And the cycle starts all over again.

Or, to put it even more succinctly, competence builds confidence, and confidence increases competence. That is how raw, inexperienced, insecure young leaders grow to be seasoned, confident, competent leaders as adults. This kind of growth doesn't simply happen with the passage of time. It happens as young leaders are given opportunities and challenges that build their skills and their faith in themselves.

Sometimes we think that all it takes to train a leader is to put a young person in a classroom, fill his or her head with knowledge, and declare, "You are now a lieutenant," or, "You are now a manager—go forth and lead." We forget that while this young person may have a lot of head-knowledge, he or she still lacks the confidence and competence to lead.

My son David, who is in the Marines, told me a harrowing story about the importance of confident, competent leadership. "I was in Iraq in 2003," he said. "Our lieutenant was leading our motor convoy on a mission when he decided to take a shortcut. As it turned out, we got lost and ended up on a very narrow dirt road with a berm on our left and a canal on our right. We had twenty vehicles and forty Marines. The road was so tight that we couldn't back out.

"We kept going forward until we ran into another canal. Now we couldn't go forward and we couldn't go back—and our lieutenant started to freak out. There were Iraqi townspeople all around, watching this in amazement.

"At that point, the first sergeant took over. He was calm and organized, and he was a very quick thinker. He assembled a team and told them, 'Dig out the berm so we can get the vehicles moving, then we'll turn around.' He had a plan and pulled us all together and got us all on the same page. Somehow we made it out of there before any Iraqi troops found us. That first sergeant was calm, confident, and competent to handle the crisis. He probably saved our lives."

How do we build the confidence of young leaders? Ronnie Floyd, Sr., pastor of the First Baptist Church in Springdale, Arkansas, told me how his high school coach elevated his confidence by encouraging him to make key decisions and call the plays.

"I was captain of the football team," he said. "Once, in my junior year, we were in a hard-fought game. Late in the final quarter, the coach called me to the sidelines. I thought he was going to tell me what play he wanted us to run. Instead, he looked me in the eye and said, 'Ronnie, what should we do?' The coach was asking for my advice! I said, 'Let's run a double reverse and put the ball into Jimmy Giles's hands. It'll work.' He said, 'Okay, go back in the huddle and give 'em the play.'"

Understand, Ronnie Floyd's coach was taking a huge risk in going with this tricky play. In a double reverse, the ball is handed off three times—and each handoff increases the chances of a costly fumble. I suspect the coach had his heart in his throat when he gave Ronnie Floyd the go-ahead. But the coach wasn't just thinking of points on a scoreboard. He was thinking about building the confidence of a young leader.

"We ran the play," Ronnie Floyd told me, "and Giles scored a touchdown to win the game. My confidence soared after the success of that play. From then on, I viewed myself as a leader."

When he told me that story, I was reminded of my own experience as a freshman quarterback on my high school football team. I attended Tower Hill in Wilmington, Delaware, a private school for the children of the DuPonts and other well-to-do Delaware families (I attended free because my father taught there). Every year, we would scrimmage with Salesianum High School, a blue-collar Catholic school.

On the first play of the game, starting quarterback Reeves Montague (who was two years ahead of me) called a play that worked magnificently, running off a twenty-yard gain. I took it all in from the sidelines, studying everything Reeves did. Finally, late in the game, the coach sent me into the game. I went into the huddle and called the same play that

Reeves had called in the first play of the game. Once again, the play worked brilliantly—touchdown!

At the end of the game, our assistant coach, former Yale center Baird Brittingham, came to me and said, "Why did you call that play?" I said, "It's the same play Reeves called, and it worked." He said, "That's the answer I wanted to hear." Well, my confidence skyrocketed—I thought I was the best play-caller since Sammy Baugh. That was a pivotal moment in building my confidence as a leader, and it all turned on a few words of encouragement from Coach Brittingham.

Leadership is a scary challenge for young leaders. Every time I've moved to the next level of leadership, I've had to accept tougher challenges and greater risks. With each new challenge, I've had to punch through another wall of fear and self-doubt.

In 1965, when I became general manager of the Phillies farm club in Spartanburg, South Carolina, I was twenty-four years old and full of enthusiasm, dreams—and fear. I had to force myself to take charge and act like I knew what I was doing. Fortunately for me, the team owner, Mr. R. E. Littlejohn, knew exactly what I was going through, and he mentored and encouraged me, building my confidence as I grew into the job.

Four years later, I was hired as the business manager of the Philadelphia 76ers. At age twenty-eight, I was in charge of the day-to-day operations of a big league basketball team. Though riddled with insecurities, I plunged into the job and fought through my fears, determined to make my mark. One year later, the call came from the Chicago Bulls, and I became general manager of that team; there, I fought my way through a whole new set of insecurities as I made trades, oversaw the draft, and had an impact on the fortunes of an NBA team.

I later moved to the Atlanta Hawks, then the Philadelphia 76ers, and finally to Orlando to build a team from scratch. At each new phase in my career, I had more doubts and fears to battle my way through. Every time I shouldered more responsibility, I made a profound discovery: *Hey, I can do this!* Year by year, my confidence grew. As my confidence was elevated, so was my competence as a leader.

Donald T. Phillips is an author, speaker, leadership consultant, and the mayor of Fairview, Texas. His books include *Lincoln on Leadership*, *The Founding Fathers on Leadership*, and *Run to Win: Vince Lombardi on Coaching and Leadership*. "I first gained confidence in my own leadership ability as a Little League baseball player," Don told me. "I played short-stop, and my coaches noticed that I seemed to have a natural gift for leadership on the field. They told me I had a number of leadership strengths, and they encouraged me to put those abilities to good use.

"I learned early on that confidence is contagious. I was eleven years old, and it was a championship game, the last game of the season. Our team was down five to two, bottom of the last inning. I was the lead-off hitter, and my teammates were sitting on the bench, dejected.

"I grabbed my bat, put my helmet on, and said, 'We're going to win this game.' The other guys said, 'Sure, we are.' I said, 'No kidding. I'm going to get on base, and then we're going to load the bases and win it.' 'Okay,' said the kid who was batting after me, 'if you get on base, so will I.' That set off a chain reaction of enthusiasm.

"First pitch, I lined a double down the left field line. Next kid up bunted for a single. Third kid up walked. Bases loaded, no outs. Next kid up popped out. Next kid up hit one over the fence. We won the game, six to five.

"My coaches instilled that kind of confidence in me when they told me I was a leader. I turned around and spread that confidence to my teammates. That's a lesson in confidence building and leadership training I have never forgotten."

Jim O'Brien, head coach of the Philadelphia 76ers, told me this story: "When I was eight years old, I was the point guard in basketball and the catcher in baseball. One of my coaches used the word *leadership* in reference to me, and I loved the sound of it and have thought about it ever since. This same coach also called me 'Coach,' because I thought I had all the answers." Jim admitted this was not intended as a compliment, "but it sounded good to me and it still sounds good today."

The Honorable Edwin Meese is former United States attorney general and currently Distinguished Fellow in Public Policy at the Heritage Foundation. "I first realized I had the ability to lead," he told me, "when I was elected to the Student Council in the seventh grade. Other opportunities came in Scouting, where I was a troop leader, and in high school, where I was elected to the Student Cabinet and made ranking officer in our high school's Reserve Officer Training Corps battalion. I had many other leadership mentors, from my junior high school coach, my high school debate coach, and several Army officers I served under, all the way to one of the greatest leaders of our time, Ronald Reagan. I learned a great deal about leadership while working for him, both when he was governor of California and when he was president of the United States.

"The experience that solidified my confidence as a leader took place when I was in college. I took a summer job as a rowing coach for a city recreation department. When I reported for work, I was asked to take a different position—director of the city's Teenage Community Center. I didn't have a clue how to run such a facility. I had no formal management training, and I hardly knew where to begin. The superintendent of recreation mentored me and helped me develop the administrative skills I needed. Also, my leadership experience from high school, college, and my ROTC training served me well.

"Even though I was scarcely older than the young people in my charge, they respected my authority, and we had a successful summer program. My success in that position increased my confidence so that I could take on increasingly bigger challenges and grow as a leader."

Young people may act cool and confident—but don't let that fool you. Inside, they are churning with insecurity and self-doubt. They hunger for a pat on the back and a word of encouragement. They desperately want to know that the people they respect truly believe in them, even when they make mistakes. So as you are building knowledge, skills, and competence in young leaders, don't forget to build their confidence as well.

■ A Commitment to Excellence

In 1958, a nineteen-year-old pianist named Liu Shi-kun took high honors at the International Tchaikovsky Competition, placing second only to Van Cliburn. Liu returned to his home in Communist China, where he received the accolades of his countrymen and became a renowned concert pianist. In the mid-1960s, however, Chairman Mao launched his Cultural Revolution throughout China. Any artistic expression deemed inconsistent with pure Chinese culture and Marxism was ruthlessly purged. Artists and musicians were jailed or killed.

Liu was caught up in the purge, since the classical music he played was considered a corrupting Western influence. Convicted as "an enemy of the people," Liu was jailed and beaten. His right forearm was fractured in one of the beatings, and he received no medical attention. For six years, Liu endured the worst prison conditions imaginable for the "crime" of being an accomplished pianist.

In the early 1970s, thanks to a thaw in Chinese-American relations, the Philadelphia Orchestra, under the direction of Eugene Ormandy, visited China on a goodwill tour. Ormandy, who remembered Liu's outstanding performance at the International Tchaikovsky Competition, requested that the pianist be allowed to perform in concert with the Philadelphia Orchestra. Embarrassed by the fact that this great talent was languishing in prison, the Chinese authorities promised that Liu would be able to perform, and Mao himself ordered Liu's release.

Liu emerged from prison for the command performance—but there was one problem: He hadn't touched a piano in six years. Even worse, the broken bone in his arm had healed improperly, causing pain whenever he moved it. How could Liu perform with such disabilities?

Yet the night of the concert, he delivered a performance that his listeners called "brilliant" and "astonishing." How was this possible?

Liu Shi-kun later explained that he had spent every day of his imprisonment doing what he loved—playing the piano. Of course, there was no piano in his cell, so he did the next best thing: He played an invisible piano. For hours and hours, his fingers danced upon thin air, and he heard the notes only in the silence of his mind. When the day came that he was finally released, it was as if he had never been away from his instrument. He preserved the excellence of his talent even through beatings and years of imprisonment.

This is precisely the kind of single-minded commitment to excellence that we need to instill in young leaders today. What prevents young people from pursuing excellence in everything they do? All too often, it is nothing more than laziness, immaturity, or the simple fact that they have never been challenged or inspired to be the best that they can be. Our job is to provide that inspiration, and awaken in them a hunger and a drive to always do their best and be the best, regardless of the obstacles in their way.

Liu Shi-kun didn't let the Cultural Revolution or a prison cell or a broken arm keep him from relentlessly pursuing excellence every day of his life. If Liu could pursue excellence from his prison cell, our young leaders can certainly become people of excellence wherever they are, no matter what obstacles they face.

Dr. Richard Armstrong, professor emeritus at Princeton Theological Seminary, recalled how his father inspired in him a commitment to excellence: "My father was my role model and the person I most admired, in addition to being a great teacher and coach. He inspired me to do my best. 'Always earn more than you make,' he said, and he lived by these words. I watched his life, and I saw that he always gave more than he took and he was admired by all."

Like Dr. Armstrong, Cathryn Cronin Cranston, publisher of *Harvard Business Review*, attributes her high standards of excellence to the influence of a father who is a leader and a man of the highest standards. She told me, "I am the daughter of James W. Cronin, recipient of the 1980

Nobel Prize in Physics, which he shared with Val L. Fitch. My parents' community was the ultimate meritocracy, where achievement was based on unassailable contributions to theories or knowledge of the physical world. Your name, or whom you knew, didn't matter.

"When it came time to start my career, I was on my own. Yet my father, consciously or not, sent me out into the world with two guiding principles: maintain the highest standards and ask the best questions, for these questions will always be more revealing than the answers. These principles have contributed immeasurably to my success and have made for what continues to be a most interesting life."

In training young people to be competent leaders, we must inspire them to pursue excellence in everything they do. We can inspire a commitment to excellence in our young people in four important ways:

First, we should preach and teach excellence on a daily basis. Dr. Armstrong never forgot the advice that his father often repeated: "Always earn more than you make." Legendary Green Bay Packers coach Vince Lombardi used to preach excellence to his players, saying, "Unless you believe in yourself and put everything you have into your pursuits—your mind, your body, your total dedication—what is life worth? The quality of life is in direct proportion to your commitment to excellence, no matter what your field of endeavor." So excellence should be a running theme in our conversations with young leaders.

Second, we should demand excellence from everything a young leader does. We should never let a young leader settle for a halfway effort. We should never let a young leader get away with turning in second-rate work. If we know that a person is capable of doing better work, we should say, "Try it again. I know you're capable of so much more. I can't wait to see what you accomplish when you really focus on excellence." We can demand excellence in a positive, encouraging, I-believe-you-can-do-it way—but we *must* demand it.

Third, we should stress the feeling of accomplishment that comes with doing work with excellence. When we do our very best work, we feel a glow of pride within. That pride of accomplishment is addictive; once we experience it, we want to feel it again and again. It is not an arrogant pride, but the kind of godly pride expressed by Eric Liddell, the missionary and Olympic athlete portrayed in the film *Chariots of Fire*; he said, "God made me fast. And when I run, I feel His pleasure." That glowing sense of pride in a job well done is the godly pleasure we take in having achieved to the limits of our ability.

Fourth, we should model excellence in our lives. We should never settle for second best in anything we do. Nothing speaks louder to a young person than the example we set. Competent leadership inspires competent leadership. Excellence inspires excellence. "The essence of coaching," says Phil Martelli, basketball coach at St. Joseph's University in Philadelphia, "is to push young guys to yearn for greatness, with no excuses for falling short. Greatness is an honorable goal."

■ Competent to Compete

"As a boy, I attended military school," recalled Dr. Richard Armstrong. "My best friend was a boy named Jamie, and he was my teammate on many of the athletic teams we played on in school. In drill competitions, however, Jamie and I were competitors. He was the captain of A Company and I was the captain of B Company, and we often competed against each other for awards.

"During one drill competition, Jamie's company went first. They accidentally forgot one maneuver, ruining an otherwise brilliant march. Going second, we had an advantage. If we just didn't make the mistake Jamie's company made, we would win—but I hated to take advantage of Jamie's mistake. If we did the maneuver, it would be obvious that Jamie had made a mistake. Before we went out, I considered omitting the maneuver so we could be on equal footing.

"Then I thought of all my young men in Company B who wanted to win. How could I let them down? When we started the march, I was still in doubt. We were doing well, and I decided to do the maneuver. Both Company A and Company B were commended—but our company won.

"I later told Jamie what I went through and how I agonized over that decision. I apologized and told him I felt I had taken advantage of his mistake. But Jamie told me that winning the way I did was right and honorable, and that he would have done the same thing. As leaders, he said, we had a duty to our men to compete and win."

A competitive spirit is an essential component of competence. In fact, you can't spell *competence* without *compete*. Every team or organization must have a competent and competitive leader in order to compete and win.

Tami Heim is the former president of Borders Books and Music Stores. Throughout her career, Tami has worked hard to mentor women and help them compete in the business world. A 1980 graduate of Purdue University, Tami Heim is a sought-after speaker and a mentor in Menttium 100, a leadership development program for women.

"During my sophomore year of high school," Tami told me, "I was asked to coach a Christian Youth Organization (CYO) kickball team for fifth and sixth graders. I enjoyed working with kids and I loved to play the game myself, but this was my first experience of being responsible for leading a group of eleven- and twelve-year-olds! This age group is just learning the ins and outs of the game, but since kickball has a fall and spring season, I knew I would have the same team over the course of the year and be able to help them develop their skill level.

"When I attended my first meeting with the other coaches, my father had to drive me since I was too young to drive myself. In fact, I was by far the youngest person in the room, giving the term *rookie coach* a whole new meaning. I was intimidated, but I hung in there and took careful notes on all the basic rules and critical deadlines.

"Next came my first practice. The qualifications were simple: If the kids showed up, they were on the team. If they consistently showed up, they stayed on the team. My biggest surprise was how little they knew about the game. I had them take their positions on the field. One very tiny girl said, 'Where should I play?' I said, 'Kim, why don't you play second base?' She looked around the field, then asked, 'Coach, which one's second base?'

"So I spent a lot of time teaching the fundamentals. The kids were all smaller than the norm for their age so, even when they knew what to do, it was hard for them to physically execute it. The fall season commenced and we took a beating—we didn't win a single game.

"I wanted to help them develop a more competitive mind-set. So when they seemed down after losing a game, I wouldn't let them stay there. I talked to them and got them to focus on what they did right during the game and how they could improve in future games. I was determined to keep them energized and optimistic about their spring season.

"We started spring training well before the season began, meeting several times a week after school—sometimes the field even had a light dusting of snow! The preseason practices gave me a clear indication of who was committed and willing to work hard to improve. Some of the parents thought I was a bit eccentric and I took my share of parental wrath, but the girls hung with it. I tried to make the drills both fun and competitive. It wasn't always easy for me to stay pumped up and motivated, but I knew I had to be enthusiastic in order for them to be.

"By the first game, they were ready to play, and they believed they could *win*! They went into the game and had a lot of fun while applying the skills they had practiced. When the dust settled, they had won their first game. Amazingly, they didn't even know they had won until it was all over—I had to tell them! It took a moment for the realization to register on their faces. Their delayed reaction was priceless and unforgettable. Winning was a new experience for them!

"Amazingly, that team, which had lost every game in the fall, ended up winning every game during the spring season. Amid all those successes, the hardest thing for me was to keep a balanced perspective—I wanted them to have a consistent attitude whether they won or lost. I didn't want them to think that competition was only about winning. I told them that competing is about working hard, doing your best, depending on each other, and enjoying the wins that followed. I pointed out to them that when we worked as a team, we made things happen.

"That was my only year as a CYO coach. After that, I started my first retail job and there were too many time constraints that prevented me from coaching. But I kept track of those girls through the rest of grade school and high school. That committed core of girls went on to become leaders in everything they did. I'm grateful that I had a chance to be a part of their lives—and I'm thankful for the lessons they taught me that have carried me through my life in the business world."

Tami Heim continues to be deeply involved in encouraging youth sports, especially for young female athletes. In 1998, Tami and her husband cofounded the Ann Arbor (Michigan) Gold Fastpitch Softball Organization, a girls' softball league that has grown from four teams to eleven teams at present. Tami builds competent leaders by building their self-esteem and motivating them to compete in sports and in life.

Mike Martin has been head baseball coach at Florida State University for twenty-five years. He told me a story from his earliest days as coach of the Seminoles: "It was 1980, and my first game as head baseball coach at Florida State was sheer misery. We were shut out, ten to nothing, by the University of Miami. We were so bad, we didn't even get a runner to third base. Then we lost the second game on an error in the bottom of the ninth.

"After that, we came back to win the third game in the top of the ninth, and I felt really good about that win. We got on the bus and were driving away from the University of Miami campus, and we saw the U.M. coach punishing his players with extra wind sprints. My assistant coach, Jim Morris (who is now head coach at U.M.), turned to me and said, 'Are we really this bad? We beat them one game out of three, and their coach punishes them!'

"Well, those wind sprints were designed to teach that team about being competitive—and it reinforced a lesson in my own mind as well. Leaders aren't content with two out of three. Great coaches are great competitors. They want to win it all."

Competition is a part of every leadership arena. Military leaders must compete for advancement within their organization—and they must compete successfully against opponents on the field of battle. Political leaders must compete for votes. Business leaders must compete in the marketplace. Sports leaders must make their teams competitive against other teams and keep them financially competitive. Even religious leaders find themselves in competition; their message about God and a moral, spiritual way of life must compete against the many opposing messages in our society—messages that promote selfishness, godlessness, hedonism, and even occultism and satanism.

It is never too early to teach young leaders to be competitive. When young leaders are willing and eager to compete, we should be careful never to suppress that competitive drive. John Merrill of the Tuscaloosa County Board of Education told me, "When I was in the sixth grade, I was the starting quarterback for the White Owls football team in the Heflin Park and Recreation League. We were an undefeated team playing the Fruithurst Devils, the worst team in the league. My coach, Don Pearce, was concerned that our team not run the score up on that team and embarrass them. But my teammates and I couldn't understand why we shouldn't try to score on every drive, on every play. Coach Pearce knew how competitive I was and how I liked to score, so he let me take only one snap in the first half, then he pulled me out.

"Finally, at the beginning of the third quarter, he let me go back in the game. He sent in the plays from the sideline. He called back-to-back running plays, with the fullback going up the middle, on the first two plays of the series. My teammate brought in the third down play, and it was another drive up the middle. I told the team that we weren't going to run that play; we were going to run a quarterback sweep right.

"The kid who brought in the play said, 'That's not the right play!' I said, 'I know, but that's the play we're going to run. All you guys need to do is block your assignments and we're going to get a touchdown.' I took the snap, and I went sixty-five yards for a touchdown.

"When I went to the sideline, I went straight to Coach Pearce and said, 'Coach, I know that's not the play you told me to run, but I knew I could score a touchdown and I didn't know if you were even going to let me play anymore.'

"He looked at me and said, 'Since you scored, there's not much I can say to you—but I will tell you this: I am the coach and I expect you to do what I tell you. Do you understand?' I told him I did, and I started to walk away with my head down, feeling chastened and dejected. But as I was walking away, he added, 'Nice run.' Well, that lifted my spirits. He found just the right balance, reminding me of his authority, yet affirming my competitive spirit. The White Owls went on to win the championship, and I never disobeyed him or any other coach again."

■ The Responsibility of Competence

These, then, are the five components of competence: knowledge, experience, confidence, commitment to excellence, and competitiveness. You might wonder why I didn't add a sixth component—talent—to that list. Well, talent is certainly a factor in making a competent leader, but talent is beyond our control. By definition, talent is a gift—a raw, untrained ability, waiting to be developed and put to use. While talent is purely God-given, the other five components are factors that young leaders can build upon and improve upon.

We can help young people gain knowledge through education. We can encourage them to take opportunities to gain the experience that will improve their level of skill. We can affirm them and believe in them, which in turn will increase their confidence. We can teach them to be committed to excellence, through our words and our example. And we can give them plenty of opportunities to test their competitive spirit. But there is nothing anyone can do to make himself or herself more talented.

Still, something needs to be said about talent: A talented person has a responsibility to develop and use those talents. People with leadership talent have a responsibility to step up and lead.

Sometimes talented people are reluctant to lead. Often, they do not recognize their talents unless a parent, teacher, coach, or mentor points them out. Sometimes they do not know that they have a talent for leadership until the responsibility of leadership is thrust upon them.

Joe Torre's quiet, intense style as manager of the New York Yankees has earned him the nickname, "The Godfather." Whether his team is winning or trailing, his stone-faced demeanor never changes. Joe's a true baseball professional—and that professionalism helped propel the Yankees to four World Series championships in five years.

I asked Joe how he came to see himself as a leader. "I wasn't a natural-born leader, that's for sure," Joe replied. "Fact is, I was pretty irresponsible in my twenties. When I think of things I did in my youth, I just cringe. When the Braves traded me to St. Louis, I began to gain more maturity, and I started to grow as a leader. When I was named team captain, I was shocked. I had never seen myself that way before. Other people saw leadership qualities in me long before I saw them in myself."

Competence qualifies a leader to lead. Competent leaders produce winning teams—and that is why competence is the fifth key to effective leadership.

Next, we will examine the sixth crucial dimension of great leadership—boldness!

| 10 |

Sixth Key:
Be Bold!

Reggie White's high school football coach once called him "a nice, big Sunday school boy who didn't want to hurt anybody." But by the time he retired from the game, Reggie had become an NFL legend. Playing for the Philadelphia Eagles, the Green Bay Packers, and the Carolina Panthers, he became the all-time NFL leader in sacks (198). As a Packer, he set a record for the most sacks in a Super Bowl game (three sacks, in the Packers' 1997 Super Bowl victory over the New England Patriots).

My writing partner, Jim Denney, once interviewed Reggie at his home in Knoxville, Tennessee. Reggie told Jim the story of how Coach Robert Pulliam of Howard High in Chattanooga turned "a nice, big Sunday school boy" into a bold leader, on and off the football field. The coach saw that one of Reggie's weaknesses as a player was that he wasn't bold and aggressive enough. So Coach Pulliam used a two-pronged approach to inspire and fire Reggie's boldness.

The first prong was affirmation. The coach took Reggie aside and said, "Reggie, I see greatness in you. I believe that you could have an outstanding career as a football player if you will just show more boldness on the field."

The second prong was physical punishment. "From the day he told me about the greatness he saw in me," Reggie recalled, "Coach Pulliam began to push and pressure me and harass me on the field and in the gym. It was baffling to me because all this rough treatment really intensified right after he had taken me aside and told me how great I could become. If he thought I was so great, why was he tearing into me this way?

"He and the other coaches used to frustrate me to the point where it made me cry—and then they would laugh at me and call me 'Crybaby'! I hated that because I was cool, man, and I didn't want to be embarrassed in front of my friends. But looking back, I realize that this experience hardened me to peer pressure and the opinions of others; it kept me from worrying so much what other people thought of me. Coach Pulliam stayed on me like that for the rest of my sophomore year and on into my junior year. It was baffling to me because I knew the coaches liked me and believed in me—but man! They sure had a funny way of showing it!

"One day, a few of us kids were playing basketball against some of the coaches—just a pickup game. We were playing man-to-man, and Coach Pulliam was guarding me. He had been pestering me and fouling me throughout the game. Finally, as I made a move to the basket, Coach Pulliam elbowed me hard in the chest. It hurt like crazy! I thought, *Man, that's it! He rassles me, he punches me, he makes me cry, and I'm sick of it!* I slammed the basketball down and walked off the court.

"I went into the locker room, sat down on the bench, and cried. I was mad and I was hurt. A little later, I looked up and saw Coach Pulliam coming down the aisle toward me. I thought, *Finally, he's gonna say he's sorry.* In fact, I found out years later that the other coaches told him he ought to apologize to me. But he bent down in front of me, grabbed the front of my tee shirt, and said, "If you think I'm gonna apologize, you might as well go in there and get ready for your next whupping. Until you start fighting me back, I'm gonna keep kicking your butt." Then he straightened up and walked away.

"I sat there and thought, *Doggonnit, he ain't gonna leave me alone!* So I took up his challenge and started fighting him back. From then on, whenever we were on the basketball court and he gave me a shot with his elbow, I elbowed him back—hard. I started playing bold, aggressive, and physical.

"Years later, I figured out what Coach Pulliam was doing in my life: He was building my confidence and courage. He knew my goal in life was to play pro football, and he knew I needed to be bolder and tougher in order to make it in the NFL. So he pounded on me to toughen me up, and it worked. I took a lot of pride in beating him, and I held on to that pride and self-confidence for a long time.

"Years later, I called Coach Pulliam. I hadn't talked to him in years, and I wanted him to know that I appreciated the boldness and toughness he had pounded into me. I said, 'It took me a while to figure out why you were so hard on me. You were trying to make me more aggressive and confident—and, Coach, you did a good job. In fact, you did such a good job, I thought you were gonna kill me!'

"He laughed and said, 'You know what, Reggie? I called the parents of all you guys and asked if I could do to them what I did to you, and your mother was the only one who said yes.'

"I was stunned. All those years, I had never known that my mother was in on what the coach was doing to me. She had the wisdom to see that I needed to step up to the next level of confidence and toughness. So she gave Coach Pulliam permission to pound some toughness into me. When Coach Pulliam told me that, I was like, 'Thank God for my mother, man!'"

Reggie White took quite a pounding from his coach, and today he thanks God for the coach who administered that pounding—and for his mother who permitted it. Though he retired from football several years ago, he is still a bold and courageous leader, a Christian minister, and a highly visible spokesman for the fight against racial and economic injustice.

Over his long career, Reggie has often relied upon the iron rod of boldness that his high school coach hammered into him. Many times, he found himself embroiled in controversy and attacked by a hostile media. In Philadelphia, his battles with the Eagles' owner were legendary. In 1992, Reggie had to play through his grief after his friend and fellow defensive lineman, twenty-six-year-old Jerome Brown, was killed in a car crash.

Reggie's toughest challenge came on January 8, 1996, when the Inner-City Church, where Reggie served as one of the pastors, was completely destroyed by fire. Racial slurs had been painted on the door. The football star received anonymous threats against himself and his family. Reggie responded by speaking out even more boldly against the racists and haters who had leveled his church and many other African-American churches across the South.

Perhaps Reggie would eventually have become a bold and dynamic leader without the pain of Coach Pulliam's elbow in his chest—but he doesn't think so. Reggie White gives Coach Pulliam, his mother, and God the credit for giving him the painful, pounding, punishing lesson he needed in order to become a Hall of Fame football player and a bold leader in the fight for human justice.

Understand, I am certainly not advocating such a physically punishing approach to developing young leaders. In Reggie's case, it was probably one of the best things that could ever have happened to him—but Reggie is a unique case. The point of the story is simply this: All leaders need boldness. If you are not bold, you are not a leader. So we need to give young people opportunities and challenges that will build their confidence and stretch their courage. We need to motivate them to take risks and take bold stands for their convictions and principles. And we need to be examples of bold leadership, giving them inspirational role models that they can remember and emulate when they face their own battles as leaders.

The sixth key to being an effective leader is simply: Be bold!

■ Boldness to Speak Up

Sometimes, leadership demands that a person be physically bold and courageous. That was certainly true of Reggie White and every other leader on the football field. But physical courage was also demanded of William Donohue, president of the Catholic League for Religious and Civil Rights. He told me, "I didn't realize I had the ability to lead until I was in the U.S. Air Force. Trained as an accountant, I was quickly promoted. This gave me the kind of confidence, at the age of nineteen, that I was previously lacking.

"A few years after I was honorably discharged, I started my teaching career at St. Lucy's School in Spanish Harlem, New York. To be a good teacher, it's important to be a good leader, especially when teaching youngsters. But in my particular instance, it was also important to defend my students from potential danger.

"For example, whenever an unauthorized person (always a male) entered the school, I was the person who searched the school looking for him—all the other teachers locked their doors. Spanish Harlem was, and is, a high crime area, and because I was one of the few male teachers (as well as being six two and 220 pounds), I was the point man everyone depended on for safety. This kind of responsibility certainly drew on whatever leadership qualities I possessed."

So sometimes the bold leadership that is needed is sheer physical courage—the courage to deal with situations of potential violence and bodily harm. But more commonly, the bold courage that is required of leaders is the boldness to take a stand, the courage to speak up.

John Schuerholz, general manager of the Atlanta Braves, described his experience: "My dad taught me to be honest, accountable, kind, committed to my principles. I broke into sports management under Lou Gorman of the Baltimore Orioles and Kansas City Royals. Lou trusted my abilities and instincts, and he gave me leadership responsibilities in the player development department. During my first year with the Royals, I reported both to Lou and to Charlie Metro, who was in charge of scouting.

"One time, when Charlie was on the road, I created a complete program of reporting procedures for newly signed players. When Charlie returned and saw the plan I had come up with, he disliked it. I defended my thought process.

"Charlie asked, 'When did you ever wear a professional uniform?'

"I said, 'When did that equate to intellect and common sense?'

"Well, that didn't go down well with Charlie. Just like that, he fired me as his assistant for scouting. I think Lou must have appreciated my boldness in standing up for my ideas. He retained me as his assistant— and a few days later, Charlie rehired me."

John Eldred, founder of the Wharton School's Family Business Program at the University of Pennsylvania, shared with me a recollection of when he discovered the boldness to speak up: "I was nineteen and working in a small manufacturing firm. We had introduced a new product line with a lot of breakthrough potential. After a few months, I noticed that our profit margins were slipping, and it coincided with the introduction of this new product.

"I started weighing the products as they were shipped, since our pricing calculations were based on a certain weight factor. Our product engineer—a hotshot who was coaching me on engineering issues (I had just started Wharton undergrad)—had dictated the pricing using standard engineering formulas. For several weeks, my daily weighing of the finished product had contradicted these formulas—the product weighed about thirty percent more than it was supposed to! That, of course, would explain the disappearing profits.

"The climactic moment occurred when I called a meeting with the owner, Mike, and the engineer. I was hesitant to show my results because I was pretty sure the hotshot engineer wouldn't take it well. My apprehension was well founded. When I pointed out the apparent mistake, the engineer went berserk and verbally attacked me, accusing me of being a 'kid' (which, as a teenager, I was) and of not being an engineer (right again but utterly irrelevant if my results were correct). I said, 'Why don't we just weigh the product and find out?'

"They led a procession to the back of the factory to weigh the products. The results of the weigh-in were threefold:

"First, we discovered that I was right. The product did weigh more than the engineer's slide rule had predicted. We adjusted the prices accordingly, and the profit margin returned.

"Second, I learned several lessons that have served me well in life: Even if you are young, inexperienced, and you doubt yourself, it is better to speak your mind boldly than to let things slide. Being young and inexperienced doesn't make you automatically wrong, nor does being a hotshot engineer make you automatically right. It is always better to speak up early and catch problems before they go too far than to wait for perfect data or absolute confidence in the facts—if you're wrong, you can simply admit it later.

"Third, I made an enemy for life out of that engineer. He saw my action as an intentional setup to embarrass him. As it turned out, his standing fell rapidly after that incident, and he was gone in six months. In the years since, I have realized that I could have found a way of handling the pricing error without embarrassing the engineer. At the time, I thought the only issue was who is wrong and who is right. Now I know that it is possible to be right and to handle it the wrong way—and it is possible to fix a wrong situation without making someone appear to be incompetent. That, too, is a lesson I have carried with me throughout my career.

"But the most important lesson of this experience is that young leaders should be encouraged to speak up boldly for what they believe is right and true. They should not be intimidated by age or experience or authority. Other people may not listen, or they may get angry, and there may even be consequences and a price to pay for speaking up. But if you are going to be a leader, you have to speak up anyway. You have to be bold."

■ Boldness to Stand Alone

To be bold, a leader must have the courage to stand alone against the crowd. Dave Hart, athletics director at Florida State University, told me about a time when this lesson was powerfully brought home to him. "My parents taught me my core values," Hart said, "and my teachers and coaches have taught me the importance of leadership and the need to take a principled stand for my core values.

"One time, in elementary school, I gave an answer in class—and the teacher opened up the issue for debate: Was the answer I had given correct or not? Some of my classmates agreed with my answer; some opposed it. As the discussion continued, the teacher suggested some arguments against my answer. The more he talked, the more he influenced the class against my answer. When students would speak up in support of me, he subtly suggested that those students might want to think about it some more.

"Gradually, all of my supporters were persuaded to the opposite position. There was no one in the class who agreed with me. I was standing all alone with my response. At that point, the teacher turned to me and said, 'Mr. Hart, would you like to change your response?' I remember that I was tempted to say yes, I was ready to abandon my answer—but I didn't. I said, 'No. I'm not going to change my answer.' He said, 'Why not? Everyone in the class agrees that you must be wrong.' I said, 'I still think I'm right.'

"The teacher then turned to the class and said, 'Class, Mr. Hart is right. He stood firm when the popular answer was the wrong answer.' And he proceeded to apply the lesson of that exercise. He told us that it is more important to be right than to be in the majority. The world needs people who are willing to stand up for what they believe is right, even if the whole world says they are wrong. That was a lesson in leadership I never forgot.

"I think one of the most important things we can do in training young leaders is to praise them and encourage them when they make tough decisions and demonstrate the courage not to follow the crowd. We should encourage young leaders to discover their core values and settle their convictions, then boldly take a stand for those values and convictions. That's what leaders do."

A leader, regardless of his or her age, must learn to take conflict, controversy, and criticism in stride. To be in leadership is to be in the eye of the storm. Max Lucado once said, "A man who wants to lead the orchestra must turn his back on the crowd." It's true. A leader has to learn to stand alone, against the crowd, against popular opinion, boldly proclaiming his or her convictions and principles to a world that usually doesn't care—and is often downright hostile.

Leadership is a lonely business.

■ Strategic Boldness

Another form of boldness that leaders need is *strategic* boldness—the willingness to take a daring strategic risk in order to achieve a worthwhile objective. "Leaders take risks," observed John C. Maxwell. "That's not to say they are reckless, because good leaders aren't. But they don't always take the safest route. Rarely can a person break ground and play it safe at the same time. Often, leaders must take others into the unknown and march them off the map."

Young leaders should be encouraged to take calculated risks, not stupid gambles. Our message should be, "Dream big dreams! Reach for your dreams and take risks to make them come true! Let go of your fears and act boldly—but leave as little as possible to chance."

Dr. Vincent Mumford of the University of Central Florida told me, "Mr. Steele was my high school computer science teacher, math teacher, and junior varsity basketball coach. He was a young teacher at the time, and he knew how to relate to young people. He was a big man with a big smile on his face and a great sense of humor. He and I were always verbally sparring with each other about our favorite basketball players—I was a fan of Dr. J, and he liked Larry Bird. He would never miss an opportunity to tell me how his team was going to mop up the floor with my team.

"As a basketball coach, Mr. Steele had a knack for building up my confidence on the court. He enjoyed pulling off a big surprise against our opponents. In one basketball game, with two seconds left on the clock, he called a time-out and designed a play for me to take the last shot. I knew I wasn't the best shooter on the team—but that was exactly the point. His play used our best shooter as a decoy. While everyone was guarding him, I would be wide open to take the shot.

"I remember walking onto the court and seeing the ball inbounded in my direction. I don't remember shooting, but I must have because the next thing I knew, my teammates were jumping on me and yelling at me that I had made the shot!

"It was a risk, putting the game into the hands of a lesser player. But the risk paid off. That taught me a lot about leadership. When the chips are down, a real leader sometimes takes a chance to save the game."

Another form of bold risk taking involves daring to attempt a challenge when all the odds are against you. Mark Rutland, president of Southeastern College in Lakeland, Florida, told me about a risk he took in high school: "When I ran for student body president, I was a relatively new student in the school. I wasn't well known, and my opponent was very popular. I decided to use superior organization to defeat local popularity.

"I recruited a campaign representative in every homeroom in the entire school. I met with those representatives every week of the campaign, which lasted six weeks. I asked each of them to recruit two assistant representatives to hand out literature and put up posters. Since each homeroom had thirty or fewer students, I already had ten percent of the votes I needed as workers for my campaign.

"On election day, I won in a landslide, even though I was a relative outsider. Going into that campaign was a long-shot risk, but I used hard work and superior organization to even the odds and defeat name recognition."

These experiences of Dr. Mumford and Mark Rutland offer insights into how we should encourage young leaders to think strategically and boldly. As we prepare and train young people to lead, let's encourage them to make bold decisions, envision bold strategies, and take bold risks. But at the same time, let's teach them how to swing the odds of success in their favor. We should show them how to do the following:

1. *Do your homework.* Knowledge is power, so research the situation. Leaders swing the odds in their favor by being well informed. Don't expect to gather 100 percent of the information you want before making a decision—be prepared to settle for 75 or even 50 percent. Get your best sense of the situation, listen to your intuition and instincts, then act decisively.

2. *Plan.* Mark Rutland knew he lacked name recognition, so he improved his odds by creating a well-planned organization. Careful strategic planning was the key to victory in a long-shot election. Young people are often impatient; we must teach them the value of wise and careful planning.

3. *Be boldly decisive.* Delaying a decision is usually more dangerous than making a bold decision based on partial information. Field Marshal William Joseph Slim, the British general who turned back the Japanese invasion of India and Burma in World War II, put it this way: "When you cannot make up your mind between two evenly balanced courses of action, always choose the bolder." Another great military leader agreed. "Decisive action is the key to success," observed General George S. Patton. "Indecision is, in fact, a decision to do nothing."

4. *Be optimistic.* Successful risk takers are optimistic. They believe in God, in themselves, in their ideas, and in a brighter future. Optimism energizes and inspires. Optimism is also infectious; it quickly spreads from leader to followers. A spirit of optimism can lift an entire team or organization. General Colin Powell was described by a former associate, Richard Haass, as "the most optimistic person [he'd] ever met. He is congenitally upbeat."

5. *Be original.* Bold leaders don't follow the beaten path; they strike out cross-country and follow their own compass. Encourage young leaders to follow the advice of *Star Trek*'s Captain Kirk: Boldly go where no young leader has gone before! Sam Walton, founder of the Wal-Mart retail chain, stated, "Swim upstream. Go the other way. Ignore the conventional wisdom. If everybody else is doing it one way, there's a good chance you can find your niche by going in exactly the opposite direction—but be prepared for a lot of folks to wave you down and tell you you're headed the wrong way."

6. *Accept losses with a smile.* There's a downside to risk taking, and it is simply this: Sometimes you lose. What then? Simple: If you lose, don't moan. Just learn the lessons of your failure and try again. Walt Disney once said, "I think it's important to have a good hard failure when you're young." Walt knew—he had many failures before his first big success, *Snow White and the Seven Dwarfs.* It's okay for young leaders to take a risk and fail. They'll survive, they'll learn, they'll grow—and they won't make that same mistake the next time.

Dr. John MacArthur, pastor of Grace Community Church in Sun Valley, California, told me, "Great leaders make great second decisions. Many times they make bad first decisions, but they learn from their mistakes and get better as a result."

Leaders make decisions. Making decisions is simply what leaders do. Every time a leader makes a decision, there is a risk involved. The decision could be wrong. It could even be disastrous. But that's why teams and organizations have leaders. A team needs to have one bold individual at the helm, one person who is willing to step up, be decisive, and accept the accolades for the brilliant decisions—and accept responsibility when things go wrong.

No team ever rocked the world on its ear by punting on every fourth-and-one situation. Sometimes you have to gather your courage and run it straight up the middle. That's a message our young leaders need to hear whenever they shrink from a challenge or a risky decision. Tell them,

"You've got to take risks if you want to be a leader. Without risk, there is no adventure."

Noted political writer Tom Wicker has observed that "ultimately, in the presidency, greatness is measured by decision making." The concept was well understood by John F. Kennedy, who remarked: "There stands the decision and there stands the president."

Jerry McMorris, chairman and CEO of Major League Baseball's Colorado Rockies, told me, "I got my start in business as an eighteen-year-old. It goes back to the day I came home from the company where I was working during summer vacation, and I told my dad all the things that were wrong at that place.

"My dad said, 'Jerry, you should be in business for yourself.' I said, 'You're right. I should.' So I found a very small trucking business and I bought it for ten percent of the asking price. My father mentored me through the process."

That small trucking business eventually became NationsWay Transport Service, Inc., which was for many years one of the largest freight companies in the nation, with around six thousand employees (NationsWay ceased operation in 1999). The success of NationsWay enabled Jerry to assemble an ownership group that acquired the MLB expansion team, the Colorado Rockies, in September 1992.

And it all began when Jerry's dad encouraged him to take a risk at age eighteen and start his own company. "Jerry, you should be in business for yourself," his father said—and the rest is history.

■ The Boldness of a Trailblazer

Stephanie Flamini is the women's basketball coach at Guilford College in Greensboro, North Carolina. "I first realized my leadership potential when I was eight years old," she told me. "That's when I started playing sports for an organized team. As an eight-year-old, I was the first female in Pennsylvania to play boys' Little League baseball. As I continued to play several sports and excel at them, I was given more and more opportunities to be a leader.

"Later, I became the first girl to play boys' basketball in my state. It wasn't easy, and I took a lot of abuse from many of the boys in the league. There were always reporters at my games, interviewing me and doing write-ups. At the time I didn't realize that I was paving the way for equality. I was just doing something I loved to do.

"We need kids who will step up, be bold, and lead. We need young leaders who want to point the way in improving the world. It's important that we support and encourage young leaders because they are taking a risk by stepping up. Leadership is a great quality, and we should encourage it and nurture it wherever we find it."

Stephanie Flamini is a trailblazer—a bold leader who led the way and opened doors for other girls to become involved in so-called boys' sports. At the time, she didn't think what she did was such a big deal—she was just playing her game. Yet she withstood the taunts and the jeers, the pressure and the media scrutiny. From the age of eight, Stephanie has been a risk taker and a bold leader.

My good friend Wayne Embry is another bold trailblazer. He was the first African-American general manager in professional sports—a title he received when he was appointed to that position by the Milwaukee Bucks in 1972. Embry remained general manager of the Bucks until 1977, when he was made a vice president and consultant. He later became an executive with the Cleveland Cavaliers, rising to the post of team president and chief operating officer (he has since retired).

Though Wayne grew up poor in Springfield, Ohio, his family bonds were strong, and his parents taught him a strong work ethic. "Whatever our family chose to do," he said, "we established goals and were proud of what we accomplished."

Raised in the 1940s and 1950s, Wayne dealt with racial prejudice on a regular basis. "You couldn't help having low self-esteem as a human being when you were told, 'You can't do this; you can't do that.' I had to grab hold of those things I was being told, and I had to use them as inspiration to work hard and succeed," he said.

"My grandfather, father, and mother helped build my self-confidence. My grandfather was the biggest influence—a real role model. He overcame great racial barriers to become a foreman at a pump factory in Springfield, back in the 1930s. I was inspired by what he had overcome and what he had accomplished.

"As I gained confidence in myself, I became an honor roll student and an outstanding athlete, and I realized that I had leadership ability. Once this happened I was able to lead my team, and I was able to have an impact on the student body—they elected me vice president of my class.

"Becoming a student leader, an African-American class officer in an all-white environment, was a challenge—and it was an unusual accomplishment for the 1950s. I had to put up with a lot of pressure and name-calling from some classmates. It reached a point where I actually quit school—but just for one day. When I announced to my class that I was not going to return, my classmates encouraged me to persevere through the name-calling and other insults. So I returned to school, and I stuck it out."

Wayne Embry became a star player at Miami University (of Ohio), where he earned a degree in education with a minor in business administration—and had his No. 23 jersey retired. He went on to an eleven-year NBA playing career with the Cincinnati Royals, Boston Celtics, and Milwaukee Bucks.

When he traded the basketball court for the front office, Wayne came under close media scrutiny—and he wasn't always comfortable with it. He didn't see himself as a trailblazer or a symbol of African-American progress. He was just a man trying to play his game and do his job.

"I've received abuse as an African-American from early childhood," he once said, "and I choose not to let that impede my progress. If I were to remain bitter and allow those scars to remain open, it would have impeded my progress."

Wayne Embry symbolizes bold leadership. As a young leader in his high school, he persevered through racial slurs and insults to become a class officer in an all-white school. As an adult, he broke the color barrier in NBA management. He is a trailblazer, opening the doors, so that others may follow where he has led.

As you raise, teach, coach, train, and mentor your young leader, make sure you prepare him or her with all the unvarnished facts. Leadership is lonely and hard. Being a leader means walking around with a bull's-eye on your chest. There will be critics who can't wait to take shots at you. It goes with the territory.

But don't forget to tell the young person that leadership is also an adventure! And life was meant to be lived as an adventure, boldly and courageously! As Helen Keller once said, "Life is a daring adventure or nothing at all." Tell that young person who is trembling with fear and anticipation, "Be bold—and be a leader!"

Next, we will examine the seventh crucial dimension of great leadership—servanthood.

| 11 |

Seventh Key:
Be a Servant

According to sports columnist Mike Burke of the Cumberland (Maryland) *Times-News*, Bill "Speedy" Morris is revered at the schools where he has coached "in much the same way Ara Parseghian is revered by Notre Damers." Speedy is currently the basketball coach at St. Joseph's Preparatory School, the Jesuit high school of Philadelphia. When he started in the coaching business, however, Speedy Morris was a reluctant draftee.

"During my senior year in high school," he told me, "I was a member of the basketball team, but I didn't play much. In the preseason I got sick and missed a few weeks. My parish priest asked me if I would be interested in coaching our grade school basketball team. The problem was that, in order to take the coaching position, I would have to quit the varsity team. Even though I wasn't playing much, I loved basketball and didn't want to leave the team.

"I asked my basketball coach what he thought, and he said, 'Billy, coaching is a great profession, and you have the opportunity to make a difference in young people's lives. I know how much you love to play the game, but if you would be willing to set aside your desire to play, I think that you would be doing a wonderful thing in the lives of those young boys. It would be a real act of service.'

"After that conversation, I made a decision to coach the youth of my parish—and I have been coaching ever since. I never regretted the decision. Next to a young athlete's own parents, few people can have a greater long-term impact on a young athlete's life than a coach."

Speedy Morris is not just a leader. He's a servant. He got into coaching to serve a team of grade school basketball players, and he continues to be a servant to high school players today. He is motivated not only by a love for the game, but also by a love for young people and a desire to influence lives.

I asked Coach Morris to name the leaders who had the greatest impact on his life. "My high school coach was my first role model of good coaching," he replied. "He was fair and always under control, and you could talk to him about anything—about life, not just about basketball.

"Then there was Dr. Jack Ramsay," he said, mentioning a name I knew well. Dr. Jack gave me my first job in the NBA. "He was also a big influence on me," Coach Morris continued. "When I coached grade school basketball, they had triple-headers in our gym. Jack Ramsay's kid was on one of the teams, and Jack would come watch the games. His son's team was not that good, nor did his son start or play much, but Jack was extremely encouraging and humble—always very courteous.

"John Wooden was another great mentor to me. I never met a finer human being. I've had the opportunity to speak with the Wizard of Westwood on three different occasions, and he is one of the wisest, most knowledgeable, most humble human beings I have ever met. He always called me 'Coach Morris,' and he said it was his pleasure to meet me. That amazed me, since he is the one who, more than anyone around, deserves to be called 'Coach'—and the privilege was all mine!"

I noticed how frequently the word *humble* came up in the conversation with Speedy Morris. Clearly, humility is a character quality that Coach Morris notices and prizes in the people he meets. And that comes as no surprise to anyone who knows him, for Coach Morris is a very humble, self-effacing leader.

But then, Speedy Morris could be such a humble man because, in his coaching career, he has so often been humbled. No, I don't mean he has been humbled by opposing teams—his winning record speaks for itself. Most of Coach Morris's humbling experiences have taken place at the sidelines—as the coach himself explained.

"During my second year as a coach," he told me, "I took my coat off and threw it behind the bench—but I threw it a little too hard. Our gym was on the third floor, and the fire escape was open. My suit coat sailed out over the fire escape and fell down three stories into a Dumpster. It was a brand-new coat—my wife had just bought it for me. When the manager retrieved it, the coat was a mess—and it smelled awful! Everyone was laughing—my players thought it was hilarious. I even chuckled. My wife, however, didn't laugh.

"A few years later, when I was in my first year coaching at LaSalle University in Philadelphia, we were playing a sold-out game at Villanova. During a time-out, I bent to speak to my team and my pants ripped. At halftime, my wife came in and sewed up my pants. While she sewed, I spoke in my underwear to my team. My wife didn't have enough thread so she used a safety pin to close the seam in my pants.

"Early in the second half, I jumped up—and I heard a ripping sound and felt a breeze and something sticking me. The pants had split again, and the safety pin had popped open and was pinching me in the butt. It was a huge rip, and the Villanova fans were chanting, 'Speedy ripped his pants!' It was embarrassing, but funny, and the blooper tapes are still being shown."

I asked Coach Morris if he thought that leaders are born or made. "The only leader that was born a leader was Jesus," he replied. "All others are made through good example and support from parents, relatives, coaches, or teachers. The best leaders are those who lead by example."

■ Leading Is Serving

I saw this same attitude of leadership-by-serving in my interview with Mel Martinez, former secretary of housing and urban development, now running for the U.S. Senate from Florida. He told me how he first discovered that he had the ability to be a leader, soon after coming to America from Cuba. "I realized that people saw me as a leader," he said, "when my teammates elected me captain of my high school baseball and basketball teams. I had only been in this country a little more than a year and was still mastering the English language, yet my teammates recognized something in me that enabled them to have confidence in me as a team captain.

"I had a lot to learn about leadership, and that's why I'm grateful for my mentors—the people who trained me, encouraged me, and gave me opportunities to lead. My father taught me to believe in myself and told me I had a responsibility to make a contribution as a leader. In the public arena, Bill Frederick and Glenda Hood, both former mayors of Orlando, gave me important opportunities to serve my community in responsible positions.

"The most important part of being a leader is being a servant. My own commitment to serving through leadership comes from my faith in the Lord Jesus Christ. He was the great example of leading by serving, and I believe that He calls us to be servant leaders."

I was impressed that both Speedy Morris and Mel Martinez cited Jesus as their ultimate role model for leadership. These two leaders, coming from two very different spheres of influence, sports and government, described almost identical views of what it means to be a leader. Both see leadership as servanthood after the pattern first laid down by Jesus Christ.

In one of his New Testament letters the apostle Paul first described this vision of leading-by-serving. He wrote,

Do nothing out of selfish ambition or vain conceit, but in humility consider others better than yourselves. Each of you should look

not only to your own interests, but also to the interests of others.
Your attitude should be the same as that of Christ Jesus:
Who, being in very nature God,
did not consider equality with God something to be grasped,
but made himself nothing,
taking the very nature of a servant,
being made in human likeness.
And being found in appearance as a man,
he humbled himself
and became obedient to death—
even death on a cross! (Phil. 2:3-8)

Authentic leadership, then, is not about being "the boss" but about being a servant. Most leadership experts agree. "If you wish to be a leader," said Frank F. Warren, former president of Whitworth College, "you will be frustrated, for very few people wish to be led. If you aim to be a servant, you will never be frustrated." Hans Finzel, Christian leadership expert and author of *Change Is Like a Slinky*, put it simply: "Leadership is a selfless journey." And author-teacher Peter Drucker observed, "No leader is worth his salt who won't set up the chairs."

Dr. Dan Gerdes is the author of *Through the Storm* and *Coaching for Character*, and founder of Renewing the Heart, a Christian ministry to people facing adversity. "Leading is a good thing," he told me, "because leadership is serving. When a young person has leadership abilities for a given situation, he or she has an obligation to use those abilities to serve others—not to gratify or satisfy the self, but to serve others. If a young person has an opportunity to serve others by leading, it would be wrong, it would be a tragedy, for that person to remain a follower.

"Too often, being self-assured in leadership is misconstrued as 'tooting your own horn.' That's a false point of view. A person can be confident in leadership, yet still humble in character. And that's what we need: more humble leaders who use their leadership abilities to help others. It doesn't help anyone if a qualified leader holds back so that an unqualified person gets the job. If a young person is qualified, then let that person serve by leading, confidently yet humbly.

"As teachers and coaches, we need to instill in young people the image of leading as a form of serving. When I played basketball in college, that was what my coaches told me: Leadership means sacrifice. It means giving of myself for the sake of my teammates and the team goals. Leadership is not just wearing a title like 'Captain.' It's not just getting to receive the attention and the glory. Leadership is also doing the hard work that others won't or can't do. It's doing all sorts of things that nobody sees, nobody notices, and nobody thanks you for. It's being a servant.

"I'm a coach, and I try to follow the pattern of the Inventor of coaching, my Savior, Jesus Christ. The Christ-centered approach to living comes down to these two commandments: (1) love God and (2) love others as you love yourself. Out of these two commandments come all the other values that are important in leadership and servanthood: work ethic, sacrifice, selflessness, self-discipline, trust, and humility."

When young people see leadership as a form of servanthood rather than a way of boosting their power, status, and egos, their entire view of life and their place in the world will be transformed. Instead of focusing on what other people can do to advance their careers, they will ask, "What can I do for other people?" Instead of focusing on what they can get out of life, they will ask themselves, "What can I give?"

■ Only Leaders Who Serve Should Serve as Leaders

The term *servant leader* was coined by a retired AT&T executive, Robert K. Greenleaf, in a 1970 essay later published as a book titled *The Servant as Leader* (Robert K. Greenleaf Center edition published 1982). Greenleaf's essay was inspired by Herman Hesse's 1932 novel *The Journey to the East* (Picador USA edition published 2003).

Hesse's novel tells of a journey taken by The League, a group of mystics, artists, and poets. Traveling with them is Leo, a servant who carries their luggage. At one point in the journey, Leo disappears. When the servant of the group can't be found, The League is thrown into chaos, torn by arguments. Leo, it seems, was the glue that held The League together. Without the quiet, almost invisible presence of the servant, the group cannot exist. By the end of the book, Leo is found—but he is no longer merely the luggage-carrying servant of the group. He is the leader of The League, dressed in a regal robe trimmed in gold.

In his essay, Greenleaf says that all truly great leaders are like Leo. We meet them first as servants, as people with a humble desire to help and serve others. Their servanthood qualifies them for leadership, for true leadership consists of serving others.

In recent years, many leadership authorities have expanded on Greenleaf's concept of servant leadership. Numerous books on servant leadership have been written by such authors as James Autry, Warren Bennis, Stephen Covey, Max De Pree, M. Scott Peck, Peter Senge, and even Pat Williams (see my book *The Paradox of Power*, Warner Books, 2002). The essential point that all of these books have in common is this: Servant leadership is the way leaders must lead in the twenty-first century. The old model of the pyramidal, boss-at-the-top hierarchy is a dinosaur, a relic of another organizational age.

Of course, the servant leadership model didn't originate with Robert K. Greenleaf in 1970 or with Herman Hesse in 1932. It originated with Jesus of Nazareth. The leadership model of the future is actually the oldest leadership model around. After two thousand years of bosses bossing people around, we have finally realized one of the oldest principles of the science of leadership: Only leaders who serve should serve as leaders.

In this world, there are two kinds of leaders: bosses and servants. Bosses wield power, give orders, and expect to be served. Servant leaders empower people, delegate authority, and serve others. Bosses elevate themselves. Servant leaders elevate others.

Dr. Paige Patterson, president of Southeastern Baptist Theological Seminary, recalled how he learned about being a servant leader when he was a teenager: "My mother and father raised me to be a leader. My mother often told me that I was an answer to prayer and that God would not have given me to the Patterson family if He did not have something strategically important for me to do in life. My father always told me he believed in me, and he urged me to seek the highest possible level of service to Jesus Christ and to others.

"When I was sixteen, my father took me around the world. I had the privilege of preaching in churches in thirteen different countries, including Korea. This was shortly after the Korean War. The plight of Korean orphans was heavy on the heart of everyone who visited Korea. My parents were instrumental in facilitating the adoption of many Korean children by people in America.

"One evening, I was preaching at the First Baptist Church in Baytown, Texas. I made an ardent appeal on behalf of the Korean children. An engineer with Humble Oil and Refining Company came up to me and asked me how he and his wife might adopt one of those children. I gave him the necessary information, and they proceeded to adopt a little boy. I was surprised to later learn that they had named the boy after me.

"That was a profound experience for a sixteen-year-old to have—the experience of being used by God to have an impact on lives around the world. I would like to see thousands of young people having that kind of experience and that kind of impact—serving God and serving others, not for personal benefits or rewards, but for the lasting joy that comes from service to others. Jesus put it best when He said, 'Whosoever among you would be great, let him be your servant.' Whoever would be a leader should begin by serving."

John Eldred of the Wharton School's Family Business Program told me, "Wherever you find people who truly understand what leadership is all about, you see servant leadership. This is true of the military, for example, which is the biggest leadership training program around. At first glance, military leadership appears to be about rank and hierarchy, with superior officers bossing the troops around. But look closer, and you see it is really about servant leadership. In the military, taking care of your followers is a critical function of leadership. The military emphasizes to its young officers that if they take care of their followers, their followers will take care of them.

"We don't see enough of this servant leadership approach in business today. There are too many bosses and not enough servant leaders. I believe that the fundamental job of leadership is to build a sense of community in which everyone says, 'We are all in this together.' The leader who selfishly places his or her own needs above those of the followers is failing, in my view. Leaders should be servants, first, last, and always."

■ Seven Insights for Young Servant Leaders

How, then, can we encourage young leaders to become servant leaders? I have assembled a list of seven insights that we can share with young leaders in our teaching and mentoring experiences with them. These seven insights form the basis of a lifestyle of servant leadership:

1. *Give up the need to control.* Servants don't control people or circumstances. Servants serve, period. Herb Kelleher, former president and CEO of Southwest Airlines, has been called "perhaps the best CEO in America" by *Fortune* magazine. He observed, "A financial analyst once asked me if I was afraid of losing control of our organization. I told him I've never had any control and I never wanted it. If you create an environment where the people truly participate, you don't need control. They know what needs to be done and they do it. The more that people will devote to your cause on a voluntary basis, a willing basis, the fewer hierarchies and control mechanisms you need. . . . I have always believed that the best leader is the best server. If you're a servant, by definition, you are not controlling."

2. *View servanthood as an end, not a means to an end.* In other words, a young leader should not serve others as a way to manipulate people to get his or her way. Servanthood is not a technique; it's a way of life. Some people seem to think, *I want power, and I'll use servanthood to get it. If I serve people, then they will be grateful and will become my followers, and*

that will give me power and control. This kind of pseudoservanthood can become a form of emotional blackmail: "I served you; now you owe me."

The mind-set of a servant is to serve without expecting anything in return. The servant does not want power or control. The servant just wants to serve, period. Even if nobody thanks you, even if nobody follows you, even if nobody recognizes your leadership, you serve because serving is what servants do.

On one of my visits to Southern California, I went to see Coach John Wooden at his Encino apartment. As I walked in the front door, I entered a hall of fame—a museum of photos, plaques, autographed books, and sports memorabilia. It was staggering and fascinating. Most interesting of all was an area that was a tribute to two people. The left-hand side of the hallway was devoted to Abraham Lincoln; the right-hand side was a shrine to Mother Teresa.

"Coach," I said, "tell me about this. Why have you devoted this portion of your home to Lincoln and Mother Teresa?"

"They are my heroes," he said. "I admire them for their wonderful character qualities—their courage, selflessness, humility, sacrifice, integrity, and servanthood. Can you think of two better heroes to have than Lincoln and Mother Teresa?" I couldn't. What leaders those two people were—and what servants!

3. *Examine and purify your motives for wanting to lead.* A young leader should not be eager for power. If leadership is about serving, then a young leader should have compassion for people and a deep sense of conviction—not an ambition to control other people. Bible teacher and author A. W. Tozer put it this way: "I believe it might be accepted as a fairly reliable rule of thumb that the man who is ambitious to lead is disqualified as a leader. The true leader will have no desire to lord it over God's heritage, but will be humble, gentle, self-sacrificing and altogether as ready to follow as to lead."

Former college football coach John Mackovic, whom I first met in 1961 when we were students together at Wake Forest, told me, "Not everyone wants to be a leader. Some are reluctant, and that reluctance can be a good sign. It shows that the young person isn't caught up in the selfish ambition of becoming a leader. Young people should know that leadership is difficult, pain and sacrifice come with it, and it should only be approached with the right motives. Those young leaders who crave the attention and admiration that often come with leadership should be handled with caution. They need to be reminded of the need for humility. They need to learn that the real reward for leadership is not an inflated ego, but the satisfaction of the accomplishment of the team."

4. *Live a lifestyle of love and caring.* You cannot love and care about people while bossing them around. Bosses don't serve; they control and intimidate. Only a servant leader is able to lead by loving and caring. Bosses say, "These people work *for* me. I'm their boss." Servant leaders say, "These people work *with* me. We're a team."

My friend and longtime writing partner, Jerry Jenkins (coauthor of the *Left Behind* series), recalled, "Growing up, I had great leadership role models in my teachers, coaches, and parents. My father was the best example of all—a truly humble, selfless leader. People loved working for him. I was often impressed by the way Dad spoke about the people under his leadership. He never said that this or that person 'works for me.' Whenever he introduced one of his employees, he'd say that this person 'works with me' or 'we work together.'

"Dad was a police chief whose command staffs tended to be hired away to become chiefs themselves. Nothing gave him more satisfaction than to see these people he cared about rising in the ranks. He believed in the principle of servant leadership, which is antithetical to society's view of leadership. Every day, he made sure that his people had what they needed to do their jobs well. Because they knew he cared about them, they in turn made him look good by being motivated to perform well.

"In 1983, when I was the youngest vice president at Moody Bible Institute, I had worked under a leader who was a champion at taking responsibility for the failures of his employees while spreading the credit for positive accomplishments. On many occasions, I experienced both the grace of his caring when he shared the negative burden and the thrill of benefiting from his public accolades. His example of servant leadership motivated me to become that kind of leader. I didn't realize how difficult servant leadership was until I tried it myself. Our natural proclivity is to do the opposite—to accept acclaim and pass the blame.

"If I could offer only one piece of leadership training advice, it would be this: Give young leaders the kind of role models I had—leaders who genuinely care about their people, who serve others, who say, 'We work together,' who shoulder the blame and spread the acclaim. That's the kind of leader we need to raise and train today."

5. *Be an obedient follower.* No leader automatically deserves to be followed. Followers must be earned. One way a leader earns the right to be followed is by demonstrating obedient followership. A leader who can obey is a leader who has walked where his or her people walk. A leader who understands followership as well as leadership will tend to treat followers as partners, not underlings. As Solon, the Athenian statesman, once said, "Learn to obey before you command."

Marriott Vacation Club executive Larry Birkes told me, "We have to be good role models for the young leaders we are raising. We need to be the world we wish to see—that is, if we want the world to be a better place, we need to be better people. If we tell our children to obey the rules, we have to be scrupulous about obeying the law. To be a good leader, you have to be a good follower. Our kids will see right through any duplicity or phoniness."

6. *Make humility your goal.* The great preacher Dwight L. Moody once said, "God sends no one away empty except those who are full of themselves." Bosses are full of themselves; servant leaders are full of humility.

Colin Powell is a humble leader with a no-frills approach as secretary of state. "I don't have to prove to anybody that I can work sixteen-hour days if I can get it done in eight," he says. "I have no food preferences and no drink preferences. A cheeseburger will do fine. I like Holiday Inns."

Mannie Jackson, owner and chairman of the Harlem Globetrotters, was born in a railway boxcar in Illmo, Missouri, and grew up in Illinois, where he earned the title of "Illinois' Mr. Basketball" and played for the University of Illinois before joining the Globetrotters as a player. He is also a charter member of the Illinois Basketball Hall of Fame. Mannie became the first African-American to own a major international sports organization when he purchased the fabled (but declining and nearly bankrupt) Globetrotters in 1993. He is also one of a dozen distinguished nominees for the Archbishop Desmond Tutu Award for Human Rights, which recognizes his work for social justice in South Africa.

Mannie orchestrated one of the most dramatic turnarounds in the history of American sports and American business when, under his leadership, the Harlem Globetrotters increased revenue fivefold and rebuilt the fan base to previously unheard-of levels. Mannie Jackson built up a list of corporate sponsors and took the Globetrotters to 117 countries where they performed for audiences of more than two million people per year. Despite all of these accomplishments, Mannie remains a humble and gracious servant leader—probably in large part because of an incident that occurred when he was a high school basketball player.

"I would not be where I am today," Mannie told me, "without the support and encouragement of my parents and my high school basketball coach, Joe Lucco. Coach Lucco pushed me to be my best, both on and off the court. The discipline and attitude I learned from Coach Lucco have made me a better business executive and have directly contributed to the revival of the Harlem Globetrotters. When I purchased the team in 1993, it was on the brink of extinction. I immediately put Coach Lucco's model into place—a model of discipline, positive encouragement, and high expectations—and the organization quickly exceeded all expectations.

"Coach Lucco was a very strict mentor regarding personal appearance. He wanted us to work together and be a team, not a loose collection of individual stars. That was tough for me at the time because I was the captain and leading scorer of the team, and I liked to dress flamboyantly in the latest style. One of my signature items of clothing was a fedora. When I first got it, I wore it everywhere.

"One day, I climbed onto the team bus for the trip to another school for a game. I was dressed in my resplendent style, including my fedora. Coach Lucco took one look at me and sent me home to change. I was surprised—but I did what I was told. When I returned to the school parking lot, the bus was gone.

"I called a cab, which took me to the other school. At the time, I was working part-time jobs and didn't have extra money for cab fare. As soon as I got to the school, I walked up to Coach Lucco and said, 'Coach, it cost me nine bucks in cab fare to get here.' He gave me a hard look and said, 'I'll make you a deal. You score thirty points and we win this game, and I'll pay back the nine bucks for the cab.'

"That night I scored over thirty points by the third quarter, and we won the game. Coach gave me my nine bucks back. This taught me an important lesson: No matter how important you think you are, when you are part of a team, you respect the rules and the other people on the team. Nobody is bigger than the organization or the rules; everyone, no matter how skilled and successful, is still just one piece of a larger puzzle. I never wore my fedora on the team bus again."

7. *Get your shoulders dirty.* I'm sure that sounds like a strange thing to say to a young leader, but it's really one of the most important pieces of advice we could offer. My friend (and fellow Wake Forest alum) Gil McGregor, announcer for the New Orleans Hornets, taught me the Dirty Shoulders Principle. Gil pointed out to me that servant leaders always have dirty shoulders—figuratively, of course. Why dirty shoulders? Because servant leaders are always lifting people up and letting them stand tall on their shoulders. Servant leaders don't care who gets the glory and recognition; they just want to lift people up.

In the old boss-at-the-top, pyramidal leadership model, the leader says, "My people exist to lift me up and make me successful." But in the servant leadership model, the leader says, "I exist to lift my people up and make them successful." Their success becomes the leader's success—but that's not the point. The leader doesn't lift people up as a means to achieve his own elevation; a servant leader lifts people up for their own sake. Servant leaders get their shoulders dirty and expect nothing in return. That's what servants do.

Gil McGregor talks to young leaders at commencements and similar functions. He always tells young people words like these: "Don't forget who made it possible for you to lead and be successful. There are people in your life who have dirty shoulders because they have lifted you up and allowed you to stand on them. Remember your parents and grandparents, your teachers and coaches, and the church and community leaders who have lifted you and supported you.

"The world is waiting for you to lead and to do some mighty big things. Some of the people who have gone ahead of you have made some big messes. But some have given you some big shoes to fill and some broad shoulders to stand on.

"So go out and make a difference—and never lose sight of what's important. Love one another; serve one another; be kind to the people around you. When you leave home and go to college, remember three things: First, stay focused on your studies. Second, find a good church and worship every Sunday. And third, don't forget to call home. And when you call, thank your mom and dad for their dirty shoulders."

■ Serving Comes First

The son of Greek immigrants, Michael S. Dukakis was born in Massachusetts. He was elected governor of Massachusetts in 1974, inheriting a record deficit and record high unemployment. He is credited with pulling Massachusetts out of one of the worst economic messes in the state's history. He was re-elected twice by wide margins, and in 1986 his fellow governors voted him the most effective governor in the nation. Dukakis won the Democratic nomination for president in 1988, but George H. W. Bush defeated him. Since leaving office, he has served as a speaker and visiting professor at schools from the University of Hawaii to the John F. Kennedy School of Government at Harvard University to Florida Atlantic University.

I asked Governor Dukakis how he became interested in leadership. "I ran for the presidency of my third grade class at the age of eight," he told me. "Don't ask me why. I just wanted to run and exercise leadership, even at that very young age. As I grew older, I received encouragement from my teachers, especially my high school French teacher, Kate O'Brien, and my basketball coach, John Grinnell. They continued to keep in touch and encourage me throughout my political career.

"I am particularly concerned these days about our ability to attract young leaders for public service. I'm concerned about a climate in our country that often paints the worst picture of public service. That's why I teach full-time on both coasts and spend a lot of time speaking on college campuses about public service and political leadership."

Then I asked Governor Dukakis what he thought was the best way to attract young people into civic leadership. "Young people want their lives to count for something," he replied. "They want to make a difference. If we can reach that spark within them, that part of every human being that yearns to make the world a better place, then we can motivate these young people to a lifetime of service. Leadership truly is service, and I hope that we can inspire a generation of idealistic young leaders who want to serve their neighbors and their world.

"There is nothing quite so personally fulfilling as being in a position where you can have a real impact on the lives of your fellow citizens, and that is what political leadership—political service—gives someone a chance to do."

George M. Leader, the former governor of Pennsylvania, told me, "At age eighty-six, I have learned that you get the greatest joy from life when you give to others. The greatest satisfaction of leadership is the capacity to help others. Without that, the burdens of leadership would be greater than the benefits."

Dr. Peter Kikins, president of the University of Arizona, told me that much of his emphasis as the head of a university is on encouraging young people to devote themselves to a lifetime of serving. "I've seen many young leaders," he said, "who experienced the thrill of winning an election, a competition, or an athletic event, and you can see on their faces that winning is a thrilling experience. It brings a wonderful emotional reward—but it's a transitory reward. A thrilling experience should not be confused with long-term satisfaction. As young people mature, they usually find that leadership is not so much about winning, but about serving—and serving brings a much deeper and more lasting satisfaction than winning. So as we train and mentor young leaders, we should make sure that they are not only competitors and winners, but true servants." When Ruth Graham, Billy Graham's wife, said to Dr. Raymond Edman, former president of Wheaton College, that the university trained leaders, he replied, "No, not leaders, but servants."

The next time a young leader asks you, "What should I do to become a leader?" here are some things you could say:

"Find some windows that need cleaning, and clean them. Find some trash on the ground, and pick it up. Find a lawn that needs raking or mowing, and make it look good. Clean under your bed; set the table; wash the family car. Clean up a mess—even if you didn't make it. Befriend and visit an elderly neighbor. Plant flowers and pull weeds. Serve a meal at a homeless shelter. Bake cookies and take them to someone who has no family or friends. Read to a child. Talk to someone about your faith. Shovel a snow-covered sidewalk. Let someone go ahead of you in line. Be a servant."

Let's teach our young leaders to be servant leaders—and being a servant always comes first.

PART III

■　■　■

How to Mentor
and Motivate

| 12 |

How to Be a Hero

Carroll Dawson, general manager of the Houston Rockets, told me about his first hero. "My father, Dewey," he said, "made no more than thirty-seven hundred dollars a year, and he fed seven people on that. He ran a Humble Oil service station in Texas. He hired a man named Percy Tate to work for him.

"One day, when I was ten, Dad said to me, 'Come, let's help Percy fix a flat tire.' With all my ten-year-old wisdom, I said, 'Let him do it—that's why you pay him.' My dad told me, 'Look, anytime you hold a job over someone's head, he'll do just enough work to keep his job and no more—and to top it off, he'll hope you fail. But if you respect a man and show him he's your equal, then that man will do more than you expect, and he'll want you to succeed.'

"That incident helped shape me as a leader, and it taught me a lot about values and how to treat your people. My dad taught me a lot of lessons like that, and that's why he was a hero and a mentor to me."

Carroll Dawson won All-Southwest Conference honors as a basketball player at Baylor. In 1963, he joined the Baylor coaching staff under head coach Bill Menefee; ten years later, he succeeded Menefee as head coach. In 1980, he joined the coaching staff of the Houston Rockets (which won two NBA championships during his tenure).

In 1989, Carroll Dawson was struck by a bolt of lightning on a golf course. The accident cost him one eye and damaged the sight in his other eye. The injury eventually forced him out of coaching and into the Rockets' front office. In 2000, he married a former Baylor classmate, Sharon Strickland Dawson, after an unplanned reunion at a Baylor football game.

Carroll Dawson believes that young leaders need heroes. They need mentors. They need older, wiser, more experienced people in their lives—people who will shape their lives, teach them values, and help them achieve their visions and goals in life. So throughout his coaching and managing career, he has been that kind of mentor and hero to hundreds of players.

"My Baylor players still call me for advice," he told me, "which makes me feel good. My wife says all the time, 'I marvel at how your old players still call you.' Well, that must mean that what I told them years ago has been validated by their experience. The things I said to them proved true. If I hadn't told them the truth, they wouldn't still call me."

Carroll Dawson continues to be a mentor because a mentor tells the truth and models the truth to young leaders-in-training. He is following in the footsteps of his greatest hero-mentor, his father.

■ The Mentoring Model

A mentor is more than just a teacher, counselor, or coach. A mentor is a person who invests his or her life in another person in a deep and personal way. The word *mentor* comes from the name of a character in Homer's *Odyssey*. In that classic tale, King Odysseus of Ithaca was going off to war, so he entrusted his only son, Telemachus, to his wise friend Mentor. Homer's Mentor demonstrated all the ingredients that young leaders-in-training need to find in a mentor today: wisdom, good character, unselfishness, compassion, and a commitment to training the next generation.

The function of a mentor is not merely to dispense knowledge to young people (though mentoring has an educational component). The function of a mentor is not merely to impart skills to others (though mentoring has a training component, too). Instead, the mentoring process is focused primarily on encouraging the growth of character, integrity, maturity, and sound judgment of a young leader-in-training. The mentor is more of an active role model than a classroom instructor. The mentoring process has more to do with what is caught than what is taught.

Rev. Theodore Hesburgh, president emeritus of Notre Dame University, told me that mentoring is the best way—perhaps the only truly effective way—of transmitting leadership qualities from one generation to the next: "I learned most of what I know about leadership from Father John Cavanaugh, my mentor and my predecessor as president. I think one discovers young leaders by identifying promising young people and placing them in tasks and situations where they will learn from others, particularly from mentors. I believe that one only learns leadership from good leaders. That's why mentoring is so important."

John Maxwell explained the mentoring process to me this way: "First, good mentors are good examples. Any child can develop into a leader, but young people need role models and positive influences. Mentors must be good examples for them to follow.

"Second, good mentors are affirmers and encouragers. They help to build children's confidence by commending them on the things they do well, by saying, 'I believe in you.' Mentors compliment young people both in private and in front of others. A mentor should find that young person's strongest traits, activities, and achievements, and encourage him or her one hundred percent in these areas.

"Third, good mentors look for opportunities to instill the qualities of a leader into young people. Those leadership qualities include character, charisma, commitment, communication, competence, courage, discernment, focus, generosity, initiative, listening, passion, positive attitude, problem solving, relationships, responsibility, security, self-discipline, servanthood, teachability, and vision. The best way to instill these qualities in others is by modeling them in our own lives. We teach what we know, but we reproduce what we are."

The greatest mentor of all time, of course, was Jesus of Nazareth. He spent three intense years pouring His life into twelve men. He preached to the masses, yet He invested Himself in a few individuals. He mentored twelve men, and through them, He changed the world.

Jesus was the ultimate role model. When He wanted to teach the Twelve about prayer, He didn't just say, "You fellas ought to get on your knees and say this and that." He took them out into the olive grove and prayed with them all night long. When He wanted to teach the Twelve about servanthood, He didn't just say, "Serve one another." He got down on His knees, took a basin and towel, and washed their feet.

Jesus mentored the Twelve not so much with words, but with deeds. He didn't just say, "Listen to Me." He said, "Follow Me." If we want to turn young people into leaders, we need to become mentors. We need to pour our lives, knowledge, skills, experience, character, and values into young leaders. The mentoring process works like this:

Step 1. The mentor says, "I work; you watch."

Step 2. The mentor says, "Let's work together."

Step 3. The mentor says, "You work; I'll watch."

Step 4. The mentor says, "Take what you've learned and be a mentor to others."

Former Dodgers general manager Buzzie Bavasi told me that his hero and mentor was Mr. Branch Rickey, the innovative baseball executive who created the modern farm system and served as general manager of the St. Louis Cardinals, Brooklyn Dodgers, and Pittsburgh Pirates. "I decided early on," he said, "that I wanted to emulate Mr. Rickey. I made up my mind to win as many pennants as he did. And I did—largely because of the lessons I learned from watching his life.

"My advice to young people is to pick out a person that you respect and want to be like. Then, whenever you have to make an important decision, ask yourself what that hero, that mentor, would do in that situation."

That's the mentoring model: one person with skills, experience, wisdom, integrity, and maturity investing in the life of an eager young learner. There is no better way to invest in the future than by investing ourselves in the life of a young leader-in-training.

■ What Mentors Do

Legendary Lakers guard Jerry West was nicknamed "Mr. Clutch" because of his cool, collected demeanor in high-pressure situations. A quiet, humble leader, he gives the credit for his amazing career to his mentors. "I grew up in Cabin Creek, West Virginia and I loved to fish," Jerry told me. "My family didn't have a car, so a kind man named Francis Hoyt took me fishing all the time. He'd drive me if I needed a ride, and we'd talk about life. Mr. Hoyt gave me a lot of support and encouragement when I was young.

"My high school basketball coach, Roy Williams, was also a huge part of my life. I was a painfully shy kid in high school, but I loved to compete. When I suddenly found myself flooded with scholarship offers to play basketball in schools across the country, Coach Williams guided me through all of that confusion. All my life, I've sought out wise people who can give me the benefit of their experience and insight. I got where I was in life because I had mentors and coaches who showed me how to get there."

When you decide to become a mentor and invest in the life of a young person, you have no way of knowing where it will lead. The person you take under your wing could become an NBA star, a president, a doctor, a scientist, a preacher, a teacher, or the first person to set foot on

Mars. If we want to produce a new generation of leaders, then we need to become a generation of mentors.

What, then, do mentors do? Here is my job description for effective mentors:

1. *Mentors exemplify good character and moral principles.* Dick Batchelor is founder of Dick Batchelor Management Group, Inc., a public policy consulting firm. "In the political realm," he told me, "I was most influenced by former Florida governor Leroy Collins. Though I was too young to have served with him, I did get to know him while I served, and I enjoyed hearing him recount personal stories of political leadership and sacrifice.

"Governor Collins once accepted President Johnson's urging that he join the march between Selma and Montgomery with Dr. Martin Luther King, Jr. His presence helped to stave off any attacks on the march, and I am impressed to this day by the governor's courage. Besides the physical danger, he knew he'd be politically punished for joining the march, but he did it because it was the right thing to do."

2. *Mentors build confidence and affirm a young person's sense of self-worth.* Robert Shafer is director of Avalon School in Orlando, a private K-12 school for students with individual differences, from kids with learning disabilities to high-achieving kids who learn best in an individualized setting. "My father was a mentor and a model of leadership in my life," Shafer told me, "and one of the most important qualities I learned from him was his sense of confidence and inner strength. You can't be a leader without confidence.

"Another person who was something of a mentor to me—though I had only one conversation with him—was Miami Dolphins head coach Don Shula. I was seventeen at the time, and an assistant coach for a YMCA tackle football team. The players were all ten years old. We were undefeated and seeded to play in a bowl game in Miami. After a twenty-eight to nothing win, I attended a party with the Miami Dolphins. Don Shula was there, and he had attended much of the game. He came up to me and said, 'You run quite an offense there!' I smiled and took it all in. To receive praise like that from the only man to coach an NFL team to an undefeated season was an incredible inspiration and a confidence booster for me."

3. *Mentors shorten the learning curve for young learners.* Jacqueline Whitmore, founder and director of the Protocol School of Palm Beach, told me, "As adults, we have to become coaches, mentors, role models, and good listeners. My own mentors in my leadership journey were my mother and the director of music in school and church. Along the way, I sought out other people to help me become a leader—people who were mature and wise, and could share their experience with me and shorten my learning curve."

Hubie Brown, head coach of the Memphis Grizzlies, told me how one of his mentors helped shorten his leadership learning curve. "Next to my dad," Hubie said, "my high school coach, Al LoBalbo, was my most important mentor. He had it all as a leader—charisma, organizational ability, and discipline. When I took my first high school coaching job at St. Mary's in Little Falls, New York, I went to Coach LoBalbo for advice. 'Hubie,' he said, 'whatever you do, don't ever use a whistle. Make them respond to your voice, not the whistle. Take them up and down with the power of your voice.' That advice has to do with how a leader communicates, how he gets his players to fly in formation, how he gets their respect. It sounds so simple, yet that advice transformed the way I coached, and probably saved me years of learning by trial and error."

4. *Mentors help young leaders make wise long-term decisions.* Susan Cox, vice president of Holt International Children's Services of Eugene, Oregon (the agency that helped us adopt eight of our children), recalled how her mentor in the 4-H program, her extension agent, helped her make a decision with long-term beneficial consequences for her life. "I especially remember going to a statewide event," she said, "and being assigned to a dorm where I did not know anyone. The rest of my friends had checked in together and were together all the time. I asked my

extension agent to request that I be moved in with my friends. He refused—and I was furious! But he wisely stood his ground because he knew what was best for me.

"He said, 'Susan, I know you are upset with me now, but you will thank me for this someday. When this week is over, your friends will have spent all their time with each other. Sure, they'll have fun—but at the end of the week, you will have met lots of new people and made new friends whose friendships you will take home with you. And you will have a better time because of it.'

"Well, he was absolutely right. That was the beginning of many wonderful experiences. I learned to get out of my comfort zone and to move beyond my circle of close friends. I have thanked him for his insight and wisdom many times, and I have used that example when I have been coaching and mentoring young people who wanted to stay in their own little insulated group."

5. *Mentors ensure their own succession and the continuation of their life's work.* Michael Markarian is president of the Fund for Animals, one of the most influential animal protection organizations in the world. The Fund for Animals was founded in 1967 by author and self-described "curmudgeon" Cleveland Amory. "I began working for the Fund for Animals at age nineteen," Michael told me, "and the organization's founder and president, Cleveland Amory, was a key mentor to me.

"Working closely with Mr. Amory for five years taught me a great deal about how to reach people with a message of compassion, how to infuse humor into an often somber field of work, how to hone my own writing, speaking, and communication skills, and much more. He was a selfless man who worked at the organization full-time without pay for thirty-one years. His example taught me a great deal about how to run a nonprofit organization and how to use our donors' dollars wisely. He passed away in 1998, and I am proud to carry on his work."

6. *Mentors fill a gap in the lives of fatherless kids.* Increasing divorce rates and the breakdown of the American family have produced more

and more fatherless kids. According to the U.S. Department of Health and Human Services, fatherless kids are more prone to sexual activity, emotional and psychiatric problems, drug and alcohol abuse, suicide, poor school performance, and criminal behavior. Kids from fatherless homes are 20 percent less likely to attend college than kids from intact, two-parent families, according to *Family Law Quarterly* (summer 1986).

So mentors have an especially important role to play in the lives of fatherless kids. Mentors provide the things that kids sometimes lack when there is no dad in the home: a positive role model, strong values, support and encouragement, and character building.

Nathan Baker coaches volleyball at Campbell University in North Carolina. "I grew up in a little town with one stoplight," he explained. "The place is called Phil Campbell, Alabama. My younger brother and I were raised in a single-parent home. My mother struggled very hard to provide for us, but she didn't have a high school diploma and finding work was always hard for her. When I entered the seventh grade, I met Coach Gary Williams. He was the high school basketball coach and the father of my first girlfriend.

"Over the next three years, Coach Williams became my friend and mentor, and practically a substitute father. He and his family would take me places I couldn't afford to go to, and they also invited me to church. Between my sophomore and junior years, I grew to six feet six inches, and I played on Coach Williams's varsity team.

"That summer, I attended a revival at their church, and I felt the Lord dealing with me, urging me to give my life to Him. I didn't go forward in the meeting. Instead, I got up and drove around for a while, and finally stopped at Coach Williams's house. I went in, and he knew right away that there was a struggle going on inside me. We talked about it, and I cried—and then the *greatest* thing in my life happened. I gave my life to Jesus Christ, and I have loved and served Him ever since.

"That decision to follow Christ was the most profound decision I ever made. I look back on that day and wonder: What if Coach Williams hadn't been a part of my life? What if I had not had Coach Williams there as my friend and mentor—someone I could trust and talk to about the spiritual struggle I was going through? Having Coach Williams as my mentor and friend made all the difference in my life. He also inspired me to become a coach and use my God-given leadership abilities in working with young athletes.

"After graduation, I went to Martin Methodist College in Tennessee on a basketball scholarship. There I met another great mentor, Rose Magers-Powell, a very special lady who was on the '84 Olympic volleyball team. She has helped to build me into a strong leader and a coach. But the first person God used to really set my life in the right direction was Coach Williams. From my own experience, I can tell you this: If kids don't have a father, they need a mentor like Coach Williams."

■ How to Be a Good Mentor

We've just looked at the role that mentors play in the lives of young leaders-in-training. Now let's consider some principles we can practice that will enable us to be more effective mentors and role models for young leaders:

1. *Let young leaders make their own decisions.* Jean-Jacques Weiler, president of Youth for Christ International, told me, "Young people need to learn how to make decisions for themselves because that's being a leader. So young leaders need mentors who will give them the freedom to make their own decisions and learn from their own mistakes. A good mentor will say, 'Set your own standards, and determine your own future. If you need my help, I'm here beside you to help you and to discuss with you. But at the end of the day, you need to make the final decision and set a course of your own choosing.'

"A young person with strong natural leadership abilities will often have weaknesses that need to be balanced. That's why it's important for mentors—people of experience, character, and spiritual maturity—to walk with developing leaders and stay beside them when they make mistakes. The mentor should not *prevent* them from making mistakes—after all, if young leaders aren't allowed to make mistakes, how will they learn? But mentors should be there to help the learner *process* those mistakes, gather the lessons from them, and regain the confidence to get up and try again. The mentor should say, 'It's okay to make mistakes. You're learning from them, and I have every confidence that you are going to be an effective leader.' "

Former attorney general Edwin Meese told me, "In order to realize their leadership potential, young people need mentors who will give them responsibility and allow them to lead. That means they will make mistakes. That's to be expected—it's part of the learning process. Adult mentors should exercise restraint in telling youngsters what to do, but they should be available to provide advice when asked. Only if a young person is about to do something that would cause serious repercussions—something that would threaten life or cause injury, cause property damage, or hurt the organization's reputation—should the adult mentor intervene. To make sure that young people learn and grow from their mistakes, adult mentors should talk to the young persons about actions and decisions, analyzing both the failures and the successes, and identifying skills that could be improved."

2. *Talk across to young leaders—not down.* Dr. William Flores, president of New Mexico State University, told me, "My second year in college, I became active in a community organization to build support for migrant farm workers. Although I had never seen myself as a leader, several students approached me to be, first, the vice president of the organization and, subsequently, its president. Through that effort I became very active in local politics within the Los Angeles area, and I quickly rose to leadership in the campaign structure.

"My aunt, Francisca Flores, editor of *Regeneración* magazine in Los Angeles, was my mentor. She took me with her to various community empowerment efforts, including the East Los Angeles Educational Rights Commission, of which she was a member. Those activities and many discussions with her and other political leaders stimulated my interest in educational and political involvement. I remember, as a teenager, having regular dinner discussions with her and other Mexican-American community and labor leaders, all of whom treated me as an equal and encouraged my participation in their discussions.

"From my own experience being mentored and mentoring others, I've learned these mentoring principles: Never talk down to youth. Treat them as adults."

3. *Watch what you say.* Jamie Brown is special assistant to the president, White House Office of Legislative Affairs. She offered this advice to mentors: "Adults need to remember how impressionable kids can be. A casual throwaway comment about a young person's potential could severely, permanently limit that boy or girl. So be careful what you say! When we talk to young people, our message should always be, 'I believe in you! I know you can do it! I'm proud of you!'"

4. *Praise in public; correct in private.* If you correct a young person in front of his peers, you'll bring humiliation, embarrassment, and shame on that individual. But affirm that person in front of his peers, and you build confidence and self-esteem. So praise is best administered in public—and correction should always be conducted in private.

"Praise young people in front of their peers," said Dr. Tony Zeiss, president of Central Piedmont Community College. "Set high expectations, praise them when they lead well, and they will astound you." Dr. Richard Armstrong, professor emeritus at Princeton Theological Seminary, agreed: "Young people are motivated best by praise and commendation. Affirm them when they do it right, and reprimand them gently and privately when they don't."

Admiral James M. Loy, administrator of the Transportation Safety Administration, told me, "As a junior officer on one of my first patrols, I found myself in the North Atlantic in the middle of a major storm. Ships often simply slow and run directly into and out of the major swell systems. Making the turn from one to the other is a crucial moment when the ship is put into its most dangerous position—beam to the sea.

"I was on watch as the officer of the deck, responsible to execute the maneuver. It was pitch dark in the middle of the night. The captain was on the bridge, where he had been for two days in the storm. I prepared for the turn. I ordered the steersman to put the rudder over in the direction of the turn, then I readied my hand to accelerate the engine that would help us through the turn.

"Just then, a hand came down over mine, lifted it, and put it on the control for the correct engine. No words were exchanged as the captain gently made sure I didn't put the ship in harm's way. I was never embarrassed or chided. No one else on the watch ever knew that the incident occurred. I learned a lot about leadership that night."

■ Kids Need Heroes

Jeb Bush, the governor of Florida, was born in Midland, Texas. He is seven years younger than his brother George W. Bush (aka Mr. President). As a boy, Jeb was accomplished in school and in sports, and very focused on a successful future. He met his wife, Columba, at the University of Texas, and they were married in 1974. Jeb graduated the following year, Phi Beta Kappa, with a degree in Latin American studies. As evidence of his focus and strong sense of purpose, Jeb completed a four-year course of studies in less than three years.

Jeb took an entry-level job in the international division of Texas Commerce Bank, and he worked his way into the executive training program. His writing skills landed him a position as administrative assistant to the chairman of the board, Ben Love. Jeb Bush's personal rule was: "Get there before the boss arrives and stay until after the boss leaves." Ben Love made it hard on young Jeb Bush—he kept long hours.

Ben Love saw strong leadership qualities in Jeb Bush, and those qualities (plus Jeb's facility in Spanish) convinced Love to send the young man to Caracas, Venezuela, to open a new bank that would specialize in loans to foreign oil companies. That was in 1977.

"I was sent to Caracas at the age of twenty-four," Governor Bush told me. "I was to open a representative office. I was ten years younger than the next youngest bank rep. It was a very difficult challenge because our two children were eighteen months and three months old, and there were shortages of every kind. Our bank did well, and that's when I knew that I could do more than I thought I could. The fear of the unknown subsided!"

Two years later, Jeb brought his family back to the States. His father, George H. W. Bush, had decided to run for president after two terms in Congress and a number of major political appointments (including CIA director and ambassador to the U.N.). So Jeb went to work for his dad—without a paycheck. The Bush for President campaign sent Jeb to forty-five states and placed a lot of responsibility in his hands. Jeb proved he could handle it. Even in his midtwenties, Jeb was a leader.

"In 1979," he said, "I took a leave of absence from my job to work in my father's campaign. The first speech I was called on to give was before two thousand people in San Juan, Puerto Rico—and I had to deliver the speech in Spanish. I was incredibly nervous, but I got through the speech and learned once again that I could overcome fear and anxiety, and I could communicate with sincerity and from the heart. It has been a lesson that has served me well over time."

Jeb Bush ran unsuccessfully for Florida governor in 1994. He came back and won the office in 1998. "There is one reason and one reason only that I'm involved in leadership today," he explained, "and that is my dad, George H. W. Bush. He's my mentor and the best role model anyone could ever have. He's my hero. Just watching him live his life has been my inspiration for success. I wish every young person could grow up with the kind of dad I've had. Every kid needs a hero, and I was fortunate that my hero was living right in my own house."

Governor Bush is right. Kids need heroes. They're hungry for role models. They are constantly looking for older people to pattern their own lives after. The person a child chooses as his or her hero could be a parent, a teacher, a coach, a minister, a firefighter, a policeman, an astronaut, a president, a sports star—or a gangsta rapper or a rock star who looks like Satan and bites the heads off of live rats. One thing you can count on, that kid is going to have a hero, whether you approve of that hero or not.

So why not be that child's hero? Why shouldn't you be the role model who has the greatest influence on that child's life? "But I'm just an ordinary person," you might say. "I'm no hero." I say you *are* a hero—*if* you'll just take the time to get involved and make a positive difference in that young person's life. Here's all you have to do:

Set a good example. Live a moral life and demonstrate integrity. Project a positive, upbeat, can-do attitude about life. Spend time with that young person, and get to know him or her. Have conversations with that young person about values, goals, faith, and important life issues. Affirm that young person and express your belief in him or her. Describe the vision you have for that young person's life: "You know, I see some terrific qualities in you. I wouldn't be at all surprised to see you someday as a great leader, maybe in business, or in the church, or in the military, or in government." And don't forget to say, "I'm proud of you," again and again.

Percy Luney is dean of the Florida A & M University College of Law, located in Orlando, Florida. He described to me how his heroes, particularly African-American heroes, shaped his life. "I realized that I could lead while I was attending a public high school in Washington, D.C.," he said. "In the tenth grade, I entered the mandatory high school ROTC program and later graduated as the number one cadet in the D.C. public school system. In ROTC, I learned about the responsibility of leadership. I was also named captain of the rifle, golf, and football teams.

"An avid reader of world history and military history, I became fascinated by World War II because my father was a member of the famous Buffalo Division. I admired Generals George Patton and Douglas MacArthur. I remember vividly the movies depicting the war heroes Sergeant York and Audie Murphy. I wanted to understand what motivated people to perform heroic acts. I admired people who led by example.

"I began searching out and studying the lives of African-American heroes. I was captivated by the Tuskegee Airmen. At the same time, I learned about the successes of great men such as Paul Robeson, Jackie Robinson, Thurgood Marshall, W. E. B. Du Bois, Booker T. Washington, Frederick Douglass, and Charles Hamilton Houston. Malcolm X and Martin Luther King, Jr., were living history in my life.

"Most important of all, I had heroes in my own home. God blessed me with two wonderful parents who provided positive influences in my life. My mother and father established the foundation of my character, especially my moral beliefs and work ethic. My parents made sure I was in Sunday school and participated in church activities until I graduated from high school and went away to college.

"As a college student in the late '60s, I had the wonderful opportunity to have Alex Haley, author of *Roots*, as a professor, friend, and mentor (he also wrote *The Autobiography of Malcolm X*). With Alex, I was able to discuss the decision-making process of many civil rights leaders, and I tried to analyze the many events that were shaping history at that time.

"The insights I gained from my friendship with Alex Haley, along with the strong foundation I had received when I was growing up, helped me to deal with the realities of campus life during the turbulent '60s. As president of the black student organization on my campus, I led a negotiation effort with the college administration to implement a number of changes on campus. We were very successful, and the three underclass students who worked with me in this effort followed me to Harvard Law. We were also able to avert the kind of building takeovers and strident student-administration confrontations that were rampant on other campuses.

"Young leaders need mentors to look up to, beginning with their own parents. As mentors, we must nurture character and a sense of responsibility, and we should make God and the church community a vital part of their everyday lives. Then we must create leadership opportunities for kids. Most of all, we have to make sure our kids can read and write because, as I did, most kids can find the lives of great heroes and great role models in the pages of books."

■ Y'all Are It

Young people need heroes. Don't you want to be a hero to your kids, to the kids you teach, coach, counsel, or mentor? I know I do. So I've put together some insights and suggestions on how to be a hero to your young leaders-in-training:

1. *Keep the lines of communication open.* Take time to talk to the young people—and take time to listen. Ask questions—and make sure they are open-ended questions, not just questions with yes-no answers. The only way you can get to know and understand a young person's feelings and needs is by communicating and listening. And that takes a serious, intentional commitment of your time.

2. *Seize every teachable moment.* If you spend time with kids, you will often find moments that lend themselves to teaching powerful lessons. News stories, TV shows, and movies provide fodder for instructive conversations about faith, honesty, integrity, and other character issues. When you read together or help a child with homework, think about character and attitude lessons that you can reinforce through that experience. Take advantage of every teachable moment in the time you spend with that child.

3. *Express your unconditional love, acceptance, and forgiveness.* Make sure the kids you are mentoring know that you are on their side, not on their back. When they fail or let you down, correct them, but that correction should take place within a context of complete acceptance and forgiveness. Always surround correction with words of affirmation and support.

4. *Be consistent and dependable.* Keep your promises. Discipline in a consistent and predictable way. Kids need to know that they can count on you. Few things threaten the security of a young person like a parent or mentor who is capricious, unreliable, and unpredictable.

5. *When you're wrong, admit it.* Turn your mistakes into lessons that your kids can learn from. Parents and mentors aren't perfect, so don't pretend to be what you're not. Be real. Kids have a surprising capacity for forgiveness—and seeing you being man enough or woman enough to say, "I was wrong," can be an important lesson in leadership for them.

6. *Never forget that you are under a microscope.* Your kids are watching you all the time, even when you don't realize it. You are their role model. They are learning what it means to be a leader by watching the decisions you make, the behavior you display, the character you have built. They will notice if there is any inconsistency between the way you live and the words you say. So be a person of integrity, especially when you think no one is watching (because kids are usually watching whether you know it or not!).

7. *Watch your mouth!* I'm not just talking about profanity—but watch that, too! Words are powerful and can cut deeper than any knife. The words you say to young people today often resonate throughout their lives, so before you say anything to a child, make sure your words will build that child up, not tear her down.

8. *Develop a vital relationship with God.* Build a habit of prayer and reading the Bible. Worship regularly. Focus on what really matters—not money, fame, status, or power, but a relationship with the Creator of the universe. Grow strong in your faith, and then pass along that strong faith to the children you are mentoring.

9. *Talk about character, attitude, and virtues.* Take time to have deep and meaningful conversations with your young leader-in-training. Let that child hear your deeply held views about such issues as self-control, work ethic, and integrity. Make character training a daily event.

10. *Talk about heroes.* Tell your kids who your heroes are and why you admire them. Ask your kids who their heroes are. If their heroes are not the kind of role models you'd like children to have, then expose them to people who have more admirable traits. Show them how real heroes affect the lives of others in a positive way, and how they demonstrate genuine character qualities. Show them what a real hero is supposed to look like.

11. *Let your kids see you sweat.* Young leaders-in-training need to learn the importance of hard work. Show them what hard work looks like. And while you're at it, show them what hard work *feels* like—put them to work alongside you. Kids enjoy participating in teamwork settings with parents and other adults. There are few better ways to be a mentor and a hero than to get into the trenches with young people and get your fingernails dirty together.

12. *Praise a good effort, even if it results in failure.* Don't let your disappointment show if the child does not perform as you'd hoped. Instead, say, "I'm so proud of you! You really worked hard! You really competed! Great job!" Praise character, attitude, and effort more than results. If you praise only results, you tempt a child to cut ethical corners to obtain your favor—and you want to build a leader of character, not a leader who will win at any cost.

13. *Set firm limits.* An effective leader attains character through discipline and good habits. That means kids should have set times when homework is done, set bedtimes, set limits on TV and computer games. Make sure that kids do their own homework, that they do it on time, and that they don't take shortcuts (such as reading summaries of the books they are assigned or swiping a research paper from an Internet Web site). Establish rules, provide consequences, and make sure kids understand that there is a cause-and-effect relationship between poor choices and unpleasant outcomes.

14. *Be involved with the child's school.* Be aware of the child's scholastic performance and behavior in class. Talk to the teachers and coaches.

Apply your family's values and beliefs to everyday realities at school. Volunteer to help the teacher by donating time or purchasing needed supplies. Be an encourager and a supporter to your child's teacher.

15. *Have fun together!* Learning should be fun and exciting. Find fun things to do with the child you are parenting or mentoring. Share laughter, adventures, and thrilling discoveries. Make a game of learning. Take trips together. Go to fun places together—the zoo or aquarium or amusement park. Use a roller-coaster ride to teach a child about adventure, risk taking, and confidence building. Make the mentoring and learning process fun, and the child will keep coming back for more.

If you do these things with the child you are parenting, teaching, coaching, counseling, or mentoring, I guarantee that young person will inevitably see you as not just a mentor, but an honest-to-gosh hero. Actress and country music star Reba McEntire once put it this way: "Our kids need heroes. Our kids need somebody to look up to. Y'all are it."

She's exactly right. All around you, kids are looking for heroes and role models, people of character and integrity, people to pattern their lives after—people who will show them how to *lead*.

These kids need heroes. These kids need mentors.

And y'all are it.

| 13 |

How to Motivate Kids to Lead

My son Bobby has been living his dream. Ever since he got out of college at age twenty-two, he has been a coach in the Cincinnati Reds farm system. At the end of the 2003 season, which he spent with a rookie club in Sarasota, Florida, the Reds organization sent him out to the Billings (Montana) Mustangs in the Pioneer League to help them finish up their season. In late August, the manager had to go home for a funeral. So Bobby got the word—he would manage the club for three games over the weekend.

The Friday night game was his debut as manager. He had a young pitcher on the mound, a kid with a lot of talent. The Reds' front office wanted this kid on a tight pitch count to keep him from overextending his arm—he could throw only so many pitches, then he had to be replaced by a reliever.

It was the bottom of the fifth. The kid on the mound had two outs and was still pitching well. The Mustangs' pitching coach turned to my son Bobby and said, "The kid's reached his pitch count. He's gotta come out." So Bobby walked out to the mound to take him out of the game.

When Bobby told the pitcher, "You've gotta come out," the kid said, "I'm not leaving."

Welcome to the wonderful world of leadership, Bobby. Here it was, his debut night as a manager, and he was faced with a decision he had never anticipated: an insubordinate pitcher. *Now, what do I do?* he wondered. *Do I get into a wrestling match with this guy right here on the mound?* Bobby thought fast.

"Okay," he said after 2.7 seconds of very rapid cogitation. "One more hitter—and then you're coming out, no matter what."

The pitcher didn't say a word, didn't nod, didn't shrug, didn't flinch. Would the kid come out after the next hitter as ordered—or would there be trouble? Bobby didn't know. He went back to the dugout and waited.

The pitcher went to work. As it turned out, he quickly struck out the batter, ending both the inning and Bobby's crisis. The kid walked off the mound, and he was happy.

I don't know what Bobby would have done if things hadn't gone that well. I don't think Bobby knew what he would have done, either. But he would have done something. He would have had to. He was a leader, and he had to assert the authority of a leader.

If you're a leader, you've gotta lead.

■ Leadership Is Scary

My friend and mentor, Dr. Jack Ramsay, coached the Philadelphia 76ers from '68 to '72, leading them to the play-offs in three out of his four years as head coach. Soon after he started coaching in the NBA, he had a phone conversation with Eddie Donovan, general manager of the New York Knicks. Jack later said, "Eddie gave me the best advice I ever got about coaching in the NBA. He told me, 'Be the boss!' I never forgot that."

What does that mean, "Be the boss!"? It doesn't mean that you have to be a bully, a despot, a tyrant, a dictator, a jerk, or a slave driver. You don't have to be Attila the Hun, Adolf Hitler, Saddam Hussein, or Leona Helmsley. The advice Jack got from Eddie Donovan was simply this: "Be the leader! Take charge! Demonstrate authority!"

When you are placed in a position of authority, people look to you to make decisions. They expect you to call the shots. That's why you are the leader. Yes, being a leader can be scary—especially for kids. If a young leader sticks his or her neck out, so many things can go wrong, and that young leader is responsible for it all!

But once a young leader makes that decision and sets the machinery of the team or organization in motion, it usually goes well. The young leader usually reflects, "Hmm, that turned out better than I thought it would! People didn't get mad at me. The villagers didn't come after me with torches and pitchforks. In fact, they appreciated having a leader in place to make the decisions. I think I'm going to *like* being the leader!"

Denny Crum has been called "Cool Hand Luke" because of his low-key personality as a motivator and coach. Mentored as a player and an assistant coach by John Wooden at UCLA, Denny went on to coach for three decades at the University of Louisville, where he led the Cardinals to six NCAA Final Fours. He retired in 2001 with a record of 675-295 and a .696 winning percentage.

"I had no idea I had the ability to lead," Denny told me, "until my high school coach asked me to serve as a player-coach on our summer league team. I was a tenth grader at the time.

"In our first summer league game, I told our center to take a rest—I was putting a guard into the lineup in his place. He said, 'I don't want to sit down—and why should I?'

"I said, 'Because I'm the coach.' He sat down." At that moment, Denny Crum found out what it means to "be the boss."

One leader who knows what it means to be the boss is Red Auerbach, who was the head coach of the most dominant franchise in professional sports history, the Boston Celtics (eight straight NBA championships, 1959-1966). I recently sat down with Red, and he told me the story of his journey as a leader.

"I grew up in Brooklyn," he said. "In basketball, I played point guard, the leadership position. I went to George Washington University and then went on to get my master's. I always got the best jobs after college and here's why: I would work at the boy's clubs and YMCAs, and the experience I got gave me an advantage when I was looking for jobs. My senior year in college, I worked at a government reform school, making twenty-five dollars a month. Those were tough kids, and I had to show leadership to get them to respect me.

"When I coached the Washington Capitals in the late 1940s, I had a player named Matt Zunic who'd been my teammate at George Washington. During a game one night, I took him out and he threw his jacket down and yelled, 'Why did you take me out?' I told him to sit down. A few minutes later, I walked over and said, 'Listen, I'm gonna succeed in this job, or I'm gonna lose it. If you are going to show emotion when I take you out of a game, then pack your bags and leave. Never question me again. If I get fired, I get fired, but not because you showed me up.' I really ripped him—but I never had that problem with him or any of my players. That was a key moment early in my leadership career.

"A few years later, I was coaching the Tri-Cities Blackhawks. One night, a player, Warren Perkins, blew a play I called and I really blasted him. He said, 'You can't talk to me like that!' I told him to take a shower. The next day at practice, I said, 'Warren, what was that all about last night?' He said, 'Coach, I was sick the day before and missed practice so I didn't know that play.' I said, 'Well, this is pro ball and you're going to get yelled at sometimes. You've got to take it.' That was another turning point for me.

"Respect is an intangible asset. It's hard to get, easy to lose. An important part of getting the respect of young leaders is teaching them to respect themselves. I knew Joe DiMaggio and Phil Rizzuto when they were with the Yankees. The Yankees always had a dress code when they were on the road. That impressed me, so one day I asked the manager, Joe McCarthy, about it. He said, 'If you dress like a champion and act like a champion, you'll play like a champion.' I never forgot that.

"Gaining respect is the most important part of leadership. Being liked is irrelevant. Not all my players liked me when I was coaching, but in time a lot of them came to appreciate the wisdom and counsel I could offer them. On my seventy-fifth birthday, all my old players came back for a big celebration. I guess that was the ultimate expression of respect."

As Celtics head coach Doc Rivers told me, "As a leader, you'd like to be liked, but you can't worry about that. Great leaders like Red Auerbach, Vince Lombardi, and John Wooden are loved in later years. While they are coaching, they're often not loved—but they're respected." And Larry Lucchino, president of the Boston Red Sox, told me that the same principle applies to young leaders. "To be leaders," he said, "young people must have an inner comfort with themselves. They can't expect people to always like them or agree with them, and they have to be okay with that. Leadership is not based on how charming you are. It's based on whether people trust you and are willing to go where you take them. You can't always worry about being liked."

Franklin Graham has a son who serves as a lieutenant in the United States Army. "I can assure you that he is not best friends with all of his soldiers," he told me. "But he is respected. Leaders are not always going to be liked, but they must be respected."

Memphis Grizzlies head coach Hubie Brown learned to be the boss as a high school basketball player. "In 1951," he said, "we were halfway to winning the state championship in New Jersey. We had a problem, however, because our best player was shooting too much. The other players came to me and said, 'Hubie, you have to tell him to stop being so selfish with the ball.' Understand, this guy was my peer, a great all-around athlete and our top scorer. Just before a game, I took him out in the hall and said, 'If you don't start passing the ball, I'll never throw you the ball on the fast break.' I was nose to nose with the guy, and I didn't know if a fistfight would erupt. As it turned out, he said, 'Okay, I'll pass the ball.' I actually got through to the guy! That was a pivotal moment for me as a young leader. We went on to win the state title."

It's not easy to motivate kids to be leaders. Few want the hassle, the hard work, the responsibility of being an example to others, the chore of giving direction to others. Most kids—even kids with a lot of natural leadership potential—would rather follow than lead. Being a leader is tough, and it sometimes puts a young person in a tough position.

Jay Carty played basketball at Oregon State, and he was on John Wooden's coaching staff at UCLA for three years. He also played for the Los Angeles Lakers. Today he is a Christian author, speaker, and consultant. Jay found out how hard leadership can be when he was senior class president in high school. "Our treasurer," he told me, "was a girl who happened to be a friend of mine. She had been elected to office, but she wasn't doing her job. I had a decision to make: Should I stick with her or impeach her? I decided to replace her. It was the first time I made a decision to place the good of the organization ahead of personal feelings. It was a decision to be a leader."

In the next few pages, I have collected the wise advice of leaders who have learned the secret of motivating young people to lead. Here are the stories and principles they shared with me:

1. Appeal to the Young Leader's Sense of Adventure

"Leadership is an adventure," said William Donohue, president of the Catholic League for Religious and Civil Rights. "I encourage young people to step up and lead because the alternative is to sit back and be led by others. No group is without a leader, no matter how small the group. If the leader isn't you, it will be someone else, so why not be a driver instead of a passenger? Isn't it more fun to be a player than a spectator? The degree of satisfaction that accompanies positions of leadership is significant and highly rewarding in so many ways. Sure, there is always the risk of failure. But since we all have only one life to live, why not go for broke? Who wants to get old and question what he or she could have become?"

"The way I look at it," said Charlie Bell, the new CEO of McDonald's, "you have three choices in life: lead, follow, or get out of the way. Leading is by far the most interesting and the most rewarding."

2. Listen to the Ideas and Dreams of Young Leaders

Jacqueline Whitmore is the founder and director of the Protocol School of Palm Beach, a company that specializes in etiquette and protocol instruction. "As adults, we have to become better listeners to our young people," she told me. "If they show an eagerness to lead, then we should do whatever we can to give them opportunities. We can make young people feel confident and worthwhile by asking them what they want to do and where they want to go in life. We should listen more, ask more questions, and talk less."

Harry Rhoads, president of the Washington Speakers Bureau, agreed: "Adults, and particularly parents, must be willing to listen to youngsters in order to build a foundation of two-way communication and trust. Kids listen better when they feel listened to. Once that feeling of trust is established, they will begin to demonstrate leadership qualities that can be nurtured and built upon."

Coach John Wooden told me the same thing. "Listen to those under your supervision and be patient with them," he said. "Encourage, support, and give guidance, but don't push them or drive them."

3. Say, "I'm Proud of You"

Val Hale, athletics director at Brigham Young University, shared a story with me that really touched my heart: "A high school basketball team from a small town won the state championship game in dramatic fashion. After the game, several players got together to celebrate in an inappropriate fashion. News of what they had done spread quickly throughout the town.

"There was one young man on the team who didn't participate in the celebration. He was very concerned because his father was a leader in the church, and he was worried that his father would think he was involved. All day at school he worried, and he couldn't wait to get home to tell his father that he was innocent.

"When the young man arrived at the house, he dashed inside to find his dad. When they met, the son didn't even get a chance to speak. The father surprised him by saying, 'I heard about what happened at the party after the game. I just wish you had been there.'

"The son was astonished. 'Why?' he asked.

" 'Because,' the father said, 'if you had been there, you would not have allowed those boys to do those things.'

"That's a great affirmation for a father to give one of his children. This story says two things about that father: First, he trusted his son so completely that he was absolutely confident his son couldn't have taken part in the event. The father didn't even have to ask, 'Son, were you there?' To this dad, such a thing was unthinkable.

"Second, he trusted his son's leadership ability and character so much that he was confident that, had his son been there, he would have put a stop to the inappropriate behavior.

"I believe one of the ways we raise trustworthy young leaders is by continually affirming to them that we believe in them and we are proud of their good character. When faced with tough choices, they will re-member that affirmation, and they won't want to let us down."

Washington State basketball coach Dick Bennett told me, "I believe in giving young leaders affirmation and compliments—not empty praise, but honest, realistic, positive feedback when they demonstrate good character, good attitude, and consistency. When you see a young leader reach out to help and encourage his teammates, tell him you appreciate it. Leaders have servant mentalities, they are looking to help others, and we need to reinforce that. We should also recognize courage and confi-dence. A good leader can positively affect the group, and with just a few well-timed words, we can do a lot to lift a young leader's confidence and motivate him or her to put out an extra effort.

"Compliments are important for building a young leader's confi-dence—but those compliments should be based on reality, on that youngster's character, attitude, and effort. A lot of adults these days just ladle out empty praise to build up a kid's self-esteem, and that's not always productive. Nobody's automatically entitled to praise, and kids shouldn't be raised to expect constant praise. But when they earn it, let's notice it and let's tell them. A few well-placed words can provide a lifetime of confidence and motivation."

4. Encourage Young Leaders According to Their Uniqueness

David Self, associate pastor of Houston's First Baptist Church (a church with an average weekly attendance of six thousand people), told me, "One of the best things parents or other mentors can do to motivate and inspire young leaders is to encourage them. Proverbs 22:6 says, 'Train a child in the way he should go, and when he is old he will not turn from it.' That passage could also be translated, 'Train a child according to his own individual bent, his own uniqueness.' In other words, we as parents, teachers, pastors, and mentors should take a good look at these kids in our care, and we should recognize the array of God-given talents, gifts, and passions they possess. Then we should encourage them to excel and develop those talents, gifts, and passions.

"It's sad that encouragement is sometimes confined to the soccer field or recital hall. Recognizing leadership potential requires spending time with your child in various settings and noticing a broad range of talents, gifts, and character traits. We should also encourage children when they try and fail, and when they compete in areas that are new to them. Above all, we need to demonstrate God's affirmation and love through our support, prayer, and unfailing encouragement."

As I've said elsewhere, I am "Dad" to nineteen kids. If there is one thing I've learned by having so many pairs of shoes lined up outside the front door and so many faces around the dinner table, it is this: No two kids are alike. Each child is a unique human soul. Each comes with his or her own unique set of personality traits, virtues, flaws, interests, likes, dislikes, ambitions, and dreams. In a very real sense, the parenting style you apply to one child is simply not transferable to the next.

Sure, you gain wisdom and acquire insights with each new child who comes into your home. But there is still a sense in which, with each individual child, you must learn how to be the parent of *that* specific child. You have to learn how to mold, guide, encourage, discipline, and love each child according to his or her own unique needs and personality type. Though you must never show favoritism, you must raise each child according to his or her own uniqueness.

Todd Shaw, president of On-Track Ministry, offered a similar perspective: "Every child is different, but every child can be a leader in his or her unique way. You can't understand your child's uniqueness unless you spend *time* with your child, observing firsthand what his or her strengths and gifts are. When we put in that daily time, talking to our kids and observing them as they pursue their interests and passions, we are able to build on their strengths and overcome their weaknesses.

"How do we build on their strengths? By encouraging them and affirming them when they do something right, when they do something well. In our home, we make a big deal of even the smallest accomplishments. When our kids make a mistake, we use it as a teaching, learning, and growing opportunity.

"Confidence is a key factor in leadership, and confidence is very fragile in young people. One time, when my youngest, Jason, made a poor decision, I said sternly, 'Jason, you're a bad boy!' I instantly regretted my poorly chosen words! Jason's little shoulders slumped in defeat. I instantly saw what a destructive thing that was to say, and I quickly corrected myself. 'Jason, I said the wrong thing,' I told him. 'You're not a bad boy—you're a good boy. You just made a bad decision.'

"That made all the difference! He could see what he had done wrong in a new light. Before, I had told him that *he* was bad—and that is like a word of condemnation. I corrected it so that he was okay, he was accepted and loved—he had simply made a poor choice. As a father, I have to remember to correct my children without breaking their confidence, without making them feel condemned."

5. Give Young Leaders Opportunities to Lead and to Serve

John Eldred of the Wharton School's Family Business Program told me, "Developing leadership capabilities is like a three-legged stool. The three legs are:

"1. *Seeing oneself as a leader.* We must help young people see themselves as leaders. We must affirm them, build their confidence, and tell them we believe in them. When we tell them, 'I know you have the ability to lead,' then they will begin to believe it themselves.

"2. *Having the skills of a leader.* This means we must train them in leadership skills, such as organizational skills, speaking skills, and people skills. We need to give them experiences that enable them to practice and refine those skills.

"3. *Being alert to opportunities to lead.* We should point them to opportunities that already exist—at school or church, or through youth programs or volunteering. We should encourage them to create their own leadership opportunities, such as starting their own volunteer project and recruiting other young people to join their cause.

"If young people have all three of these factors working together—if they see themselves as leaders, and are honing their skills, and finding or making opportunities—then everything works together, and leadership takes place."

Major league outfielder and baseball coach Danny Litwhiler told me how he made his own opportunity to become a leader: "I first realized I had the ability to lead in 1937. I had just finished my junior year at Bloomsburg State Teachers College, and I reported to the Charleston Senators in the Class C Middle Atlantic League. On the first day with the team, I had a hairline fracture of my right ankle. I went back to my home in Ringtown, Pennsylvania, for rehab. Ringtown was a little town of about eight hundred people. The kids had nothing to do during the summertime, so I organized a Little League of four teams who played two times a week. I coached all four teams. I kept those teams together from June until August when I had to report back to Charleston."

A couple of years later, one of Danny's mentors, Dr. E. H. Nelson, gave him a leadership opportunity that would change the course of his career. "In 1939," Danny said, "I reported to the Toledo Mud Hens [Detroit's AAA ball club] at their spring training camp. I was put in right field. The first day of practice, a batter hit a lazy line drive out to me. I thought I could make a shoestring catch, then realized I couldn't so pulled up to catch it on the bounce. The force of that sudden stop tore the cartilage in my left knee. My 1939 season was over.

"I went back home to recuperate. I received a call from Dr. E. H. Nelson, my baseball coach from Bloomsburg State Teachers College. He asked if I could help coach the college team. That spring and the next fall I helped him, and that coaching opportunity convinced me that coaching was the job for me."

A highly successful playing career in Major League Baseball delayed his entry into coaching, but in the early 1950s, Danny Litwhiler began coaching and managing in the minors, and later for Florida State and Michigan State. Danny was also instrumental in bringing a number of innovations to the game, including the use of radar guns to measure pitching speed, a drying agent (Diamond Grit) for wet baseball fields, and an unbreakable mirror used by pitchers to perfect their throw.

Jack Gregory, a former high school and college football coach, told me about a leadership opportunity that was given to him by my own father, Jim Williams. He said, "Two prominent community leaders in the Wilmington, Delaware, area—Mr. Bob Carpenter, owner of the Philadelphia Phillies, and Mr. Jim Williams, a former high school coach—asked me to serve as the first full-time director of the Delaware All-Star High School Football Game (the Blue-Gold Game), a benefit for the Delaware Foundation for Retarded Children. I was twenty-nine at the time, and the annual game was only in its second year. Mr. Carpenter and Mr. Williams had a dream of using this annual event to raise awareness and raise funds for research to help retarded children. They asked me to coordinate all aspects of this great event.

"They wanted me to work with coaches throughout the state and to help in organizing efforts to make this dream come true on an annual basis. I didn't consider myself a leader at the time, and I had never taken on a challenge of this kind before, but I must have done something right in helping to launch the event because this dream of Mr. Carpenter and Mr. Williams is still going strong almost fifty years later. The Blue-Gold Game is still played every year to benefit the same cause, and it uses the same format it used when the game began in 1956.

"Mr. Carpenter and Mr. Williams had a great influence on me in developing any leadership qualities I may have. By giving me an opportunity to lead, they helped lay the foundation for my forty-two-year career in coaching and athletic administration."

Lisa Maile, founder and owner of Lisa Maile Modeling, told me that some of the best leadership opportunities for young leaders are found through volunteerism. "If you want to provide leadership opportunities for young leaders," she said, "there is no better way than by encouraging them to volunteer. Young people are always needed and welcome in a variety of situations—tutoring younger children, teaching sports to younger kids, reading books or teaching crafts to smaller children. Everyone needs to feel capable, useful, and important at something, and volunteering can provide that experience for young leaders!

"And if we want to see our kids volunteering their time, then we should lead by example. Young people do what they see, not just what we tell them. If they see that we are motivated to help and to serve, they will be, too."

6. Don't Leave Anyone Out

Todd Shaw reminded me that you sometimes have to look hard to find the leadership qualities in some kids, but the qualities are there. We need to make sure that no kid with leadership potential gets left out or left behind—or all of that wonderful potential will go to waste.

"As a youth pastor," Todd said, "I have asked teens, 'How would you like to lead? What would you like to do?' The sky's the limit! No dream is too big. No idea is too weird. When that is our approach, kids flourish! Their motivation soars! Why? Because we have given them permission to dream. We've given them a place where they can pursue their own unique interests and passions.

"We had one kid in our youth ministry who I thought would never last. He was kind of different and just didn't fit in. Other kids couldn't relate to him, and when I tried to talk to him, I couldn't relate to him, either. He was a computer geek and a science-fiction fan who could actually speak Vulcan. He was the last kid you would have naturally picked as a leader. Even so, he wanted to be on our youth leadership team. I was dubious, but I said, 'What would you like to do?'

"He said, 'Computers. I want to do something with computers.' To make a long story short, we made him a leader in an area where he was strong and had an intense interest. In no time flat, he had our own youth program Web page up and running—something I had been trying to do for years, to no avail. He recorded every Wednesday night youth service, converted the recordings to computer files, and placed them on our site that night so that others could go and download the message. He made movie shorts called 'trailers' to promote our upcoming events.

"Soon, this kid who hadn't fit in before was a real leader—he even had his own cult following! It was an amazing transformation. Today, he works for several churches in town, producing their Web and video work.

"The clincher is this: The kid's mom called my office one day and thanked me for the change in her son. Her exact words, which I'll never forget, were, 'I thought my son would never find a place to serve God, much less be a leader anywhere. But look at him now! I am so proud of him. Thank you!' She said this while fighting back tears.

"The moral to the story: You should never assume that this kid or that kid can't be a leader. Kids will surprise you every time! I'm reminded of the story of David and Goliath. Here's this skinny little drink of water named David going up against a guy who'd make Arnold Schwarzenegger cry, 'Mama!' As David was getting ready to meet this man-monster, King Saul tried to put his big, bulky suit of armor on the boy. David shrugged off the armor and said, in effect, 'I'm going to face this giant my way and God's way, not your way.' And David went out and killed the giant, not with a sword and armor, but with a sling and a stone.

"If we give kids a chance to show what they're made of and the freedom to lead according to their own uniqueness, if we encourage them and support them, then those giants had better look out!"

7. Empower Young Leaders to Make Their Own Decisions

"There were two times in my early life that it really hit home to me that I could be a leader," John Eldred told me. "The first such moment was when I was in the seventh grade at St. Timothy's parochial school. I was the captain of the safety patrol, and we were holding a disciplinary hearing of a fourth grader who had run into the street, ignoring the direction of one of our crossing guards. At one point in the hearing, the nun turned to me and asked, 'What do you recommend, Mr. Eldred?'

"I just about swallowed my tongue! After all, the nuns were in charge, weren't they? I remember feeling stunned by the realization that some of the awesome decision-making power of leadership was being placed in my hands.

"The second moment came during my ROTC training, when I was battalion commander for the day. At the end of my orientation, the training NCO said, 'Well, it's all yours.' And a thousand men turned to me for leadership and decision making—I was in complete charge!

"Those two moments helped me realize that I had the capacity and legitimacy to lead. I still had to acquire the skills and confidence, but those things would come over time. The point is that in order to build young leaders, we need to empower them with genuine decision-making power. If they are going to be leaders, we have to let them lead."

San Antonio Spurs head coach Gregg Popovich agreed: "We can't just give young leaders a meaningless title and pretend to let them lead while we make all the decisions. If we want to motivate young leaders to lead, we have to give them the ability to make real decisions. We have to allow them the space to decide how they will spend money, what activities or projects they will be involved in, and how they will carry them out. Once young leaders make those decisions, we need to avoid interfering or trying to steer them into making the decision we would make. Let their decision stand, let it play out—then, at the end of the process, sit down with the young leaders and talk about the consequences of that decision: What were the positive and negative outcomes of that decision?

"Above all, at every point in the process, we need to avoid being judgmental. If the young leader feels, 'I have the power to lead, I'm making real decisions, I'm being trusted to truly lead in this situation, even if I make a mistake or two,' then that young person will be motivated to continue building his or her skills. Nothing raises young people's confidence level like knowing their parents and mentors trust them with real power to lead."

Steven Sample, president of the University of Southern California, put it this way: "Do you want to raise *real* leaders? Then delegate *real* authority to them! You can't expect young leaders to learn how to lead unless you give them the opportunity to make real decisions that have real consequences. They will never lead as long as some adult supervisor is hovering over them, second-guessing their every move. As adults, we are uncomfortable giving them that much autonomy. We're afraid to entrust untrained, untested young people with a large amount of authority. And remember this: While we can delegate authority to that young person, we still have to take ultimate responsibility for the results! So raising young leaders is risky for us adults—but it's a risk well worth taking."

One of the most important mentors in my life was Mr. R. E. Littlejohn, a businessman and co-owner of the Spartanburg, South Carolina, minor-league baseball team. In February 1965, I arrived as the twenty-four-year-old general manager of the ball club, and Mr. R. E. gave me full rein to run the team. We had four wonderful years together, and he loved me like a son. He let me operate the ball club as I saw fit. Even when I was making rookie mistakes (and I made plenty of them), he almost never interfered.

I would do expensive promotions and book athletes for personal appearances at the games—stars like Johnny Unitas and Bart Starr. Mr. Littlejohn knew we would never get our money back on those promotions, and he knew that if I overspent, it would affect my bonus at the end of the year. But he let me do my thing because he wanted me to learn by experience (the hard-won lessons stick with you for life). He understood the need to let young leaders make decisions—and make mistakes. I couldn't have asked for a better, wiser leadership coach.

I can recall only two times when he intervened in a decision I had made. The first time occurred when I booked an ad in our baseball program. The ad was for a tavern, and Mr. R. E.—who was a deacon at the First Baptist Church—refused to advertise alcoholic beverages or taverns in his programs.

The other time he intervened involved a car-giveaway promotion. Every year, we gave a new car to one lucky fan. I thought, *Gee, this is such a great idea. Let's give away two cars!* The prize was always an American-made sedan, but I decided that the second car we gave away would be an inexpensive Volkswagen Beetle. So I made an arrangement with the VW dealer without checking with Mr. R. E.

When he found out what I had done, he was not happy. It wasn't the cost of the promotion that bothered him. It was the fact that he thought that VW Beetles, being so small, were not safe cars. Mr. R. E. cared about his customers, and he was afraid I would be putting one of our fans at risk!

So that's where Mr. R. E. drew the line when delegating: If one of my decisions violated his moral and ethical sense, or if it endangered one of his fans, he brought me up short. But if it was only money, he let go of the reins and let me lead.

8. Challenge Young Leaders—But Don't Overwhelm Them

Young people are motivated and energized by a challenge, but they can quickly become discouraged and overwhelmed if they discover that the challenge is simply too great. Dr. Richard E. Lapchick, director of the DeVos Sport Business Management Program at the University of Central Florida, told me, "I would advise any adults who have a responsibility for young people—whether they be parents, coaches, counselors, or teachers—that they provide young people with exciting challenges. They should treat all young persons as potential leaders and talk to those young leaders about the problems confronting society and the fact that young people have an opportunity to find solutions to those problems. Tell them, 'I believe that you have the potential to make a contribution.'

"At the same time, we have to be careful not to make the challenge seem too overwhelming. Our message should not be, 'You must change the world,' but 'You have a part to play.' We shouldn't make young leaders feel that they have a personal responsibility to fix everything that's wrong with the world, but we do want them to know that they can do their part and they can help bring about meaningful change. And the way they can do that is by becoming a leader."

9. Inspire Young Leaders to Seek Satisfaction, Not Material Rewards

The biggest motivation for young people to become leaders involves the rewards of leadership. It is not unreasonable for a young person to ask, "If I choose to be a leader, what do I get out of it?" Asking this doesn't mean that the young person is approaching the question selfishly or with a mercenary attitude. Don't be afraid to say, "The most important rewards of leadership are largely intangible—a sense of accomplishment, satisfaction, increased confidence, and the knowledge that you are making the world a better place." In fact, you'd be surprised how many young people will find an intangible reward much more attractive than, say, money or fame.

Legendary basketball coach Pete Newell won a gold medal as coach of the U.S.A. Olympic basketball team in 1960, and he has coached college basketball at the University of San Francisco, Michigan State, and the University of California. He has also served as general manager of the San Diego Rockets and L.A. Lakers.

"For me, the motivation to be a leader comes from a sense of satisfaction," Pete said, "not money, prestige, or material rewards. When I was a young teenager, I organized pickup games and was always a captain. I liked a good, challenging game, and I always wanted the sides to be even, so I usually gave the other team captain first pick. I derived the greatest satisfaction from winning as the underdog and coaching my fellow players to work together and play above their own skill level.

"When I began coaching professionally, I wanted to make sure I was coaching for the right reasons. When I took my first NCAA Division I coaching job, I took it on as a challenge. I was in charge of basketball, baseball, and golf, though I made a fairly small salary. I have never made a decision based on money. I did it all because I love to coach and teach. If you love the game, if you love the challenge of leadership, if you relish the idea of making other people better, if you don't care about feeding your ego or getting rich, then you have the right motivation to be a leader."

Bill Vogel, superintendent of Seminole County Public Schools, told me, "One of the most satisfying aspects of leadership is the sense of belonging it creates. Leaders work in a team environment, and they bring others into the fold. Leaders share their vision and their values, and they focus the efforts of the entire team on a single goal. This creates a shared sense of belonging to something bigger than any one individual. That sense of belonging is, in itself, an intrinsic reward. The satisfaction of leading the group, of accomplishing goals, of belonging to a larger cause, of influencing situations and events—these are intangible rewards, but they are appealing to kids.

"We don't have to bribe kids with tangible rewards in order to motivate them to lead. We can inspire them to seek the intangible rewards and the sense of satisfaction that are part of the leadership journey. Kids hate boredom, and leadership is exciting; it's an adventure. Give young leaders the freedom to pursue their interests and become involved in a cause they care about, and they will be motivated to lead."

10. Show Young Leaders That Leadership Is *Fun*!

Mike Anderson became head men's basketball coach at the University of Alabama at Birmingham in the spring of 2002. In his first season, he guided the UAB Blazers to the best single-season improvement in school history, finishing with a record of 21-13. "I think we sometimes forget the best motivation of all to be a leader," Mike told me. "It's simple: Leadership is *fun*. I don't care what the arena is, whether sports, business, government, education, or whatever, when people are having fun at what they do, they always do it better.

"We were preparing to play in the National Junior College Championship game against Nolan Richardson's Western Texas Junior College. We were huge underdogs to a team that was undefeated. I went to the team with a confident smile on my face and said, 'Look, we've got nothing to lose. We're not even supposed to be here, so let's go out and have some fun.' And we did. Those guys had a lot of fun on the court, and we led by six at the half. We ended up losing, but we played to win and competed at a higher level because we were having fun.

"There's nothing that creates a more positive spirit than a sense of fun. Fun builds confidence. Fun makes you fearless. Fun motivates. Young people are our future, and we need to encourage them to approach the problems of this fast-changing world with a positive attitude and confidence."

■ Activities and Organizations That Build Leaders

If you want to build young leaders, the best place to begin is athletics. Through sports, kids learn a wide range of lessons and principles that contribute to a lifetime of success: being part of a team and offering mutual encouragement; setting goals; acquiring a strong work ethic; being self-disciplined; having focus, dedication, and commitment; taking risks and dealing with pressure situations; attaining self-confidence and a healthy self-esteem; developing sportsmanship and a competitive spirit; following healthy habits, such as proper nutrition, rest, and exercise; having a positive mental attitude; bouncing back from losses and failures; and overcoming adversity.

In addition to these lessons and principles that we all need to understand in order to have a happy, healthy, successful life, sports teach kids the seven keys of effective leadership that we've discussed throughout this book: having a vision of winning; communicating with each other on the court or field; relating to teammates with good people skills; building good character; being competent to compete; exhibiting boldness; and being a servant to the team.

Randy Mobley, president of the AAA International Baseball League, told me, "The first evidence of leadership in my life occurred as a result of athletics. I was not the best athlete in any sport, but I was one of the better athletes in just about everything I participated in. This gave me visibility and caused many of my peers to look up to me as a leader. Sports gave me the confidence to tackle other leadership arenas, such as involvement in Student Council. Each leadership success increases your competence and confidence to go to the next level. For me, it all began with sports."

But what if your young leader-in-training isn't interested in sports? That's okay. There are many other programs and organizations for training young leaders—and there is almost certainly one that is a perfect match for the abilities and interests of your young person. For example, the National Youth Leadership Network has programs for inspiring and training young leaders with various disabilities. The 4-H International program works primarily with young people who have an interest in farming and raising animals, but also meets the needs of kids who are interested in science, shooting sports, intercultural exchange, and more. The Rotary International encourages young leaders through its RYLA (Rotary Youth Leadership Award) program.

Rick Goings, CEO of the Tupperware Corporation, spoke of a program that holds a special interest for him: "I have been deeply involved in the national leadership of Boys and Girls Clubs of America, and was selected to serve as national chairman. This is a program that looks at each young person's unique gifts and gives young people an environment where they can express their leadership ability in ways that match their passions and interests."

Congressman Mark A. Foley is a five-term representative from Florida's Sixteenth Congressional District. He told me about a youth leadership program that impacted his young life: "When I was a senior at Lake Worth High School in Lake Worth, Florida, I ran for Mayor of the Day, a youth day organized by the American Legion. That experience showed me that I could play a significant role in the life of our city. I wanted to enrich the lives of our students through participation in city government, and I wanted adults to see that young people could be a positive force in our community."

What about kids who would like to be leaders in the world of science and technology? Karen Howe, CEO of the Internet company Singingfish, told me, "One of the best programs I've participated in, both as a coach and as a judge, was Odyssey of the Mind. I saw children of all ages compete as teams in amazingly creative ways, and I watched as each child demonstrated leadership ability in various ways. It was fascinating to see what I call 'fluid leadership' taking place—kids passing the baton of leadership around the team, from child to child as appropriate."

Our churches and other houses of worship can and should be giving young people opportunities to discover and exercise their leadership ability. Kids should be given responsibility to lead their own youth groups, Bible studies, retreats, and sporting events; to take an active part in the worship service; to plan and carry out ministries and outreach efforts;

and to conduct fund-raising activities such as bake sales and Christmas tree lots. All too often, paid staff members provide the leadership, and kids are herded around or simply entertained. Forward-thinking churches, however, aggressively seek ways to put decision-making and leadership power in the hands of the kids.

As young people start looking to the future, we should consider encouraging them to think about military service as a way of building their leadership skills. In fact, I would say that the United States Marine Corps is the greatest leadership training program ever invented for young people between the ages of seventeen and twenty-nine. No less a leadership authority than Fred Smith, the founder of FedEx, said, "Nothing has prepared business leaders better for their roles in business and society than the lessons they learned in the Corps—lessons of discipline, organization, commitment, and integrity."

Dick Batchelor, founder of Dick Batchelor Management Group, Inc., told me, "I began to see myself as a leader during high school, but the real eye-opener came while I was completing my Marine Corps boot camp at Parris Island, South Carolina, in 1966. Before I went, I would not have believed I could run several miles, memorize the Uniform Code of Military Justice, be able to dismantle, reassemble, and fire assault weapons, and be able to assist in commanding a platoon.

"I give credit to the Marine Corps for enabling me to see myself as a leader, for giving me the motivation, confidence, and training I needed, and for teaching me how to be a decision maker and an initiator. These lessons served me well during my eight years in the legislature (where I was elected at the age of twenty-six), as well as in my civic, business, and family responsibilities."

My son Peter is a Marine Corps veteran. "Leadership training is centrally important in the Marines," he said. "Young people grow up fast in the Corps. You are handed a lot of responsibility, and you are expected to meet the challenge. Most do. Occasionally, you see a guy rushed into a leadership position too quickly—he gets a promotion and tries to act like a leader, but he's not ready. When people see he's not a real leader, no one wants to follow him. Leadership has to be earned. Fortunately, most Marines do earn it.

"Every day in the Corps was a lesson in leadership. I believe every leadership lesson I've learned in the Corps is transferable to civilian life. A lot of people think that leadership in the Corps consists of a drill instructor barking and snarling at a bunch of raw recruits. But Marine Corps leadership training is far more sophisticated than that. Marines are expected to be rigorously professional in everything they do; to take responsibility and be accountable; to live a lifestyle of continuous learning and self-improvement; to demonstrate decisiveness and good judgment; to communicate and work as a team; and to practice absolute integrity at all times. If you want a proven leader, you want a Marine."

Another son, David, is currently in the Marines and a veteran of Operation Iraqi Freedom. David told me that the leadership training he received in the Marine Corps has impacted his life forever. "There are fourteen leadership traits that all Marines aspire to," he said. "Those traits are bearing, courage, decisiveness, dependability, endurance, enthusiasm, initiative, integrity, judgment, justice, knowledge, loyalty, tact, and unselfishness. A Marine is expected to exemplify these traits. Any person who exemplified those fourteen traits, whether in the Marines or in civilian life, would be, by definition, a leader.

"Leaders in the Corps made a big impression on my life. When I was stationed at Camp Pendleton in California, I met a Marine named Sergeant Miller, a fair and honest man. What made him unique was this—he didn't have to do the hard work, but he did. He got his hands dirty along with the rest of us. He didn't just tell us what to do and then leave. He was right there with us the whole time. We all knew that he cared about our success, and we respected him for that. He was a rare leader, and I will always remember him."

When I told General Tommy Franks that my son David was a Marine and that he had seen combat in Iraq in 2003, the general said to me,

"You tell your son that someone else loves him besides you." Both of us got lumps in our throat when he said that.

I was never in the Marines, but I had my own "Sergeant Miller," only his name was Sergeant Enrique Fishbach. It was September 1964, and I had just finished the baseball season with the minor-league Marlins in Miami. I was twenty-four years old, and the Phillies organization had invited me to come to Philadelphia to help prepare the team for the 1964 World Series. Well, as things turned out, the Phillies collapsed by the end of the season, and they didn't get to the World Series.

Meanwhile, Uncle Sam called and said, "Pat, remember when you signed up for the Army Reserve a year ago? Remember that we told you there'd be some basic training? Well, on the nineteenth of September, you are to report to Fort Jackson, near Columbia, South Carolina." So I reported for eight weeks of basic training. During those eight weeks, I received a crash course in leadership.

The sergeant in charge of our unit was a Cuban-American named Enrique Fishbach. Picture the ultimate spit-and-polish drill sergeant—a steel-rod stance, boots so glossy you could use them for rearview mirrors, steely eyes, square jaw. He issued commands in a clear, crisp, powerful voice that you couldn't possibly disobey or ignore. I can picture him to this day—an impressive model of military leadership, and let me tell you, that bunch of scared recruits responded to him with unquestioning obedience.

There was another fellow in our unit, a recruit named Don Wehde. He came from the opposite end of the spectrum from Sergeant Fishbach. Don was a six-foot four-inch disk jockey, the life of the party, a hail-fellow-well-met, an entertainer with a lot of charisma, one of the boys. But shortly after we arrived for basic training, the powers that be announced that good ol' Don was going to be our squad leader. The transformation that came over Don was nothing short of amazing. He instantly went from the Life of the Party to Mr. Military—a tough-as-nails squad leader who barked orders, marched us around, and chewed us out for every little infraction.

This went on for a number of weeks until Don messed up. I don't recall what he did, but I do know that Don got busted from squad leader back to a government-issue grunt like the rest of us. Don was kind of embarrassed about being sent back into the ranks. I can still see him—he ended up in the last row, and his attitude was, "Let's get the rest of basic training over with so I can get outta here." I'll never forget the words he said when he came back to our ranks after being busted: "Well, I'm back—just bopping along with the troops."

Whenever I'm watching a youth sports event or a school activity, it never fails—I always spot some kid who reminds me of Don. I see that look on a kid's face that says, "Well, here I am, just bopping along with the troops." There are so many young people with so much leadership potential, so many talents, so many undiscovered abilities. If their parents, teachers, or coaches just knew how to reach them, how to motivate them, how to give them some challenging opportunities, those kids might become like Sergeant Fishbach—real leaders, people who inspire respect and admiration, people who make a difference in this world.

What a waste—what a tragic, awful waste—that so many kids are just marching along at the rear, marking time, just bopping along with the troops.

You and I have a challenge before us, my friend. We need to spot these kids, snatch them out of the ranks, and show them we believe in them. We need to hold a mirror up to them and show them the possibilities and potential we see in them—potential they can't even imagine.

Let's keep our eyes open for the kids with potential, kids who are just bopping along through life, kids whose lives could make a difference in this world if they were just given the chance. Let's take advantage of every teaching, coaching, and motivating opportunity. If you and I don't do it, who will? And if we are willing to let these kids slip through the cracks and waste all of that glorious potential, what kind of leaders are we?

It's up to us to coach these kids to become leaders.

Let's get going!

Epilogue

It's Your Turn

As I was putting the final touches on this book, I came across a story in *Sports Illustrated* (February 10, 2004) that says a lot about what can happen when we coach young people to become leaders. The story, written by Michael Bamberger, is called "Full Nelson," and it tells the story of Jameer Nelson, possibly the best college basketball player in the nation—and he plays at one of the smallest schools in the country, tiny St. Joseph's University, a Jesuit school in west Philadelphia.

Jameer is a young man with all the qualities we've been talking about in this book—a kid who never had any advantages in life, yet he's clearly a young leader on the way. He's got it. He understands it. He leads. "I was always the best player on my team," Jameer explained, "so I had to lead. The other guys wanted to follow me."

Jameer is always looking out for every member of his team, thinking of ways to keep them involved, helping each of his teammates to contribute toward the team goal. Jameer noticed one quiet, red-haired freshman from Allentown, Pennsylvania, who was working hard to make the team as a walk-on. The freshman, Andrew Koefer, worked very hard, but after three practices, St. Joe's tough-minded head coach, Phil Martelli, decided it was time to cut Koefer from the team.

Martelli called Koefer into his office and started giving him the same speech he had given many other times over the years. "Kid," he said, "you've been working hard out there, but we're going to have to cut you from the team. You can try again next year."

Martelli had just barely started giving Koefer the bad news when the phone rang. He picked it up, and it was Jameer Nelson.

"Coach," Jameer said, "is that red-haired kid in your office right now?" Jameer didn't even know Koefer's name—but he knew Koefer's heart as a player.

"Yeah," Martelli said, "he's in here."

"I think you should keep him."

"Oh? Why is that?"

"The guy works hard, Coach, and he makes the rest of us practice harder."

"You think it's important we keep him?"

"Yes, sir, I do."

"All right. We'll do that."

Martelli hung up the phone, looked at Koefer, and said, "I've decided to keep you on the team." He didn't mention that Jameer Nelson had called on his behalf.

Later that season, Coach Martelli sent Koefer into the game at guard in the final seconds of the game. Koefer collected an assist, his first of his college career. As Koefer came off the court, Jameer Nelson told him, "That was a good look, my man!"

Bamberger later asked Jameer Nelson why he interceded with Coach Martelli on behalf of a freshman walk-on player whose name he didn't even know. "A lot of dreams don't come true in life," Jameer replied. "If you can make somebody's dream come true, you should."

I asked Coach Martelli his opinion of Jameer Nelson, and he replied, "Jameer is the best player in college basketball because he is the best leader in college basketball. And from the day he came back to play his senior year, he demanded in a very quiet way from his teammates and his coaches that we pursue excellence. And that is what we have done."

Jameer Nelson is a leader. He's a young man with a vision; he's a communicator with a big heart for people and great character; he's a competent young leader, destined for a big future in the NBA; he showed boldness in calling his coach on behalf of another player; and he's a servant, always looking out for other people and their dreams. Jameer is everything we want all young leaders to be.

And one more thing: Jameer Nelson is from a little town called Chester, Pennsylvania. I know that town. It's located about twenty miles from my hometown of Wilmington, Delaware, and I have driven through Chester many times. I'll tell you something—the town of Chester, Pennsylvania, is not the kind of place you would consider a launching pad for success and leadership. Chester is a rough place. Most kids don't make it out of that town. So for Jameer Nelson to come from Chester and to be the kind of leader he is tells me that someone has done a fine job of coaching this young man to be a leader. (In June 2004, the Orlando Magic drafted Jameer, as the 20th pick of the first round.)

Our communities need young leaders. The future of our nation and our world depends on whether we can raise a new generation of leaders to tackle the increasingly complex problems we face. This is not an option. This is an absolute necessity.

In every period of history, it has always come down to leadership. Will we produce the kind of bold, visionary leaders who will take us into the future—or will our society sink under the weight of such problems as poverty, racism, ignorance, ecological destruction, political division, corporate corruption, spiritual and moral bankruptcy, terrorism, global economic and political instability, and more?

Our young people are under relentless attack. They face incredible pressures. We've got to get them ready for the challenges of today and the opportunities of tomorrow. So take these principles, my friend. Learn them, apply them, and teach them to others.

In this book, you've heard the stories and inspiring ideas of some of the greatest leaders of our day, from all walks of life, from all segments of society. Now let me leave you with one final inspiring story, as told to me by a twenty-four-year-old leader, a graduate of Jay Strack's Student Leadership University, currently working on her master's degree at George Washington University. Her name is Nikki Finch.

"In the past eight years," she said, "I have traveled to twenty-six states and three countries, speaking out on health and safety issues that affect my peers. I've held over forty press conferences, from the Capitol building to the White House, and I've appeared on news programs from the *Today* show to CNN. I've met with President Clinton, lobbied Congress, and sat on the boards of directors of three national nonprofit organizations. I earned a bachelor's degree from Florida State and spent a year serving in the D.C. inner city schools with AmeriCorps.

"It has been one awesome ride, and I've had a number of coaches and mentors who've helped me along the way—friends and family, my youth minister, my high school guidance counselor, and others. But the story begins in July 1996, when I was seventeen. That's when I attended Student Leadership University 101 in Orlando. There I first grasped what can happen in my life if I would simply believe what Philippians 4:13 tells me: 'I can do everything through [Christ] who gives me strength.'

"In one session, Dr. Strack looked each student in the eye and asked, 'If you had no limits on your life, what would you do? What goals would you set for your life?' He gave us ten minutes to write down our thoughts. Some students wrote that they would lose some weight, read more, or try harder in school. Good goals—but I told myself, *Nikki, think big! Dr. Strack said, 'No limits!' What would that be like—living life without limits?*

"I wrote down that I would like to meet the president of the United States and talk to him about Jesus Christ. Then I wrote that I would like to work undercover for the CIA. Then I wrote that I would like to be a national speaker for Students Against Drunk Driving (I was a leader in my high school's SADD chapter at the time). When I read my goals to the class, some thought they were unreachable. But I walked away from SLU 101 with the realization that nothing is unreachable when I have Jesus Christ at my side. I decided that I had all the resources of the God of the Universe at my disposal, and I wasn't going to limit what He could do through me.

"Even though I had set high goals and I believed I could reach them, my thinking was still limited in one way: I thought that I would not reach these goals for many years. I soon learned that God does not have an age requirement. He's ready to use us as soon as we start taking Him seriously. Within a year of SLU 101, I reached many of the goals I set.

"Though I still haven't gotten an assignment from the CIA yet, most of the so-called 'unreachable' goals I wrote down at SLU 101 proved to be within my reach. I was selected to be the National SADD Student of the Year, and I traveled around the country speaking out on alcohol abuse. I met with the president to push for a national blood alcohol standard of .08.

"Next, with the encouragement of family, friends, and mentors, I took on a new alcohol abuse issue. I teamed up with New York's attorney general, Dennis Vacco, to end the practice of selling alcohol to minors over the Internet. I helped set up sting operations and lobbied Congress for federal legislation. We stood toe to toe with the alcohol industry—and we won.

"Young people *can* make a difference in the world if they will just open their minds to what God has planned for them. And parents, teachers, coaches, business leaders, and ministers have a big part to play. Adults can help young people envision the possibilities. They can encourage young people to reach for the 'unreachable.' So what are you waiting for? God's ready to use us! The only question is: Are we ready for God?"

That's quite a challenge that Nikki Finch has set before us. How about you? Are you ready to leave your mark on the next generation?

Just imagine the leadership adventure you are about to undertake. Imagine the impact you are about to have on the young lives within your circle of influence. Imagine the impact you are about to have on the world through the young leaders you are mentoring right now.

In the days and years ahead, as you see lives changed and new leaders stepping up to the challenge of the future, I hope you'll send me an e-mail or pick up the phone and call me. Tell me your story.

I can't wait to hear what happens next!

▪ Acknowledgments ▪

With deep appreciation I acknowledge the support and guidance of the following people who helped make this book possible:

Special thanks to Bob Vander Weide and John Weisbrod of the Orlando Magic.

I am especially grateful to my assistant, Diana Basch, and my intern, Doug Grassian, who have poured both heart and soul into this book. Highest gratitude also goes to those who have given so much time and effort in helping me research this book: Peggy Matthews-Rose, Carol Winston, Suzanne London, Lisa Zolnier, Nasreen Ahmad, and Shaimallah Ahmad.

Hats off to my advisor, Ken Hussar, and my ace typist, Fran Thomas.

Hearty thanks are also due my publisher at Warner Faith, Rolf Zettersten, who originated the idea for this book; my editors, Stephen S. Wilburn and Bob Castillo, who shaped and refined it; and my writing partner, Jim Denney. Thank you all for believing that I had something important to share and for providing the support and the forum to say it.

Special thanks and appreciation go to my wife, Ruth, and to my wonderful and supportive family. They are truly the backbone of my life.

Finally, this book is the product of the experiences and wisdom of literally hundreds of people who generously shared their stories with me. If

I could have used all of the wonderful material they shared with me, this book would be thousands of pages in length. Many of the interviewees and contributors whose names are on the following list do not appear in the text, yet their insights shaped the ideas and principles shared in this book. I am profoundly grateful to every one of these leaders, from all walks of life, who truly "wrote the book" on coaching kids to be leaders:

Kareem Abdul-Jabbar

Dick Abel

José Abreu

Ernie Accorsi

Val Ackerman

John Adams

Luis Aguayo

Danny Ainge

Steve Alford

Jim Allen

Craig Anderson

Mac Anderson

Mike Anderson

David Andrews

Dan Angel

Andy Appleby

B.J. Armstrong

Richard Armstrong

Murray Arnold

Joe Ash

Mark Atteberry

Red Auerbach

W. Sherrill Babb

Pete Babcock

Rob Babcock

John Bach

Ed Badger

Dwight Bain

Nathan Baker

Gary Balanoff

Dr. Robert Ballard

Cass Ballenger

Sal Bando

Sal Bando Jr.

Ed Barks

George Barna

Gary Barnett

Colleen Barrett

Robby Barrett

Gene Barton

W. Todd Bassett

Dick Batchelor

J.T. Battenburg III

George Bauer

Renee Baumgartner

Don Baylor

Buzzie Bavasi

Kevin Beary

Jim Beattie

Charlie Bell

Sam Bell

Adrian Benepe

Tony Benford

Fred Bennecke

Dick Bennett

Arnie Beyeler

Buddy Biancalana

Bernie Bickerstaff

Jay Bilas

Dallas Billington

Larry Birkes

Dr. Hollis Bivens

Michael Black

Dr. Henry Blackaby

Richard Blackaby

Bill Blackwell

Vanessa Blair

Marty Blake

Dr. Ken Blanchard

Frank Blethen

Theodore Blunt

Daniel Boggan, Jr.

Bobby Bonds

Mike Bone

Dean Bonham

Cam Bonifay

Dr. Rita Bornstein

Pam Borton

Larry Bowa

Bobby Bowden

Jim Bowden

Terry Bowden

Kathy Boyd

Sylvia Boyd

Bill Bradley

Bobby Bragan

Myles Brand

David Brandon

Gregg Brandon

Jim Brewer

Mike Brey

Lynn Bria

Bill Bright

Brad Bright
General Leo Brooks
Dale Brown
Gen. Doug Brown
Hubie Brown
Jamie Brown
Larry Brown
Sen. Michael Brown
Dave Budd
Rick Burleson
Jeb Bush
Sal Butera
Howard Butt
Jim Calhoun
Sherry Campbell
Jack Canfield
Dom Capers
Eddie Cardieri
M.L. Carr
Pete Carril
John Carroll
John Carry
Gary Carter
Dr. Carol Cartwright
Jay Carty
Brian Cashman
Charley Casserly
Michael Castle
Truett Cathy
Larry Catuzzi
John Celona
Ed Cerny
Matt Certo
Alan Chambers
Maurice Cheeks
Bruce Chesser
David Cicilline
Fred Claire
Tony Clark

Stan Cliburn
H. Boyd Coffie
Dr. Jordan Cohen
Jerry Colangelo
David Colburn
Barry Collier
Chuck Colson
Tinker Cooper
Barbara Corcoran
Pat Corrales
Dave Coskey
Bobby Cox
Susan Cox
Tom Craddick
Roger Craig
Cathryn Cranston
Pat Croce
Bill Crockett
Gary Cromton
Tom Cronin
Rich Crotty
Bill Crouch
Denny Crum
Billy Cunningham
Kevin Cushing
Chuck Daly
Alvin Dark
John Dasburg
Nancy Davies
Johnny Davis
Tom Davis
Carroll Dawson
Carol Deady
Joe Dean
Fred Decker
Patty Dedominic
Dr. Jim Denison
Paul De Podesta
Ben Despain

Bing Devine
Doug DeVos
Rich DeVos
H. William Deweese
Glenn Diamond
Marty Dickens
Jamie Dixon
John Doleva
Andy Dolich
Dave Dombrowski
William Donohue
Vince Dooley
Silne Dorlus
Eddie Doucette
Steve Downs
Moe Drabowsky
Jimmy Draper
Homer Drew
Scott Drew
Karl Droppers
Phillip Dubois
Bill Dugan
Michael Dukakis
Joe Dumars
Todd Duncan
Ericka Dunlap
Mike Dunleavy
Hugh Durham
Dr. Gerald Durley
Stina Duve
Douglas Holtz-Eakin
Mel Eaton
Mike Eaves
James Edwards
Dr. Harry Edwards
John Eldred
Lee Elia
Don Elliman
Wayne Embry

John Erickson
Carl Erskine
Glen Esnard
Rob Evans
Tony Evans
Charlie Evranian
Jack Falluca
Janice Farley
Gerry Faust
Bill Fay
Jay Feaster
Tom Feeney
Charles Feghali
Bobby Ferguson
Mark Few
Arnold Fielkow
Steve Fisher
Bill Fitch
Paul Fixter
Stephanie Flamini
Royce Flippin
Venera Flores
Dr. William Flores
Paul Flory
Bobby Floyd
Ronnie Floyd
Jeremy Foley
Mark Foley
Gordon Forbes
P.J. Forbes
Danny Forshee
Bill Foster
David Foster
Skeeter Francis
Terry Francona
Lawrence Frank
Carl Franks
Gen. Tommy Franks
Dave Frantz

Mike Fratello
Herman Frazier
Jim Fregosi
Bill Gaither
Mike Gannaway
Lydia Gardner
Mike Gaudy
Matt Geiger
Dan Gerdes
Scott Gilbert
Steve Gilbert
Bill Giles
Mike Gillespie
Raymond Gilmartin
Newt Gingrich
Dimitry Givans
Richard Glas
Joel Glass
Tommy Glavine
Rich Goings
Taylor Jo Goldsmith
Oscar Goodman
Mark Gottfried
Franklin Graham
Vincent Grasseti
Dallas Green
Dennis Green
Andrea Greene
Jack Gregory
Karen Greifenstein
Bob Gries
Grant Griesser
Jon Gruden
Eddie Grunfeld
Almon Gunter
Matt Guokas
Eugene Habecker
Dr. John Haggai
Val Hale

Jane Hames
Michael Hammond
Hank Hanegraaff
Jim Haney
Heidi Hanna
Christopher Hansen
Jack Harbaugh
Bob Harlan
Jim Harrick
Del Harris
James Harris
Jim Harris
Larry Harris
Charlie Harrison
Dave Hart
George Hartwell
Rick Hartzell
Chris Hatcher
Ken Hatfield
Bill Heath
Tami Heim
Roland Hemond
Solly Hemus
Jim Henry
Lou Henson
Rich Herrara
Whitey Herzog
Rev. Theodore Hesburg
Paul Hewitt
Jack Hibbard
Rich Hilgert
Armond Hill
Rev. Chris Hill
Grant Hill
Leroy Hill, Jr.
Greg Hillard
Dr. John Hitt
Dana Hobart
Stu Holt

Gene Hooks
Marianne Horinko
Ed Horne
Paul Houston
Dwight Howard Sr.
Art Howe
Karen Howe
Mike Huckabee
Brian Hug
Dan Hughes
Gary Hughes
Gerry Hunsicker
David Hunt
Johnny Hunt
Randy Hunt
Bobby Hurley
Asa Hutchinson
Stu Inman
Mannie Jackson
Phil Jackson
Vini Jacquery
Randall James
Ron Jaworski
Jerry Jenkins
Toni Jennings
Jack Jensen
Dick Jerardi
Martin Jischke
Jay John
Bob Johnson
Brent Johnson
Ollie Johnson
Randy Johnson
Bobby Jones
Charlie Jones
June Jones
Eddie Joost
Deloris Jordan
Eddie Jordan

Joe Jordan
Walter Kaiser
Ronald Kamm
Paul Karofsky
Stan Kasten
Saul Katz
Gene Keady
Larry Keenan
Art Kehoe
Kevin Kennedy
Carolyn Kilpatrick
Ben Kinchlow
Jerry Kindall
Bruce Kindy
Billy King
Clyde King
Shaun King
Joe Klein
Charlie Kleman
Patrick Knapp
Billy Knight
Bob Kobielush
Jim Kroll
John Kuntz
Lou Lamoriello
Steve Lanham
David Langdon
Lawson Lamar
Bryant Lancaster
Lee Landers
Richard Lapchick
Knute Larson
Tony LaRussa
Tom Lawless
Frank Layden
George Leader
Jim Leavitt
Jeff Lebo
Gregg Legg

Fred Leonhardt
Rich Levin
Marv Levy
Robert Levy
Marvin Lewis
Todd Lickliter
Dr. Peter Likins
Dick Lincoln
Tom Lindh
David Littlefield
Danny Litwhiler
Jim Livengood
Herbert London
Candace Long
Donna Lopiano
Honorable J.M. Loy
Larry Lucchino
Don Lund
Percy Luney
Bobby Lutz
Jimmy Lynam
Bill Lynch
Michael Lynch
Dr. John MacArthur
John Mackovic
John MacLeod
Kyle Macy
Lisa Maile
Edward Malloy
Rich Maloney
Kip Marchman
John Margaritis
David Markarian
Tim Markham
Phil Martelli
Charlie Martin
Mike Martin
Mel Martinez
Alex Martins

Jose Marzan
Craig Masbach
Rollie Massimino
Jim Mastandrea
John Masiarczyk
Nancy Matowitz
Thad Matta
Joel Maturi
Robert Maxson
John Maxwell
Larry McCarthy
Ian McCaw
Red McCombs
Clyde McCoy
Jack McCloskey
Joe McDonald
Matt McDonald
George McGovern
Dick McGuire
Kevin McHale
Jack McKeon
John McLaren
Pat McMahon
Nate McMillan
Jerry McMorris
Hal McRae
Steve McWhorter
Michael Means
Edwin Meese
Betty Mekdeci
John Merrill
Ron Meyer
General Richard B.
   Meyers
Ron Michalec
John Mica
Don Miers
Todd Milano
Dave Miley

Bruce Miller
Jay Miller
Jon Miller
Paul Miller
Rob Miller
Ron Miller
Randy Mobley
Sam Momary
William Monahan
Charlie Monfort
Dan Monson
Mike Montgomery
Rev. Don Moomaw
Terrence Moore
Speedy Morris
Stan Morrison
Mike Mueller
Pat Mullen
Chris Mullin
Jeff Mullins
Vincent Mumford
Pat Murphy
Eric Musselman
Andrea Myers
Richard Myers
Vince Naimoli
John Nash
Vince Nauss
William Nelsen
Don Nelson
Jameer Nelson
Drew Nemec
Pete Newell
C.M. Newton
Frank Neumann
Kim Nichols
Jon Niednagel
Thomas Nielsen
Amy Niles

Russ Nixon
Robert Nolan
Dickie Noles
Dan O'Brien
Jim O'Brien
Tom O'Brien
Kevin O'Connor
Martin O'Connor
Dave Odom
Mike O'Koren
Lute Olsen
Buck O'Neil
Steve Orsini
Bob Ortegel
Joel Osteen
Tim O'Toole
Danny Ozark
Billy Packer
Rod Paige
Donald Palmisano
Tom Palombo
Sunny Park
Larry Parrish
Rev. Jesse Lee Patterson
Paige Patterson
Steve Patterson
Rev. John Pawlikowski
J.P. Pawliw-Fry
John Paxson
Danny Peary
Tom Pecora
Richard Peddie
Tom Penders
Bruce Perkins
Jim Petro
John Peyton
Don Phillips
Tom Phillips
Wintley Phipps

Anne Pierson
Lou Piniella
Bill Polian
Wesley Poling
Ron Polk
C. William Pollard
Gregg Popovich
Terry Porter
Bill Posey
Ned Powell
Terry Presto
Skip Prosser
Robert Prunty
Keith Pugh
Dr. Jack Ramsay
James Ramsey
Clifford Ray
Ken Rector
Colonel George Reed
Jerry Reiger
Chuck Reiley
Brian Reily
Jerry Reinsdorf
Kevin Renckens
Edward Rendell
Harry Rhoads
J.P. Ricciardi
John Rice
Tim Rice
Mark Richt
Pat Richter
Wayne Rickman
Jim Riggleman
Bob Rikeman
Dawn Riley
Michael Riley
Mark Rivera
Doc Rivers
Dr. Phil Roach

Rick Roach
Steve Roadcap
Brooks Robinson
Frank Robinson
Rachel Robinson
Lt. Col. Thomas
    Robinson
Pete Roby
Jack Roeder
Lorenzo Romar
Phil Roof
Judy Rose
Rev. Marvin Rosenthal
Ernie Rosseau
Vern Ruhle
Mark Rutland
Jeff Ryan
Steven Sample
David Sampson
Kelvin Sampson
Steve Scanlon
Bernie Schaeffer
Danny Schayes
Carl Scheer
John Schnatter
Nick Scheele
Linda Schefstad
John Scheurholz
Joanie Schirm
Mike Schmidt
Jim Schnorf
Patricia Schroeder
Peter Secchia
Bob Seddon
Bill Self
David Self
Bud Selig
Andy Seminick
Tim Seneff

Bud Seretean
Robert Shafer
Mark Shapiro
Bill Sharman
Todd Shaw
Dal Shealy
Gary Sheffield
Tommy Shepherd
Rev. Mike Shirle
Tom Shirley
Mike Shula
Tony Sidoti
Paul Silas
John Silber
Jim Silver
Scott Skiles
Jerry Sloan
A. J. Smith
Bev Smith
Dan Smith
Dick Smith
Julie Smith
Otis Smith
Ozzie Smith
Sonja Smith
Tubby Smith
Jeff Smulyan
Jerry Solomon
Norm Sonju
Dan Sparks
Dick Spears
George Spelius
Kirk Speraw
Charlie Spoonhour
R.C. Sproul
Jack Stallings
John Stearns
Jerry Steele
Eddie Stefanski

Brandon Steiner
Charlie Steiner
Vera Steinfeld
Tom Stemberg
David Stern
Chuck Stevens
Scotty Stirling
Terry Stotts
Jay Strack
Cameron Strang
Chris Sullivan
Rick Sund
Scott Suttles
Bill Sutton
Dr. David Swanson
Chuck Tanner
Ed Tapscott
Mary Taylor
R. Scott Taylor
Pastor Ted Taylor
Diana Taurasi
George Tenet
Claude Terry
Tom Teti
Jeanine Klem-Thomas
Geraldine Thompson
Mike Tice
Joe Tomaselli
Jim Tooley
Jeff Torborg
Joe Torre
Carlos Tosca
Brian Tracy
Jim Tracy
Alan Trammell
Jeff Turner
Ron Turner
Dave Twardzik

John Tyson
Peter Ueberroth
Jack Uldrich
Wes Unseld
Hal Urban
Rick Van Arnam
Stan Van Gundy
Norm Van Lier
Tara Vanderveer
Kiki Vandeweghe
George Vavelides
Mike Veeck
Dick Vermeil
Dick Versace
Fay Vincent
Bill Vogel
Dave Walker
Dr. Leroy Walker
Wally Walker
Chris Wallace
Donnie Walsh
Pam Walters
Jeff Ward
Kurt Warner
J.C. Watts
Reg Weaver
Jean-Jacques Weiler
Norman Weinstock
John Weisbrod
Phillip Wellman
Jim Wells
Bob Wenzel
Jerry West
Paul Westhead
Paul Westphal
T.K. Wetherell
Richard Wexler
Jeff Wheeler

Steve Whitaker
Dr. Alan White
James White
Steven White
John Whitehead
Jacqueline Whitmore
Donald Whitney
Sheila Widnall
Morlon Wiley
Dominique Wilkins
Bobby Williams
David Williams
Jimmy Williams
Michael Williams
Peter Williams
R. Murphy Williams
Ruth Williams
Stephen Williams
Thomas Williams
Fred Wilpon
Bill Wilson
Ralph Wilson
Rod Wilson
Tex Winter
Adam Witty
Bill Wood
Dan Wood
John Wooden
Dennis Worden
Al Worthington
Jay Wright
Danny Wuerffel
Ed Young Jr.
Dr. Johnathan Zaff
Dr. Tony Zeiss
Don Zimmer

You can contact Pat Williams at:

Pat Williams
c/o Orlando Magic
8701 Maitland Summit Boulevard
Orlando, FL 32810
(407) 916-2404
pwilliams@orlandomagic.com

Visit Pat Williams's Web site at:

http://www.patwilliamsmotivate.com/

If you would like to set up a speaking engagement for Pat Williams, please call or write to his assistant, Diana Basch, at the above address or call her at (407) 916-2454. Requests can also be faxed to (407) 916-2986 or e-mailed to dbasch@orlandomagic.com.